The Prison at Philadelphia
CHERRY HILL

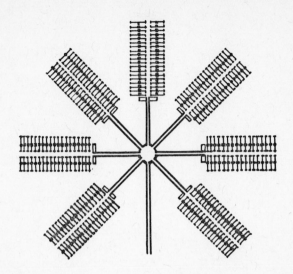

The Prison at Philadelphia
CHERRY HILL

THE SEPARATE SYSTEM OF PENAL DISCIPLINE: 1829–1913

By NEGLEY K. TEETERS and JOHN D. SHEARER

Published in New York   1957

For TEMPLE UNIVERSITY PUBLICATIONS

By COLUMBIA UNIVERSITY PRESS

© 1957 COLUMBIA UNIVERSITY PRESS, NEW YORK

PUBLISHED IN GREAT BRITAIN, CANADA, INDIA, AND PAKISTAN
BY THE OXFORD UNIVERSITY PRESS
LONDON, TORONTO, BOMBAY, AND KARACHI

LIBRARY OF CONGRESS CATALOG CARD NUMBER: 57-6211
MANUFACTURED IN THE UNITED STATES OF AMERICA

The Pennsylvania System is a Divine System

—DON JOSÉ SANTIAGO RODRÍGUES
Penal lawyer, Caracas, Venezuela
(Minutes, Philadelphia Society for Alle-
viating the Miseries of Public Prisons,
July 9, 1832)

Introduction

IT IS an exciting task for a European criminologist to write an introduction to an American history of the Eastern Penitentiary of Pennsylvania. For the better part of the nineteenth century, Cherry Hill was a symbol of American influence on European penology. It was a favourite subject in the continuous and universal process of proposing, testing, and criticising new ideas for the treatment of prisoners. The model prison of Philadelphia was the goal of a long series of pilgrimages from the old world. Alexis de Tocqueville and Gustave de Beaumont, Demetz, the founder of Mettrai, and the architect Blouet came from France; J. J. Gurney, brother of Elizabeth Fry, and William Crawford, one of the first prison inspectors, came from England; Dr. Nicolaus Julius, collecting materials for the first lectures on prison discipline delivered at Berlin, came from Germany. Not only experts came to Philadelphia. Authors of contemporary prose like Charles Dickens, Harriet Martineau, and Captain Marryat (known to generations of boys for his sea stories) wanted to see for themselves the treatment of prisoners under the new regime. E. Ducpetiaux, himself a political prisoner in an old-fashioned congregate prison, became head of the Belgian prison service and converted the prisons of his country into the model institutions of the separate system in Europe. Nearly all the great figures in the penitentiary movement of the last century had much to say in praise of the dignified, humane, and advanced methods implied in what they called "the Pennsylvania System." These views, though by no means unopposed, preceded a triumph of separate confinement in Europe which left a lasting effect on the architecture of most of the prison buildings still in use in European countries.

Prison history, as Karl Krohne, one of the leading prison administrators about the turn of the century, said, is a history of ideals and errors. It is in this spirit that we, some distance removed from the passionate struggle for *the* penitentiary system, look back not only to a literary controversy of bygone days but also to the true aspirations and the actual achievements of those who carried on the hard work of administering prisons and of dealing with the hazards and difficulties of the day-to-day prison routine in those model establishments which were so much in the forefront of contemporary discussion. The interest in unbiassed empirical evidence is characteristic of present-day criminology. In prison history, too, we want to know the facts and to learn what actually happened in the old penal establishments rather than to repeat idealistic speculations and polemical arguments of a literary movement of the past.

It is for these reasons that not only students of American social and legal history but penologists in America as well as in the Old World will be grateful to the authors of this book. Much has already been done in the study of Pennsylvania prison history. Professor Teeters has given us a history of the Pennsylvania Prison Society, which was the first of its kind, a noble forerunner of similar organisations founded in Europe under the influence of Elizabeth Fry. He also gave us an account of the once famous Walnut Street Prison in Philadelphia, *The Cradle of the Penitentiary*. The present study is a most welcome sequel to H. E. Barnes's study of Pennsylvania prison history. On the strength of new documentary evidence, it brings to life the story of the Eastern Penitentiary which was once the world's most famous prison.

Prison history is more than an account of architecture and a survey of statutory and administrative regulations. In its achievements and in its failures, penal reform is first and foremost a history of men and women, of their plans and work, their successes and their failures. In this book we meet a colourful variety of persons, all concerned, at different levels, in the bold experiment of a revolutionary new prison system. They all seem to come to life again—Dr. Benjamin Rush, with his bold conception of a new approach to the treatment of prisoners; Haviland, the English-born architect who had family connections with a personal friend and admirer of John Howard;

the wardens, chaplains, and medical officers of the new prison; the inspectors; and, among the latter, the powerful figure of Richard Vaux. There are the distinguished visitors, both from abroad and from America, including the antagonist of the Pennsylvania System, the Reverend Louis Dwight, forceful champion of the New England–Puritan case for congregate work against the Quaker concept of reflection in solitude. Last but not least we see a mixed lot of prisoners, an interesting reflection of the social structure of Pennsylvania before the War of Secession, numerous immigrants from Germany and Ireland, and southern Negroes, some of them noteworthy for their bold attempts to escape from the impregnable fortress.

Interesting as all these details are, the principal question is this: How do we, separated by more than a century from the opening of the Eastern Penitentiary and with the knowledge of all the facts brought to light by the authors, assess the merits of solitary confinement as it was devised and practised by the Pennsylvania reformers? On the whole we are inclined to stress the absurdities of the system: the miniature individual exercise yards, the masks, and the religious service to which the prisoner listened through the peep-hole of his cell door. At the same time, it would be easy to argue that even in the model prison, a complete isolation of prisoners was never accomplished. We hear constantly of successful attempts of prisoners to communicate with one another. Certain work had to be performed for the maintenance and the management of the prison which made it unavoidable that prisoners mixed with some of their fellow prisoners and with free workers. This fact in itself testifies to the impracticable, because unnatural, character of solitary confinement.

The judgement of history leads to a more balanced assessment. Solitary confinement was a necessary stage in the development from the unhealthy promiscuity of the pre-Howard gaol and, in the case of Philadelphia, the scandal of chain-gangs working in public, to a well-ordered, disciplined, and dignified prison administration, capable of serving the ends of criminal justice. Only a forceful idea could move human inertia and stir up lawgivers and administrators to a resolute reform of unbearable prison conditions. When we today complain of the lack of proper workshops in our traditional cellular prisons, we are at least capable, short of emergency measures in over-crowded prisons, of separating prisoners at night. We know today that the isolated existence of a prisoner in his cell has little if any relation to his reaction to the stimuli for good or for evil, of real life. But in the old penitentiaries, the prisoner was kept at least alive, and a first, if distorted, opportunity arose for the study of the prisoner's personality.

The root of the failure of the Pennsylvania System was the very fact that it was intended to be a system. There is a strong rationalist element in the struggle between the three rival systems of the nineteenth century, the Pennsylvania, the Auburn, and the Progressive-Stages Systems. It was still the idea that there must be a "system," which, once introduced and administered in accordance with precepts, should guarantee the desired results almost automatically. A prison regime can, at best, be only a framework which facilitates the personal efforts of those who are engaged in the day-to-day work with prisoners. This experience is strengthened by the evidence of this book. When and where the Pennsylvania reformers succeeded in making the treatment of prisoners humane and sensible, it was due to the work of devoted personalities. It was neither the cellular structure of the building, nor the prison regulations, but the provision of regular work for the cell inmates, still possible at the time of the hand loom, the practice of prison visiting, the somewhat belated appointment of a chaplain as a "moral instructor," and the beginnings of a medical service which justify, to a certain extent, contemporary panegyrics. It is a common human experience that in prison, as in many other institutions, helpful efforts alternate with weakness and failure.

In the end, therefore, this book leads to the conclusion that the merits of the Pennsylvania reformers are due not so much to the conception and consequent administration of their "system," but to the unobtrusive personal work with individual prisoners. Beyond this general statement it must be left to the reader to find what lessons for our tasks we can learn from one of the most fascinating chapters in prison history.

MAX GRÜNHUT

Oxford University
November, 1956

Foreword

On October 25, 1954, the American Congress of Correction held its eighty-fourth annual meeting in Philadelphia. By coincidence, on that same date, 125 years earlier, in 1829, prisoner No. 1 entered the Prison at Philadelphia to serve a two-year sentence for larceny. Since that date fully 56,000 convicted felons have served terms of imprisonment in this institution. On several occasions during the last quarter century it has been recommended that the formidable old bastille be demolished, but it still survives. It will probably continue with its grim responsibility for many more decades.

This book, dealing with the greater part of the history of Cherry Hill prison, has been in process over a long period of years. The writers, who have been friends for 30 years, have spent many hours together talking about the Eastern State Penitentiary's architecture, administration, prisoners, wardens, and other of its characteristics. Both writers know this prison, each in his own field of competence, with a certain intimacy. This book has grown out of this association.

Much of the material has its sources in the voluminous records that, until 1954, were stored in the towers of the prison. In that year the more significant documents were transferred to the State Record Office at Harrisburg, the capital of the Commonwealth.[1] Mr. Henry Howard Eddy, Chief Record Officer of the Commonwealth, has stated that the records of both the Eastern and Western State Penitentiaries of Pennsylvania, the latter located at Pittsburgh, are remarkably complete. This is a tribute to the many inspectors and wardens of the prisons who must have approached their guardianship as a sacred trust. The president of the Board of old Eastern for 40 years, Richard Vaux, writing in 1872, stated that one of the two volumes of the minutes of the Building Commission had been

[1] See Appendix I, pp. 235–36, for a list of these records.

"mislaid and not yet been found." The volume was in the prison as he was writing this. It was found by Mr. Shearer in 1952, carefully tucked away among the records in one of the towers.

A word of appreciation to helpful people is always a pleasure to record in a preface. Former Warden C. J. Burke showed more than a passing interest in the compilation of this book. He made it an easy task for the writers to have access to the many volumes of records. The late Frank G. Martin, who died while this book was in press and who retired only recently as warden, was especially interested in the history of the prison. He was identified with its administration for over 30 years and on many occasions expressed his opinion about the unique significance of Cherry Hill. He was highly regarded by the staff and by hundreds of the prisoners who valued his wise counseling. Joseph Brierly, major of the custodial staff, has also shown his interest.

For the pictures that embellish the book appreciation is extended to: the Metropolitan Museum of Art, New York, for the excellent painting of the architect, John Haviland; to the editors of *Pennsylvania History* for the use of a cut of the prison in its early days, which is a reproduction of an oil painting still found in the prison; and to the Pennsylvania Prison Society for the use of several cuts reproduced herewith.

To the Faculty Research Committee of Temple University for a fund to assist in pre-publication costs, a word of appreciation, and to Temple University Publications for financing the printing of the work, deep appreciation is due.

For the Introduction a word of thanks to Professor Max Grünhut of All Souls', Oxford University. Professor Grünhut has long been interested in historical penology and shares with the writers a genuine scholarly attachment to the old system of separate confinement as an experiment in penal discipline.

NEGLEY K. TEETERS
JOHN D. SHEARER

Philadelphia, Pennsylvania
November, 1956

Contents

List of Illustrations

The Prison at Philadelphia
CHERRY HILL

☰1
The Pennsylvania System of Penal Discipline

On October 25, 1829, an eighteen-year-old youth was taken from the Delaware County Pennsylvania jail, conducted to Philadelphia, and placed in the newly constructed penitentiary of the Eastern District of the Commonwealth, the Eastern State Penitentiary. Thus, Charles Williams, convicted of larceny, became prisoner No. 1 in this famous prison. Known throughout the world as the "Prison at Philadelphia," it has always been locally referred to as Cherry Hill because its site had once been a cherry orchard.

When this prison was built it was not merely a prison; rather it epitomized one of the most unique philosophies of penal treatment ever conceived by man. Its founders created this prison on the principle of separate, or solitary, confinement, by which each prisoner could be separated from all others. This was accomplished by providing an individual cell for each inmate in which he worked, slept, and ate alone. His only contacts were his keepers, the chaplain, and a few interested citizens from the city of Philadelphia, who, by law, were permitted to visit him.

The Cherry Hill prison did not become a reality without considerable opposition. Many sincere citizens of Pennsylvania, some of them well informed in the infant science of penology, were opposed to the philosophy of separate confinement. They were impressed with another concept of prison discipline, at the time in operation in the Auburn and Sing Sing prisons of New York State, known as the "congregate" or "silent" system. In this system prisoners were permitted to mingle together at work, under a rule of strict silence with scrupulous surveillance. At night they were placed in individual cells.

The Pennsylvania reformers who were responsible for the system of separate confinement were resolute men. They were unalterably opposed to any form of penal treatment by which convicted felons could have any social intercourse with one another. They contended that such communication resulted in contamination which impeded rehabilitation. They were also aware that blackmail often resulted when a man, after leaving prison, wanted to go straight.

The prison at Philadelphia and the prison at Ossining, New York, known as Sing Sing, competed for recognition throughout the nineteenth century. European commissioners as well as American legislators visited both institutions in an effort to ascertain which system was better for disciplining and reforming criminals. The two systems became known as the Pennsylvania and the Auburn.[1] Each had its advocates, among whom were the outstanding students of prison discipline of their day.

The Pennsylvania System failed to win much support in this country, but it was adopted, in principle, by practically every country in Europe and in most of South America. Pennsylvania alone persisted in clinging to its system, although there were some states that experimented with it for short periods of time.[2] Even Pennsylvania was obliged to abandon it through special legislation in 1913, when it was obvious to all that it had failed.

The Eastern State Penitentiary is no longer operating under the philosophy of separate confinement. Up to the turn of the century some 20,000 convicted felons from the eastern counties of the state spent their dreary sentences there, most of them housed in individual cells, working and eating alone, with few contacts from the outside world. From 1900 down to the present another 40,000 prisoners have served time in the old institution, but they have reaped the benefits that have gradually developed as a more liberal interpretation of the congregate Auburn System unfolded.

[1] The prison at Auburn, New York, was less accessible to visitors than was the Sing Sing prison. Thus the latter institution became the model for the system.

[2] See p. 201.

The system of separate confinement, as applied in the "model prison" at Philadelphia from 1829 to 1913, represents a fascinating story in the annals of penology. It was not abruptly conceived; rather it evolved in the thinking of many persons who were opposed to the older and more brutal forms of punishing criminals. It had its roots in European concepts of penal treatment, but it found its tangible realization as a result of the deliberations of Philadelphia reformers.

Who were these reformers? How and under what conditions did they develop this strange philosophy of separate or solitary confinement as a mode of punishing, or treating, convicted criminals? To what degree was it a punitive philosophy and to what extent was it conceived as a reformatory measure? Was the system one of "solitary" confinement, as it was many times referred to, or one of "separate" confinement, as it eventually became to be known?

An examination of the literature written and published prior to the opening of the Cherry Hill institution demonstrates the confusion existing in the minds of both the protagonists and critics of the Pennsylvania System. In view of this confusion and the fact that the system, in modified forms, survives in several European countries, it seems important to devote some space to the controversy that raged during the decade prior to the opening of the institution.

Certainly no one will quarrel with the thesis that the philosophy of the penitentiary was first implemented in Philadelphia through the efforts of the Philadelphia Society for Alleviating the Miseries of Public Prisons. This Society was founded May 8, 1787. While its story has been told often, it seems necessary to include here an abridged account of its activities since it played such a prominent part in establishing the concept of separate confinement for disciplining criminals.[3]

The reasons for the thiry-seven charter members banding

[3] The history of the organization may be found in Negley K. Teeters, *They Were in Prison* (Philadelphia, 1937). Throughout this book this organization will be referred to as the Philadelphia Prison Society, although since 1887 its official title has been the Pennsylvania Prison Society. It functions today as a professional case working agency.

together to discuss the status of penal treatment in Philadelphia at that time are to be found in the records of the
Society. Some months earlier an act had been passed by the
Pennsylvania legislature, dated September 15, 1786, which
called for all felons lodged in the jails throughout the Commonwealth to be subjected to hard labor. The object of this law
was "to correct and reform offenders, and to produce such
strong impression on the minds of others as to deter them from
committing like offenses." The new legal requirement called
for "continued hard labour, publickly and disgracefully imposed . . . in streets and cities and towns, and upon highways
of the open country and other public works." [4]

This law was the special interest of the Chief Justice, Thomas
McKean. He and others looked upon it as a reform measure
since it provided work for the inmates of the Philadelphia
Walnut Street Jail.[5] But there were many other intelligent
citizens who considered the implementation of this act as debasing and humiliating.

The bands of convicts who were taken from the jail and
publicly worked were referred to as "wheelbarrow men." They
were employed at digging ditches, excavating cellars, and
grading and filling ponds. The presence of these groups in the
narrow streets of the city, clothed in a garish and degrading
garb, was considered by some substantial citizens as unwhole-
some. Roberts Vaux, writing in 1826, made this comment:

The sport of the idle and the vicious, they often became incensed,
and naturally took violent revenge upon the aggressors. To prevent
them from retorting injuries still allowed to be inflicted, they were
incumbered with iron collars and chains, to which bomb-shells were
attached, to be dragged along while they performed degrading service, under the eye of keepers armed with swords, blunderbuses, and
other weapons of destruction.[6]

[4] For the wording of this act, see the *Pennsylvania Mercury* (September 8,
1786), p. 2.
[5] While much will appear in this chapter concerning the Walnut Street Jail,
a more complete story of this establishment will be found in Negley K. Teeters,
The Cradle of the Penitentiary (Philadelphia, 1955).
[6] *Notices of the Original and Successive Efforts to Improve the Discipline of
the Prison at Philadelphia, and to reform the Criminal code of Pennsylvania:
with a few observations on the Penitentiary System* (Philadelphia, 1826), p. 21.

It is little wonder that the Philadelphia reformers were outraged at the results of this law. These men were spiritual descendants of William Penn, the founder of the Commonwealth of Pennsylvania, who, in his Great Law of 1682, had devised a humane penal code. In this historic document he had called for fines and imprisonment in a workhouse as the only penalties for most offenses, flogging for adultery, arson, and rape, and the death penalty only for premeditated murder. The Great Law was maintained until 1718 when the Anglican code, known as the Code of the Duke of York, was forced upon the colonists. This code was extremely severe since fully thirteen capital offenses were recognized. It remained in operation until 1786 when the law of September 15 went into effect.

The man who seemed to have especially disapproved of this law was Dr. Benjamin Rush, distinguished colonial physician and signer of the Declaration of Independence. Aside from his many contributions in the fields of medicine and politics, the talented Dr. Rush made two contributions to the field of penology. He was opposed not only to public punishment as codified by the law of 1786 but to capital punishment as well. He penned two scathing denunciations of these penalties that deserve recognition even today.[7]

The first pamphlet by Dr. Rush, which dealt with public punishments, was read at a meeting of the members of the Society for Promoting Political Inquiries held at the home of Benjamin Franklin, March 9, 1787, only six months after the law Rush so disliked had been in operation. This was only two months prior to the organization of the Philadelphia Prison Society.

The gist of Dr. Rush's arguments may be summed up in his own words: "All public punishments tend to make bad men worse, and to increase crime, by their influence upon society." Another significant thought expressed by this progressive penologist was: "As such punishments are always connected with

[7] *An Inquiry into the Effects of public punishments upon criminals and upon Society,* 1787; and *Considerations on the injustice and impolicy of punishing murder by death,* 1792. These pamphlets have been republished by the Pennsylvania Prison Society in *A Plan for the Punishment of Crime* (Philadelphia, 1954).

infamy, they destroy in him [the criminal] the sense of shame
which is the strongest outpost of virtue."

Rush was undoubtedly the leading spirit behind the formation of the Philadelphia Prison Society. Although there is
nothing in his commonplace book, or diary, to indicate that
he even belonged, his name appears first on the list of charter
members in the minutes of the first meeting. Dr. James Mease,
writing in 1811, implied that Rush was the man responsible
for the Society's inception.[8]

It was in such an atmosphere that these citizens of Penn's
city, moved by no small degree of humanity as well as civic
pride, met to consider the law of the previous September. They
were aware that this law was championed by the Chief Justice
of the Commonwealth and had the appeal of economy since
it put idle prisoners to work, even if on the public thorough-
fares. The Society was also greatly disturbed by the appalling
conditions existing in the Walnut Street Jail, the gray stone
edifice standing directly across the street from the State House
(now Independence) Square. This jail was begun in 1773 [9]
but was only partially completed when war with England was
declared. During this struggle it was used to house prisoners
of war, first by the British during their occupation of Philadelphia in 1777 and later by the colonial government for captured British prisoners.

In 1786 conditions in the new jail were abominable. All types
of prisoners were thrown together promiscuously so that members of both sexes shared the same facilities. The swaggering
keeper extorted fees from the helpless prisoners and, to aug-
ment his ill-gotten income, maintained a bar within the walls.
This sounds incredible today, but such practices were traditional in jails throughout Great Britain as well as in the
colonies.

The ancient practice of garnish, by which a newcomer to the

[8] Mease, *Picture of Philadelphia* (Philadelphia, 1811), p. 161.
[9] Prior to the erection of the Walnut Street Jail all types of criminals were
housed in the Old Stone Prison, a typical colonial jail, standing at the corner
of Third and High Streets. The pillories and stocks were directly across the
street from this old structure.

jail was ordered by the other prisoners "to strip or pay," was tolerated by the keeper. A man thrust into jail was obliged to treat the group or be deprived of his clothing which was traded with the barkeeper for rum. As a result many prisoners were nearly naked. Moreover, there was no work for the prisoners. Novices in crime, young boys, old men—all were thrown together in one sordid mass of humanity. Perhaps the most serious situation in the Walnut Street Jail was that the jailer, normally responsible to the county sheriff, refused to obey his orders and was practically a law unto himself.

The members of the Philadelphia Prison Society were aware of the difficulties involved in cleaning up the jail. They also appreciated the problem involved in repealing the law of 1786. But at the October (1787) meeting they began their task. A committee was appointed "to inquire into the effects produced by the late penal law in the Criminals now at work in our streets, and also on its Influence upon Society." At the January (1788) meeting it was agreed that a Memorial should be sent to the legislature protesting public punishments. It is in this first Memorial that the Society suggested, as a substitute, "punishment by more private or even solitary labour" which would "more successfully tend to reclaim the unhappy objects." [10]

This petition, together with a later one sent to the Supreme Executive Council of the Commonwealth, dated December 15, 1788, laid bare the abuses of current penal practices. A bill of particulars describing the shameful conditions existing in the jail was presented. In the second document the Society again took its stand in favor of solitary confinement in these words:

The Committee think it their duty to declare, that from a long and steady attention to the real practical state, as well as the theory of prisons, they are unanimously of the opinion that *solitary confinement* to *hard labour*, and a total abstinence from spirituous liquors, will prove the most effectual means of reforming these unhappy creatures. (*Italics added.*) [11]

The effects of this Memorial were highly gratifying to the Society. The legislature passed the act of March 27, 1789,

[10] In Teeters, *They Were in Prison*, pp. 448–49.   [11] *Ibid.*, pp. 448–51.

which designated the Walnut Street Jail as a place for the reception of more serious offenders from all parts of the Commonwealth and enacted all of the Society's recommendations. But it was the act of April 5, 1790, stipulating solitary confinement for the more "hardened and atrocious offenders," that marks the legal origin of the Pennsylvania System of prison discipline. In fact, it marks the beginning of the penitentiary system in this country.

This act directed the commissioners of the county of Philadelphia to erect, in the yard of the jail, "a suitable number of cells six feet in width, eight feet in length, and nine feet in height," which "without unnecessary exclusion of air and light, will prevent all external communication, for the purpose of confining the more hardened and atrocious offenders, who have been sentenced to hard labour for a term of years."

The three-storied cell house subsequently constructed became known as the "penitentiary," not only for the county of Philadelphia, but for the entire state of Pennsylvania. It can truly be referred to as the first penitentiary in the world for the housing of convicted felons.

Solitude and labor were the chief features of this new plan of treatment, or at least these were implied in the law, but they were difficult to implement. Solitude formed only a part of the sentence imposed by the court, and solitary labor was difficult to furnish. Thorsten Sellin contends that the "experiment was highly overrated." For instance, after examining the dockets of the jail he found that in 1795, out of 117 convicts admitted, only four arrived with sentences requiring that they spend part of their time in solitary confinement; in 1796, of 139 admitted, only seven received such sentences from the courts.[12] All other offenders, not specifically sentenced to solitary confinement, worked in association and were still housed in "night rooms." This distinction between "hardened criminals" and all others should be remembered, since so much of the argument and discussion of separate confinement and convict labor hinged on this differentiation.

[12] "Philadelphia Prisons of the Eighteenth Century," in *Historic Philadelphia* (Philadelphia: Amer. Philosophical Soc., 1953), Vol. 43, Part I, p. 329.

It is a moot question whether the advocates of the system of solitary confinement were concerned with the reformative value of solitude or with its segregative value in protecting other prisoners from the more hardened offenders. Conceivably, solitary confinement, as understood in those early days, had a two-fold objective: first, to punish and yet reform hardened criminals, and second, to protect the casual or accidental offender from contamination by those who lived by crime and violence.

The act of April 5, 1790, which provided for solitary confinement for the more "hardened and atrocious offenders," definitely marks the turning point in American penal philosophy. A completely new concept of penal treatment was introduced into the thinking of those who were perplexed by the problems of crime.

After 1790 the Walnut Street Jail became the show place of the penal world. Visitors from Europe and from other states went through the establishment and witnessed for themselves the various innovations that were developed by the newly appointed Board of Inspectors. Improved conditions for debtors were initiated in 1791; the prison keeper was placed on a salary rather than dependent fees in 1792; and in that same year a complete revision of the penal code was inaugurated. During the period between 1794 and 1799 several other important reforms were effected by the legislature. The act of April 22, 1794, abolished the death penalty for all crimes except premeditated murder; in 1795 the jail's dungeons, which had not been used since the renovation, were legally abolished. In short, this decade represented the golden era of Pennsylvania penology.

ORIGINS OF THE CONCEPT OF SOLITARY CONFINEMENT

We know that the members of the Philadelphia Prison Society were familiar with the writings and convictions of the great English prison visitor and reformer John Howard (1726–90). This intrepid man dedicated his life to bettering the lot of the prisoner, not so much through personal contact as by boldly condemning contemporary prison practices and de-

manding reform. After surveying the prisons in practically
every European country, he wrote his great work, *State of
Prisons,* which was published in 1777. In this work Howard
strongly urged a form of prison discipline that would have
separation of prisoners as its main objective. He advocated that
small rooms or cabins should be supplied the prisoners so that
they could sleep alone. He preferred that they should be kept
separated at all times but did not advocate "absolute solitude."
He believed this separation to be conducive to reflection and
thoughtfulness, both of which were necessary in rehabilitation.

As one reads Howard's work one is impressed with his deep
convictions concerning the reformation of criminals and with
the methods he suggested for its realization. He believed that
only long term prisoners should be separated, since, in his
judgment, five years of incarceration were necessary to produce the reflection and expiation needed to induce reform.

Howard, however, did not originate the concept of solitary
confinement for prisoners. He admitted that he was impressed
with such a practice carried out on a limited scale in some of
the countries of Europe, notably Holland and Switzerland. He
was also much impressed with the Hospice of San Michele,
erected in Rome by Pope Clement XI in 1704 for the treatment
of incorrigible youths.

The Hospice resembled a monastery in its design and program. The delinquents worked in association in a central hall,
spinning and weaving. Chained by one foot to their work
benches, they were charged to strict silence while monks of
the order droned through religious tracts. Flogging was the
penalty for "past mistakes" as well as for infractions of rules.
Over the door of this prison was the inscription: "It is in-
sufficient to restrain the wicked by punishment unless you
render them virtuous by corrective discipline."

Important as Howard's contribution was, the fundamentals
of solitude or separation are monastic in origin. Perhaps the
earliest mention of solitary incarceration as a means of effecting
reform or repentance may be found in the writings of a Bene-
dictine monk of the Abbey of Saint Germain, in Paris, Jean

Mabillon (1632–1707). He suggested that penitents should be secluded in cells like those of the Carthusian monks. Employment at various types of labor could be carried on and, for exercise, they could be let out into small gardens where they could cultivate the ground. He further suggested that worship could be provided in small, separate stalls. Mabillon strongly advocated unbroken solitude except for visits from the Superior or some person designated by him to "exhort and console" the victim.[13]

In England the earliest allusions to solitude or separation for criminals as beneficial to repentance or reformation are: 1710, a Dr. Thomas Bray of the Christian Knowledge Society of London in his "Essay Toward Reformation of Newgate and Other Prisons About London" advocated separate confinement for prisoners under sentence of death, but to be restricted to them; [14] 1740, Bishop Joseph Butler, in his *Hospital Sermon*, recommended "the discipline of solitude with labour and low diet"; and in 1772, a clergyman named Samuel Denne in a letter to Sir Robert Ladbroke stated that "good effects [can be] expected from the confinement of criminals in separate apartments." Later, in 1776 Jonas Hanway (1712–86) published a special treatise on "solitude in imprisonment, with proper labour and spare diet, the most humane and effectual means of bringing malefactors to a right sense of their condition." [15]

These tracts suggest that separation of prisoners had two diverse objectives: on the one hand, a form of retributive punishment for hardened offenders; on the other, a period of time in solitude for those susceptible of reform. It is doubtlessly true that these two objectives were endorsed by many people throughout the eighteenth and nineteenth centuries, since we find the system advocated by some as punishment for "hardened and atrocious" criminals and by others as preparation for release. It is in the light of this confusion of objectives that we may understand the arguments for and against solitary

[13] Frederick H. Wines, *Punishment and Reformation* (New York, 1895), p. 143.
[14] *Ibid.*, p. 144.
[15] See Max Grünhut, *Penal Reform* (London, 1948), pp. 30–31.

confinement in Pennsylvania as well as in some other states.

We know that Howard's recommendations had considerable influence in England. In 1778, the year following the publication of Howard's work, Sir William Blackstone and Sir William Eden drafted and submitted to Parliament the Penitentiary Act, which was passed in 1779. This act permitted the establishment of penitentiary houses throughout the realm. The basic tenets of this act were to reform "by sobriety, cleanliness and medical assistance, by a regular series of labour, by solitary confinement during the intervals of work . . . to inure them [the prisoners] to habits of industry, to guard them from pernicious company. . . ."

Because of financial difficulties resulting from England's war with her American colonies and because of sheer inertia, the objectives of the Penitentiary Act could not be realized and no penitentiaries were constructed. However, there were a number of reforms initiated in several of the counties where jails were renovated or, in some cases, rebuilt.

Perhaps the most significant of these reforms was that conceived and put into operation by Sir Thomas Beevor in the small village of Wymondham in the county of Norfolk in 1785. It is especially pertinent because what was done in this small jail became known to the members of the Philadelphia Prison Society who described it in a pamphlet published in 1790.[16]

The "gaol" at Wymondham actually embodied the features endorsed by John Howard. The sexes were segregated, and each prisoner was provided an individual cell not only for sleeping purposes but also for labor throughout the day. This solitary confinement was said by Sir Thomas Beevor, the director of the establishment, to be more effective than flogging and to be that part of the punishment "from which reformation is chiefly expected."

The new system was found to be effective in every way. With hard labor provided for all on six days of every week, many prisoners earned more than double the cost of their

---

[16] *Extracts and Remarks on the Subject of Punishment and Reformation of Criminals* (Philadelphia, 1790).

maintenance. As a reformatory measure, the results were not less satisfactory. For instance, it was found that the use of irons was no longer necessary as a form of punishment, and furthermore the deterrent effects of the system were gratifying since there were fewer commitments recorded after the system began to function.

This small jail is still standing, but it is now used as the headquarters of the village police. Its historical significance is known to very few people even in England.[17]

THE BREAKDOWN OF THE WALNUT STREET JAIL

The Pennsylvania legislature of 1790 changed the Walnut Street prison from a county jail to a state penal establishment, although it was necessary for it to serve in a dual capacity until the state penitentiaries at Pittsburgh and Philadelphia began to receive state prisoners in the 1820s.

There were many problems inherent in the dual functions of the jail. The question of housing and segregating vagrants and misdemeanants from the county and convicted felons from the state taxed facilities and the ingenuity of the administration. The cost of maintaining the prisoners was shared between the counties and the state, and this situation precipitated many differences of opinion and even bad feeling. Overcrowding of the institution, due largely to the increase of population, pressed the limited space of the prison to the danger point. Riots, mass escapes, and deadly assaults on the keepers by the embittered convicts resulted from these wretched conditions. The problem of securing adequate labor for the prisoners was also serious.

There was a sharp difference of opinion as to the function of labor among those who eagerly watched the development of the penitentiary system as it evolved in the Walnut Street Jail. Some believed that labor should be a reformative device; others viewed it as a means of supporting a prison; while still others considered it only as a form of punishment.

[17] For further details regarding this jail, see Negley K. Teeters, "Gaol at Wymondham, Norfolk," *Prison World,* Vol. XII, No. 2 (1950), pp. 22 f.

While many citizens of Philadelphia willingly accepted appointments as inspectors of the new prison, some despaired that any ultimate good might develop in such a structure. They early recognized that architecturally it was inadequate to maintain a program of sound penal discipline. The cherished philosophy of separate or solitary confinement for prisoners could not develop in an institution that served both as a county jail and a state penitentiary.

Protests from the counties of the hinterland regarding the high cost of transporting convicts to and from the Philadelphia jail were frequent. It was the responsibility of the sheriffs of the various counties to see that convicted criminals were safely deposited at the penitentiary house, and travel was not only costly but a real hardship. The trip had to be taken by stagecoach. Since protests were made by passengers of the coaches, the prisoners often had to be carried up beside the driver. The convicts were shackled and watched at overnight taverns by extra guards.

After the sheriff returned home he was obliged to present, in person, to the auditor-general at the state capital his record of expenditures. Many of these were in excess of $300 per prisoner and it was not unusual to find the costs as high as $500. County commissioners and legislators alike protested that transportation costs often exceeded the total maintenance of the prisoner during his entire sentence in the jail.[18]

A discouraging note of impending failure may be read between the lines of the minutes of the Philadelphia Prison Society as early as 1799. It is doubtful that at this time the members fully realized the extent to which the deterioration would eventually go, but as years went on the futility of patching up the system or the prison was obvious. In their report for 1799 we find the statement that "the state of the prison was one of idleness, dirt and wretchedness exceeding anything of the kind which they have observed there for some years past."

For the next few years both the Society and the prison board hoped for the erection of a Bridewell or vagrants' prison to re-

[18] Teeters, *Cradle of the Penitentiary*, pp. 73–81.

lieve the situation. This was eventually realized in 1817 in the Arch Street Prison, which stood on the ground now known in Philadelphia as Reyburn Plaza directly across from City Hall. This prison only afforded temporary relief.

In the interim the Society had time to reflect on its philosophy of penal discipline. While little appears in the minutes of their meetings that would indicate all the areas of their thinking, it is clear that the members at least held one opinion strongly: that no relief could be expected until suitable state penitentiaries were constructed wherein a strict separation of convicts could be developed.

THE EMERGENCE OF THE PENITENTIARY SYSTEM

As early as 1801, in a Memorial sent to the legislature, the members of the Society expressed their hope that a penal institution might be created in which the principle of solitary confinement with labor could be given a fair trial. They asked the legislature "to devise such means as may appear . . . most adequate to separate the Convicts from all other descriptions of prisoners in order that a full opportunity of trying the effects of Solitude and Labour may be afforded."

During those years New York State had also been wrestling with the problem of penal discipline. The reformers of that state, particularly those living in New York city, were disturbed by the gross evils of association of all types of criminals in the Newgate Jail situated in Greenwich Village. They had seen the remarkable system in operation in the Walnut Street Jail during its successful period (1790–99) and were much impressed. They too were opposed to the contamination of one prisoner by another and were strong advocates of some form of separation.

In time, the legislature of New York appropriated funds for the establishment of a penitentiary centrally located at Auburn. The evils of the congregate system of confinement had not been appreciated in New York State when construction at Auburn began, so that double cells and large cells or apartments, each capable of housing ten or more inmates, were provided. By 1819 sentiment for the Philadelphia plan of separate, or solitary, confinement influenced the New York legislature to direct the inspectors of the Auburn prison to confine certain classes of prisoners to separate cells and to construct a second wing for the solitary confinement of each prisoner.

This prison, and the later Sing Sing prison, were totally unsuited for the development of the philosophy of separate confinement as conceived by the Philadelphia reformers. The Auburn prison finally consisted of five-tiered cell blocks with extremely narrow cells built purposely for separation at night only. Little sunlight or fresh air ever entered the cells. The concept of the builders and administrators, William Brittin, Elam Lynds, and John Cray, was to work the convicts in association, separating them at night only. It was believed that contamination could be prevented through a strict system of silence. The slightest breach of this system resulted in a strict flogging for the culprit.

This Auburn System was to become the rival of the one conceived by the Philadelphia Prison Society and its friends. It had the advantage of being first in the field, preceding the Pennsylvania System by a few years. But its greatest appeal was economic. By the introduction of contract labor by the prisoners working in association, it was believed the prison could pay for itself. In its early days Auburn failed to achieve this objective, but after the administration gained the confidence of the contractors who were permitted to push the convicts to greater production, it developed into a relatively self-sufficient institution.[19]

By 1818 the Pennsylvania legislature was prepared to meet the requests of the Philadelphia reformers for a state penal institution. In an act dated March 3 of that year, the lawmakers appropriated $60,000 for the construction of a penitentiary at Pittsburgh on the principle of solitary confinement. No mention was made of labor for the prisoners and we know that the establishment was built with no such provision. This same act au-

[19] See Ralph S. Herre, "The History of Auburn Prison from the Beginning to about 1867" (unpublished Ph.D. dissertation, Pennsylvania State University, 1950).

thorized but did not command the sale of the Walnut Street Jail, the removal of prisoners to the Arch Street Prison, and the erection of a new penitentiary in Philadelphia with the proceeds of the Walnut Street site.

Later, on March 20, 1821, influenced again by a Memorial from the Society, dated January 22, the legislature appropriated $100,000 for the erection of a prison at Philadelphia. This act stated that the Philadelphia institution should "be constructed on the plan of the Penitentiary at Pittsburgh [and that] the principle of solitary confinement of the prisoners be preserved and maintained." Again there was no provision for labor. The Western Penitentiary at Pittsburgh was ready for occupancy in July, 1826; the one at Philadelphia in October, 1829.

At this late date we have no way of knowing which specific members of the Philadelphia Prison Society persisted in urging a system of "separate confinement with labour." From the days of the first Memorial sent by the Society to the legislature, January 29, 1788, to the last one dealing with the penitentiary, December 27, 1827, a period of 40 years had elapsed.[20] Many of the original members of the Society were dead by 1827. Much of the opposition to the provision of labor came from persons who were members of the Society as well as members of the Board of Inspectors of the Walnut Street Jail. Thomas Bradford, for example, was one of these.

In 1821 the Board of Inspectors of the jail petitioned the legislature to hasten the erection of the Philadelphia prison (Cherry Hill) and to inaugurate the system of strict solitary confinement:

The effects of a pure solitary system have not yet been exhibited in Pennsylvania. Enough has been seen, however, to justify the belief that its effects will be to reform entirely or to deter from the commission of a second offense. . . . To be shut up in a cell for days, weeks, months and years, alone, to be deprived of converse with a fellow being, to have no friendly voice to minister consolation, no friendly bosom on which to lean or into which to pour our sorrows and complaints, but on the contrary, to count the tedious hours as

[20] See Appendix II, p. 237, for partial wording of these Memorials.

they pass, a prey to the corrodings of conscience and the pangs of guilt, is almost to become the victim of despair.[21]

The Board continued by recommending "such an entire seclusion of convicts from society and from one another, as that during the period of confinement no one shall see or hear, or be seen or heard by any human being, except the jailer, the inspectors, or such other persons as, for highly urgent reasons, may be permitted to enter the walls of the prison."

The inspectors went further. They called for solitary confinement without labor in the county jails until the state's penitentiaries could be built. They suggested that a sentence of one year without labor would be equivalent to three years in solitary confinement with labor. Their reasoning was that "employment diminishes in a very great degree the tediousness of confinement and thus mitigates the punishment, [thus] it may be a question whether labour ought not to be abandoned altogether, except as an *indulgence* to penitent convicts and as a relaxation from the much more painful task of being compelled to be idle." This document was signed by Peter Miercken, president, and Thomas Bradford, secretary.

The period between 1821 and the opening of the penitentiary at Philadelphia is punctuated by much debate and by several significant reports. The question most under discussion dealt with the provision of labor for the prisoners and, if furnished, under what conditions. Men of great learning, judgment, and experience entered the controversy. European as well as American scholars participated.

So great was the division of public opinion and so earnestly did the advocates of conflicting theories urge their favorite views, that in March, 1826, a board of commissioners was appointed by the legislature to revise the penal code and to carry out this revision according to the system of imprisonment "at hard labour and solitary confinement." [22]

---

[21] From the minutes of the Board of Inspectors of the Walnut Street Jail, January 15, 1821; found also in *Report of the Penitentiary System,* published by the Pennsylvania Senate, January, 1821; republished 1913.

[22] Resolution of the Assembly of 1825–26, *Report of the Commission on the Penal Code* (Harrisburg, Pennsylvania, 1828), p. 413.

This commission was composed of three distinguished jurists, Charles Shaler, Edward King, and T. J. Wharton. While engaged in their labors they came under the spell of the Reverend Louis Dwight, secretary of the Boston Prison Discipline Society, who was perhaps the most zealous and influential supporter of the Auburn System of penal discipline. As a result of his advocacy of the Auburn "silent" but congregate system of labor and the favorable impression of it derived from personal visits to Auburn and Sing Sing prisons, these commissioners recommended in a two-hundred-page report that the new penitentiaries at Pittsburgh and Philadelphia be altered in their construction so that they might be administered along the lines of the Auburn System.

While this influential commission was working on its report, the legislature passed a resolution (April 14, 1827) requesting the Building Commissioners, who had earlier been appointed to superintend the construction of the Eastern Penitentiary, to state their views on the modifications of the penal code and to submit a plan of organization and discipline for the penitentiary. The first commission filed its report (hereinafter referred to as the Wharton-King) in December, 1827. The report of the Building Commission was filed January 4, 1828.

Both documents were alarming, so far as some members of the Philadelphia Prison Society were concerned. The Wharton-King report advocated the Auburn System. The second recommended with great force the principle of solitary confinement without labor, and the words were unequivocal: "The solitary confinement we recommend, *is absolute, without any employment,* except the study of the Scriptures, connected with affectionate religious instruction. We say *without* any employment, because less time will be requisite to produce a beneficial result on the mind of the prisoner unemployed than when employed.

At that date, January, 1828, the Eastern Penitentiary was well under construction with three cell blocks practically completed and designed for the principle of solitary confinement, as decreed by the act of March 20, 1821.

We know from later testimony of Thomas Bradford, a member of the Building Commission, that there were sharp differences of opinion among the members. He stated before an investigating committee in 1834 that "Wood [later warden at Cherry Hill] was in favor of separate confinement with labour and religious instruction; [Roberts] Vaux, [John] Bacon and Bradford, with other members of the Commission, were against labour." [23] It would seem, therefore, that it was Samuel R. Wood who influenced the legislature in favor of providing labor at Cherry Hill.

This is further substantiated by the action of the Philadelphia Prison Society on hearing that the Building Commission was against the provision of labor and that the Wharton-King report favored the Auburn plan. The Society first sent a committee composed of Vaux, Bradford, and Wood to Auburn to ascertain the merits of its system. To offset the arguments of the Building Commissioners, Mr. Wood was sent to Harrisburg to labor with the chairman of the judiciary committee of the legislature, Mr. Garrick Mallory. We have no documents to show the persuasiveness of Mr. Wood, but apparently his arguments won over those who were empowered to make the final decision.

The Wharton-King report, a thorough and scholarly document, set forth many arguments against the separate system. After investigating all angles of the matter of prison discipline, its authors felt obliged to conclude: "We entered upon the performance of our duty with a belief and wish that the system of solitary confinement proposed to be pursued in the new prisons at Pittsburgh and Philadelphia, would be found, upon examination and experience, to be sound in theory, valuable as respects convicts, and not inconveniently burdensome to the finances of the state." But they stated:

Our belief, in the value of solitary confinement, as a punishment for crime, has gradually given way before the irresistible conviction, which a thorough examination of the subject has forced upon us; and however the conclusion may be at variance with the sentiments

[23] Vaux was willing to introduce labor in order to save the system.

of a highly respectable portion of our fellow citizens, as well as with our own pre-conceived impressions, we should be unfaithful to our trust, and to our consciences, if we hesitated, for a moment, to declare our deliberate opinion.[24]

To offset the influence of this report, the president of the Building Commission Thomas Sparks wrote in his annual report, dated February 6, 1829, "Notwithstanding all that has been written and urged against the adoption of the great principle of separate or solitary confinement of criminals, adopted in Pennsylvania almost a half century ago, the Board remains undivided as opinion and undiminished in their confidence of its ultimate and successful operation."

The legislature brought the controversy to a close by passing the act of April 23, 1829, which definitely specified "separate or solitary confinement at labour."

CONFUSION IN PENAL PHILOSOPHY
AMONG THE EARLY REFORMERS

It is not surprising that the early reformers were confused concerning the treatment of criminals. Penal philosophy during the first two decades of the nineteenth century reflects both punishment for confirmed criminals and reformative treatment for the less serious offenders. Yet all who wrote on the subject were deeply disturbed by the conditions that contaminated the prisoners as they strolled about in the congregate prisons and jails of that day. Consistency would have suggested the separation of all prisoners immediately following arrest, but few writers of that day ever advocated such a complete and thoroughgoing policy.

It must be remembered that these were momentous days in penal reform. All who understood the rudiments of penology (the word was not even invented at the time) [25] were con-

---

[24] For an analysis of the two reports bearing on this knotty problem, see *Journal of Prison Discipline and Philanthropy*, Vol. I, No. 1 (1845), pp. 1–15. This is the official publication of the Philadelphia Prison Society and is now known as the *Prison Journal;* publication has been continuous since 1845.

[25] Dr. Francis Lieber is given credit for coining the word penology. Charles R. Henderson, ed. of *Correction and Prevention* (New York, 1910), I, 146,

vinced that the barbarisms of an earlier day were gone, it was hoped, forever. They were casting about for a system—one that would prove a worthy substitute for anything that had previously been practiced. Imprisonment seemed to be the answer, but the details that would be instrumental in effecting both punishment and reformation were quite nebulous. They were all feeling their way, groping for answers.

We have mentioned thus far only the views of some of the reformers of Pennsylvania and of New York State. But others wrote on the perplexing subject. One of the famous exponents of the concept of solitary confinement was Edward Livingston (1764–1836), great statesman and jurist of New York and, later, of Louisiana. Sir Henry Maine, noted British historical jurist, called Livingston "the first legal genius of modern times." He is best known to penology for his *System of Penal Law*, or Livingston's Code, which was drawn up for his adopted state of Louisiana but which was rejected because of its mild and remedial character. Yet Livingston penned the following words, which he wished inscribed over every murderer's cell door:

In this cell is confined, to pass his life in solitude and sorrow, A.B., convicted of the murder of C.D.; his food is bread of the coarsest kind, his drink is water, mingled with his tears; he is dead to the world; his cell is his grave; his existence is prolonged, that he may remember his crime and repent it, and that the continuance of his punishment may deter others from the indulgence of hatred, avarice, sensuality, and the passions which led to the crime he has committed. When the Almighty, in his due time, shall exercise toward him that dispensation which he himself arrogantly and wickedly usurped toward another, his body is to be dissected, and his soul will abide that judgment which Divine Justice shall decree.[26]

---

states, "In 1834 Lieber mentions in his diary, among the subjects continually in his head, that of 'penology.' He coined the word from his brain; later he defined it in a letter to de Tocqueville, as 'that branch of criminal science which occupies itself . . . with the punishment of the criminal, not with the definition of crime, the subject of accountability and the proving of the crime, which belongs to criminal law and the penal process.'"

[26] Wines, *Punishment and Reformation*, p. 145 n.

Despite these terrible words, Livingston was opposed to the death penalty. He believed wholeheartedly in solitary confinement without brutality or flogging. He advocated the teaching of trades in prisons and suggested that a day-by-day record be kept of each prisoner. He even advocated remuneration for work performed by convicts. He seemed to have had great faith in the reformation of criminals. Thomas Jefferson wrote Livingston that his code would place his name among the sages of antiquity.

Livingston seems to have been the only person writing at the time who grasped the significance of separate confinement, since, in a letter he wrote during the year 1828, he warned,

But above all do not force those whom you are obliged to imprison before trial, be they innocent or guilty, into that contaminating society from which, after they are found guilty, you are so anxious to keep them. Remember, that in Philadelphia, as well as in New York, more than two thousand five hundred are annually committed; of whom not one-fourth are found to be guilty; and that thus you have introduced every year 1,800 persons, presumed to be innocent, into a school where every vice and every crime is taught by the ablest masters; and we shut our eyes to this enormous evil, and inconsistently go on preaching the necessity of seclusion and labour, and industry after conviction, as if penitentiaries are the only places in which the contamination of evil society were to be dreaded.

He continued by admonishing Pennsylvania to take the lead in establishing a *complete* system of separating all following arrest "instead of patchwork legislation, that can never be effectual." [27]

One of the founders and first warden of the Maine state prison at Thomaston was Dr. Daniel Rose a physician. About 1822, with apparently no knowledge of penology, he became obsessed with ideas of the reformation and treatment of criminals. Where he got his concepts of penal "reform" is not known, but they were embraced in these words:

[27] Quoted by Richard Vaux, *Brief Sketch of the Origin and History of the State Penitentiary for the Eastern District of Pennsylvania at Philadelphia* (Philadelphia, 1872), p. 26.

State prisons should be so constructed that even their aspect might be terrific, and appear like what they should be, dark and comfortless abodes of guilt and wretchedness. No mode or degree of punishment which ever has been made or which ever can be adopted is in its nature so well adapted to purposes of preventing crime and re- forming a criminal, as close confinement in a silent or solitary cell, in which, cut off from all hope of relief during the term for which he shall have been sentenced, the convict shall be furnished with a hammock on which he may sleep, a block of wood on which he may sit, and with such coarse, though wholesome food as may be best suited to a person in a situation designed for grief and penitence; and shall be favored with so much light from the firmament, as may enable him to read the New Testament, which shall be given him as his sole companion and guide to a better life. There his vices and crimes shall become personified, and appear to his frightened imagi- nation as the co-tenants of his dark and dismal cell. They will sur- round him as so many hideous spectres, and overwhelm him with horror and remorse.[28]

The Maine prison was unique in its construction. It was the only prison in this country, if not in the entire world, in which the "cells" were holes in the ground. The only entrance was an aperture two feet square in the top so that a ladder could be lowered for the prisoner to descend to his subterranean abode. But solitary confinement was the lot of only those convicted and thus sentenced by the court. Others were sentenced to "hard labour" only. It is obvious then that in Maine solitary confinement was considered as a punishment, not as a reforma- tive device.

Many other outstanding citizens throughout the country wrote on various concepts of prison discipline during the period between the opening of the Auburn and Sing Sing prisons in New York State and the two penitentiaries in Pennsylvania. But it is the writings that were published prior to 1829 that have most meaning so far as the opening of the prison at Philadelphia is concerned. The Wharton-King report of 1827, mentioned earlier, quoted William Roscoe, noted English

[28] From the minority *Report of the Commissioners on the Removal of the Maine State Prison* (Augusta, 1891).

scholar and penal reformer of Liverpool. Roscoe (1753–1831) was an ardent advocate of the abolition of the slave trade and author of several historical works, the most important of which are *The Life of Lorenzo Di Medici* and the *History and the Life and Pontificate of Leo X.* Washington Irving included a short account of Roscoe in his *Sketch Book.* This English reformer looked upon the separate system as "destined to contain the epitome and concentration of human misery, of which the Bastille of France, and the Inquisition of Spain, were only prototypes and humble models." He further condemned the system as "the most inhuman, and unnatural, that a tyrant ever invented." [29]

Roscoe excoriated both the Pennsylvania and Auburn Systems of prison discipline. It was his contention that both were cruel in their concepts of discipline. He maintained that the early Philadelphia reformers quite correctly visualized the reformation of criminals in the renovated Walnut Street Jail (1790–99). He endorsed the practice of placing only confirmed criminals in solitary confinement until they would improve and stated that all other prisoners should be worked at associative labor during the day under the "vigilance of their keepers" and housed in individual cells at night.

Roscoe's pamphlet reflects his state of confusion as he pondered the various plans submitted by far-off Philadelphians. For instance, he took it for granted that the convicts were not to be supplied with labor in their cells. He was justified in this interpretation since he quoted from the report of the inspectors of the Walnut Street Jail which we mentioned earlier. He referred to General Lafayette's experience in the French Bastille where that glamorous revolutionist was kept in complete solitary confinement for a period of three years. Roscoe quoted from a friend's letter which expressed Lafayette's views concerning the Pennsylvania System. The great soldier compared the system to the regimen of the Bastille in these words:

[29] William Roscoe, *A Brief Statement of the Causes which have Led to the Abandonment of the Celebrated System of Penitentiary Discipline in Some of the United States of America* (London, 1827).

I am told that they [the prisoners] are to be without the least employment, and are not to be allowed the use of books. . . . Another feature chilled me [when] I saw the turrets which flank the corners of the wall, from which the sentries are to overlook the establishment [Cherry Hill]. I have been subjected to all of this; and of all the sufferings of my life, none have exceeded—none have equalled that single oppression of being, for three whole years . . . exposed to the view of two eyes, watching my every motion, taking from my very thoughts every idea of privacy.

Lafayette's view of prison discipline was to use solitary cells at night only and to provide the prisoners labor during the day in "common rooms small enough to enable the managers to keep distinctions among the men to be reclaimed, according to the state of their morals and behavior."

Roscoe had also engaged in an extensive correspondence with the prominent Philadelphia physician Dr. James Mease. In his essay he credited Dr. Mease as being the person "who first proposed this mode of punishment" and who called for the subjection of "criminals to solitary confinement, both by day and by night, without permitting them to labour." [30] It is true that Dr. Mease was an advocate of strict solitude for criminals. In his work *On the Penitentiary and Penal Code of Pennsylvania*, published in 1828, he wrote, "To give the reforming system a fair trial, the seclusion of the prisoners ought to be complete, day and night, during the whole period of confinement; nor ought the smallest intercourse to take place with any other individuals than their keepers during the week, and the preacher of the Gospel on Sunday." However, it was inaccurate for Roscoe to give Dr. Mease the credit for being the first to propose this "mode of punishment."

Roberts Vaux, one of the chief spokesmen of the Philadelphia Prison Society and later one of the Commissioners appointed by the governor to erect the Eastern State Penitentiary, answered William Roscoe. He pointed out that the cells or rooms of the new institution were commodious, "judiciously lighted from the roof, ingeniously provided [with] a continual supply

[30] Mease, *Picture of Philadelphia*, p. 27.

of excellent water," and to be "inspected without a military guard usually, though not necessarily employed in establishments of this kind in most of the States." Vaux attempted to allay Roscoe's fear "that a great number of individuals will be put to death by the superinduction of diseases" or that the treatment would "cause the mind to rush back upon itself." He insisted that rather than punish a criminal by unusual or barbaric devices, the system would punish through his separation from all evil associations.[31] He further insisted that this same separation would tend to reform even the most hardened. Without committing himself to the introduction of labor or even to permitting visitors from the outside, Vaux hinted at a variety of plans by which it was hoped reformation might result. He stated, "Some prisoners may labour—some may be kept without labour—some may have the privilege of books— others may be deprived of them—some may experience total seclusion—others may enjoy such intercourse as shall comport with an entire separation of prisoners." Referring to disciplinary measures that might be adopted he continued, "Denying the refractory individual the benefit of his yard, by taking from him his books or labour, and lastly, in extreme cases, by diminishing his diet to the lowest rate. By the last mean, the most fierce, hardened, and desperate offender can be subdued."

It is these statements by Roberts Vaux that best described the philosophy of penal discipline most desired by the majority of the members of the Philadelphia Prison Society. Such a philosophy represented the ideal since it supplied a variety of disciplinary measures for varying types of offenders. Only partially was this flexible philosophy adopted and carried out when the system was put into effect at the Philadelphia institution in 1829.

Others who wrote during these years defending the proposed system were John Sergeant, eminent jurist of Philadelphia, who recommended that the system of solitary confinement at least be given a fair trial since in that way only could

---

[31] Vaux, *Letter on the Penitentiary System of Pennsylvania addressed to William Roscoe* (Philadelphia, 1827).

some of the dire predictions expressed by the critics be tested; [32] and George Washington Smith, "cultivated student and investigator," who wrote his *Defense of the System of Solitary Confinement of Prisoners* in 1829.

A few years later, after the Cherry Hill prison was functioning, the friends of the separate system found an influential champion in the person of Dr. Francis Lieber, prominent political economist and German refugee. As he did not arrive from his native Prussia until 1827, his partisan interest in separate confinement did not flourish until the prison was opened. He wrote vigorously on the merits of "uninterrupted solitary confinement at labour" and voiced his opinions in several letters written to friends of the Pennsylvania System during the 1830s. [33]

LAY VISITING AS A COMPROMISE TO SOLITARY CONFINEMENT

The act of April 23, 1829, resolved the conflict concerning the disciplining of convicted felons in Pennsylvania. This act provided that persons convicted by "the proper court [should] suffer punishment by separate or solitary confinement at labour." It should be noted that even the legislature could not or would not distinguish between "solitary" and "separate" confinement.

Another provision of this act had far-reaching effects. This was the section which authorized the visiting of prisoners in their cells by "the Governor, Speaker and members of the

[32] John Sergeant and Colonel Samuel Miller, *Observations and Reflections on the Design and Effects of Punishment, in letters addressed to Roberts Vaux* (Philadelphia, 1828).

[33] See *A Popular Essay on Subjects of Penal Law and on Uninterrupted Solitary Confinement at Labour* (Philadelphia, 1838). See also a letter written by Lieber to the Honorable Charles Penrose which is perhaps the best defense of the Pennsylvania System, found in *McElwee's Report*, pp. 60–68. This report is known as *A Concise History of the Eastern Penitentiary of Pennsylvania, together with a Detailed Statement of the Proceedings of the Committee Appointed by the Legislature, December 6, 1834* (Philadelphia, 1835). It was privately printed by Thomas B. McElwee of Bedford County, Pennsylvania, who was one of the members of a Joint Legislative Committee to investigate the administration of the Philadelphia prison. The story of this investigation will be told in a later chapter. Throughout this book this report will be referred to as *McElwee's Report*.

Senate, the Speaker and members of the House of Representa-
tives, the Secretary of the Commonwealth, the Judges of the
Supreme Court, the Attorney-General and his deputies, the
President and Associate Judges of all the Courts of the State,
the Mayor and Recorder of the cities of Philadelphia, Lancaster
and Pittsburg, Commissioners and Sheriffs of the several counties, and the Acting Committee of the Philadelphia Society for
Alleviating the Miseries of Public Prisons."

While the appointment of these public officials as visitors
may have been a mere formality, the selection of the members
of the Philadelphia Prison Society was of particular significance.
It was this provision that gave the Pennsylvania System its
strength. Having lay visitors enter the cells of the prisoners as
friendly counselors gave the system its uniqueness.

It is not clear just how this interesting provision was determined by the framers of the act. There is nothing in the Minute
Books of the Philadelphia Prison Society that would suggest
a hope that its members would be appointed as legal visitors.
Nothing appears in the writings of the advocates of the separate
system that visitors from the outside would strengthen the
proposed system.

The immediate reaction of the members of the Society to
their selection as official visitors was to state in their minutes
of May 2, 1829, that they were "deeply sensible of the high
trust and confidence reposed in them by the legislature; and
whereas, it is due the legislature and to the Public that the said
Quest should be discharged with zeal and fidelity . . . resolved, that it shall be the duty of the Visiting Committee . . .
to visit the Penitentiary . . . at least once in each week." The
Society called on the Visiting Committee to keep a book in
which pertinent information regarding each prisoner visited
should be recorded.[34]

Forty years were to elapse—from 1790 to 1829—before the
Pennsylvania System of prison discipline was to become a
reality. During that painful period of discussion, engaged in

[34] See pp. 161–69 for an account of the activities of the lay visitors from the
Society.

by men of ability, great integrity, and unselfish civic consciousness, the cardinal principles were hammered out. These pioneers knew generally what they wanted but they became
confused over specifics. Some of them, such as Judges Shaler,
Wharton, and King, were forced by conviction to abandon
their original concepts in favor of the rival system developed
at Auburn and Sing Sing prisons. Still others, such as Thomas
Bradford and Dr. James Mease, held out without compromise
for solitary confinement without labor.

While most of the original members of the Philadelphia
Prison Society who worked to secure the system in 1790 were
dead in 1829, their true descendants, Roberts Vaux and Samuel
R. Wood, held firm in their insistence on separate confinement
with labor in the prisoners' cells. When in 1829 the prison gate
at Cherry Hill opened to its first prisoners, it was these salient
features plus the provision of friendly visiting by citizens from
the free community that pointed up the distinctiveness of the
Pennsylvania System of prison discipline.

☰2
The Building of Cherry Hill

ORGANIZATION OF THE BUILDING COMMISSION

THE members of the Building Commission appointed in 1821 by Governor Joseph Hiester to supervise the erection of the Philadelphia prison realized the significance of their task. Consequently, they labored long and faithfully to bring into being a structure which would measure up to the aspirations of the pioneer reformers.

The only stipulation laid down by the legislative act of March 20, 1821, calling for the erection of the penitentiary for the Eastern District of the Commonwealth, was that the prison be designed on the principle of solitary confinement with a capacity of 250 cells, to be constructed similar to the plan of the penitentiary at Pittsburgh, "subject to such alterations and improvements as the Commissioners, or a majority of them, with the approval of the Governor, approves and directs." The Commissioners were to receive no compensation for their labors.[1]

The members appointed to the Building Commission were as follows: Samuel R. Wood, manufacturer (later to be first warden of the prison); Peter Miercken, sugar refiner; George N. Baker, lumber merchant; Thomas Bradford, Jun., lawyer; John Bacon, city treasurer; Caleb Carmalt, conveyancer; Thomas Sparks, shot manufacturer; James Thackera, engraver, Academy of Fine Arts, Philadelphia; and Daniel R. Miller, hardware merchant. Two men appointed by the governor refused to serve. These were Thomas Wistar and Dr. Samuel Powell Griffitts.

Of the above, Bacon, Bradford, Carmalt, and Wood were

[1] The material in this chapter is taken from the Minute Books or Journal of the Building Commission. These volumes, together with most of the records of the prison, may be found in the State Records Office at Harrisburg, Pennsylvania.

members of the Philadelphia Prison Society for a long time. Bacon, Bradford, Miercken, Miller, Sparks, and Wood had served at one time or another as members of the Board of Inspectors of the Walnut Street Jail and brought to their task a knowledge of prison management.

The vacancies existing on the Commission after Thomas Wistar's and Dr. Griffitts's refusal to serve were not filled for some time after deliberations began. On December 12, 1821, fully eight months after the initial meeting, Roberts Vaux and Coleman Sellers, a wire manufacturer, were appointed to fill the vacancies. The following July, Peter Miercken, who had been elected president by the members, died, and his place was filled by William Davidson, a broker. Thomas Sparks was then elected president. On April 6, 1824, George N. Baker resigned and the governor appointed Michael Baker, lumber merchant, in his place.

The task which these men faced was a difficult one. For 12 years from April 6, 1821, to December 27, 1833, they met over 400 times and acted on countless ramifications of the building program. Their fidelity, civic interest, and dogged perseverance in the face of much discouragement and bitter internal strife are probably unparalleled in the field of penology. It took 14 years to build the prison at Philadelphia.

Most of the Board's meetings were held in the Walnut Street Jail, Sixth and Walnut Streets. There, in the inspectors' meeting room, they argued in accord with the time-honored procedure of parliamentary debate; they met with architects, the master builder, and contractors; and they made decisions of great moment in penology.

The first two matters disposed of were the selection of a suitable site and a capable architect. In selecting a site for the new prison, the Commission advertised in the local papers. The legislative stipulation was made that the ground could not exceed twelve acres or be less than eight and that it should not be further than "two and a half miles from the state house." [2]

[2] For a list of the possible sites see Appendix III, pp. 239–41.

At the second meeting of the Commission, on May 1, it was decided to "invite architects to furnish a plan of the prison comprising 250 solitary cells." A premium of one hundred dollars was authorized for the plan "to be adopted by the Commission, subject to the approval of the Governor." At the meeting held July 10, the members busied themselves with the reading of the documents accompanying the plans submitted. These plans were those of three Philadelphia architects, William Strickland, John Haviland, and Samuel Webb (listed in the city directory of 1820 as a carpenter), and one New York architect, Charles Loos, Jr. The plans of Webb and Loos were apparently given little consideration since no further reference is made to them.

At the outset, Strickland's plan met with favorable response from all members of the Commission. There is evidence, however, that one member, John Bacon, showed some partiality from the beginning to Haviland's plan. Strickland (1788–1854) had been appointed in 1818 by the Board of Inspectors of the Walnut Street Jail to build the Pittsburgh penitentiary.[3] He was an eminent architect and had already made a reputation in the revival of the classical Greek architecture. Today he is remembered best for designing the Second Bank of the United States, the United States Naval Home, the old Exchange Building, all in Philadelphia, and the Tennessee State Capitol in Nashville. He was also noted for his engineering skill in the building of early canals.[4]

When the Building Commission was appointed, the Pittsburgh prison was already under construction.[5] As it was being

[3] It has long been assumed that Haviland submitted a plan for the Pittsburgh prison, but there is no evidence to substantiate this. It is true, however, that, in 1819, both architects did compete for a commission to build a proposed prison for Philadelphia County, as provided by the act of March 3, 1818. This prison did not materialize. For details see Negley K. Teeters, *The Cradle of the Penitentiary* (Philadelphia, 1955), pp. 109–12.

[4] Agnes A. Gilchrist, *William Strickland, Architect and Engineer* (Philadelphia, 1950).

[5] Strickland's design was based on the bizarre plan of Jeremy Bentham, noted British political economist, known as the *Panopticon*, or "inspection house." This plan was in the form of a huge lantern, circular in shape. It was repudiated in England but, with modifications, adopted by Strickland's mentor, Benjamin Latrobe, in the penitentiary at Richmond, Virginia, in 1800. This may have

erected on the principle of solitary confinement without labor, its philosophy did not come under attack until 1829 when the law was passed calling for "solitary confinement with labour" in both prisons. By then it was universally agreed that the arrangement and size of the cells were not adaptable for labor. In 1833, therefore, the legislature ordered the interior of the Pittsburgh institution to be rebuilt. Because of the controversy between the Strickland and Haviland factions in the erection of the Eastern Penitentiary, it was ironic that Haviland was called upon to consummate the renovation.[6]

It was eventually decided that the outer wall of the Philadelphia prison should be rectangular instead of octagonal like Pittsburgh's, and that the ranges of cells should be on the radial design rather than, as at Pittsburgh, built around the outer wall. By the time these major decisions were made, there was a division in the Commission. The minority composed of Bacon, Carmalt, Sparks, and Wood showed signs of favoring the Haviland plan. But with the appointments of Coleman Sellers and Roberts Vaux in December, 1821, to fill the original vacancies, the Haviland group became the majority. The sudden shift from a majority position to that of a minority embittered the champions of Strickland. From that time on, this group, consisting of Baker, Bradford, Miercken, Miller, and Thackera, used every parliamentary device to checkmate the majority on the important problems of construction.

Strickland was much better known in the community than was Haviland, and because of his experience in building the Pittsburgh prison, his position as a competitor was more favorable than that of the new comer, Haviland.[7] From the minutes of the Commission we know that much bitterness and rancor

---

prompted Strickland to use the plan for the Western Penitentiary at Pittsburgh. Many years later, a more faithful *Panopticon* was utilized in the Stateville, Illinois, penitentiary.

[6] For a discussion of the difficulties concerning the Western Penitentiary, see Le Roy De Puy, "The Triumph of the 'Pennsylvania System' at the State's Penitentiaries," *Pennsylvania History*, XXI (1954), 7 f.

[7] For a discussion of Haviland's importance in the field of prison architecture as well as a short biographical sketch, see pp. 57–62.

arose and continued until the prison was eventually finished.[8]

Apparently none of the decisions of the Building Commission was influenced in the least by improper political pressure. It is known that Roberts Vaux (a member of the majority group) was a kinsman of Governor Hiester, and from the minutes we know that Vaux, among others, went to Harrisburg, from time to time, as a member of a committee to obtain the approval of the governor on important architectural matters. But there seems not the least suspicion that improper politics had any influence on decisions dealing with architectural design or in the placing of contracts.

Charges of fraud and waste were made against the men who were responsible for building the prison. However, aside from one mysterious irregularity by which the first president of the Commission, Peter Miercken, "lost" $1,000 of the state's appropriations (discussed below), there is no evidence that fraud played any part in the erection of the prison. So far as extravagance is concerned, it is fairly obvious that sums of considerable size were spent unwisely and that injudicious contracts were let. How much of this was due to the zeal and ambition of the architect who wanted to erect a monument to his talent and how much can be laid at the door of inexperience of the members of the Commission would be hard to determine. There were many items of expenditure which, at this distance, demonstrate extravagance. Today as one examines the records of construction, it is easy to concur with those who, at the time, charged the Commission of waste and unwise spending.

THE THOUSAND-DOLLAR LOSS

The only tangible evidence that there may have been fraud connected with the establishment of the new prison may be deduced from the minutes of the Building Commission itself.

[8] There is no evidence that the two architects entered into this bitter strife personally. They must have respected each other and must have worked in community activities quite closely. For example, when General Lafayette visited Philadelphia in 1824, he was entertained in the Chestnut Street theater. Strickland made the design for the painted floor and Haviland was in charge of the decorations. They both belonged to the same architectural societies.

It involves an alleged loss of a sum of money that was sent to the president of the Commission, Peter Miercken, by the auditor-general of the Commonwealth. The details of this bizarre episode in the history of the Commission's activities make interesting reading even today.

It seems that Mr. Miercken was in the habit of sending his servant to the post office each Sunday morning to receive a letter from his son, who was attending Princeton University. On Sunday, December 2, 1821, the servant conveyed a draft drawn to Miercken for $20,000 for use in building the state prison. On the following day, Miercken, thinking the Commission was to meet that evening, went to the Bank of Pennsylvania and cashed the draft, taking twenty notes of $1,000 each. On his way home he stopped at the Farmers and Mechanics Bank and exchanged a $1,000 note for two $500 notes, offering no reason.

He recollected some time during the day that the meeting of the Commission was not until the next night—Tuesday, December 4. Thus he carefully placed the notes in a private drawer in his desk. On the evening of the meeting, he "took them out . . . and wrapped them in a piece of paper, twisted each end and put them in his right hand pantaloon pocket." On arriving at the prison where his colleagues were assembled, he discovered "that the paper containing the money was missing." He "immediately retraced his steps, examining his way carefully back to his dwelling house." Enlisting the aid of his son-in-law, they walked back to the prison "searching the gutter and every place that seemed likely the paper could have fallen or been kicked into but without success; that on searching his pocket he there found a hole through which the paper must have escaped." He then notified the other members of the loss. He expressed his deep concern and solicited their advice.

The members of the Commission immediately went into action. They adjourned and "proceeded to look for the lost money." And with Peter Miercken in the lead "the other members taking proper distance they proceeded to his home at 37 Shippen Street and back again to the prison examining the way in hope of finding the lost parcel but failed in their endeavor."

It was only natural that the Commission would call on its counsellor, Horace Binney, for advice. He recommended that a committee be sent to Harrisburg to lay the matter before the governor.

At the next meeting on the following evening, Mr. Miercken appeared "much elated." He took from his pocket "a wet paper having the appearance of a letter opened, having a wafer affixed to it, containing a number of Bank Notes which on being counted amounted to fifteen thousand dollars." He stated, apparently quite gleefully, that "being in his parlour this evening his little servant girl came running in and stated there was a man in the warehouse that frightened her." He proceeded to the warehouse but saw no one. But he discovered a "paper that had been shoved under the door which on taking it up struck him that it contained Bank Notes" which "so agitated him that he could not open it. He ran upstairs to his wife who was sick in bed, when his daughter took the paper and upon opening it found fifteen thousand dollars . . . and observed that he was never so happy in his life as having it in his power to hand it over to the Board."

On December 12, Mr. Miercken told this amazing story:

About seven o'clock this evening my brother David on opening the warehouse door picked up a note addressed to me. On entering my office shortly thereafter he asked me if I knew the handwriting of Tom Find; asking his reason he handed me a note which on opening I found contained the following words: "acknowledge the balance put into the window, Tom Find, December 11." Search was instantly made by the members of my family at all the windows of the dwelling and sugar house cellar but without effect. On preparing to empty the water out of the cisterns of the sugar house cellar immediately under the window a letter containing four notes of one thousand dollars each was found back of a scum bottom and blood churn by the chambermaid near the cistern containing these words: "I take the reward of $500, the other $500 should be enclosed but I want it— on the honour of a Mason it shall be returned. Brother Tom Find, Dated 6 of December."

This was Peter Miercken's story. He and two other members of the Commission journeyed to Harrisburg to report the loss to the governor. Their report stated, "After an interchange of sentiments with him, we were informed that he had referred the documents to the attorney-general for further proceedings."

No more word was had of the missing thousand dollars or of the mysterious Tom Find. On July 7, 1822, six months later, Peter Miercken died insolvent. The Commission took the loss, reporting it periodically in its accountings to the auditor-general, and finally, in 1827, the Commonwealth apparently gave up hope of locating the elusive Mr. Find and adjusted the books of the Commission. It is significant that in each report sent up by the Commission, the missing thousand dollars was always referred to as the "alleged loss of Peter Miercken." [9]

CONTROVERSY OVER ARCHITECTS AND PLANS

The chief differences between Strickland's and Haviland's plans for the prison were the position of the cells in relation to the wall, the size of the front or administration building, and the shape of the outer wall. From the minutes of the Building Commission we may assume that Strickland was eager to cooperate in all matters. He presented the plans of the Pittsburgh prison to enable the Commission to make comparisons. He submitted figures of costs and professional services. He set his own fee at $2,000 per annum or $1,400 at half-time, that is, for visiting the site and consulting with the master builder, Jacob Souder, three times per week.

Haviland's original design employed the arrangement of outside-cell construction in long blocks, or ranges, radiating from a common center. There were to be seven ranges, each with 36 cells.[10] His design of a front building for administrative purposes was vastly more ornate than Strickland's. One of the aspects of the controversy that marred the deliberations of the Commission dealt with this front building.

[9] This interesting story was brought to light from the records by De Puy "Triumph of the 'Pennsylvania System,'" pp. 9–10.

[10] John Haviland, *A Description of the Plan for a New Penitentiary* (Philadelphia, 1824), p. 4. See plan p. 66.

By October, 1821, the Commission seemed ready to appoint an architect but only for the purpose of superintending the work of construction. Strickland was appointed with the stipulation that "it be understood . . . the Board does not adopt the plan furnished by the said William Strickland."

After this action was taken, the Commission busied itself with such matters as letting contracts for the erection of the wall, so that nothing appears in the minutes at this time regarding the status of the two architects. Since Strickland was not to be employed until the following March, he went to Europe to make a study of prisons, canals, and public works. Upon his return in February, 1822, the questions of architect, plans, and compensation had to be faced by the Commission.

The minority group pressed for Strickland's plan. They attacked Haviland's design for the front building, which they regarded as much too showy and expensive. They referred to it as "more suited for the dwelling of a nabob than the keeper of a prison" and said that the legislature did not intend that funds "should be expended in building Palaces for the Keepers or Costly Towers for Cart Houses."

By this time Strickland was actually on the job although the extent of his duties is somewhat obscure. By May of 1822, fully a year after the original plans were submitted by the competing architects, the controversy came to a head. A committee was appointed to call on Strickland to advise him of his tenuous employment as superintendent of construction but not necessarily as architect. We can see from the following letter that he believed he had actually been appointed:

May 28, 1822

Gentlemen:

By a resolution of the Commissioners for the erection of the state penitentiary passed in September last I was appointed the architect of the Board and by a subsequent resolution passed on the 7th instant my salary was fixed and my duties were prescribed. I have accepted the appointment according to the terms mentioned in the said resolution; who or how many of the Board were present or absent when these resolutions were adopted I can neither know nor enquire. They were duly communicated to me and I have entered upon the duties of the appointment on the faith of them.

I have had conferences with the Building Committee respecting the work avowedly under my direction without a suggestion until the receipt of your letter that there was any thing informal much less invalid in the manner of my appointment. I must therefore hold myself not only entitled but bound to go on with the Building until an authorized legal authority shall declare the contract under which I am proceeding to be void. I could not be justified in abandoning this contract on the grounds contained in your letter—it would be to admit that the majority of the meeting by which my services were required and my salary fixed had abused their trust and taken advantage of accidental circumstance to violate their duty.—It is not for me to pass or in any way countenance such an imputation upon these respectable gentlemen. It is for them and not for me to vindicate themselves against the charges preferred against them and to reply to the detail set forth in your letter and I may presume they will be found fully competent to their own justification.

As to your proposal of a written contract I am ready to execute it with such security for the performance of the duties as architect as can be rightfully required of me and I shall certainly hold myself obliged to render the services which may be necessary to the whole extent of my contract as now made and hereafter to be accordingly reduced to writing.

I take this opportunity to remark that while I shall not object to erect the building on such plan as the proper authority shall adopt and direct, it must not be expected that I will be responsible either for its success in the main object or economy in expenditure unless the plan is proposed or approved by myself. Neither can I assume the responsibility of the contracts and expenditures that have been purchased without my knowledge or approbation.—This is but common reason and justice.

Respectfully submitted,
William Strickland

Despite the fact that Strickland had some reason to believe that he had been chosen superintendent-architect and that his plan for the prison had an even chance of being adopted, the records show that he was eventually not appointed or was his plan adopted. The painful steps by which the Commission finally arrived at a decision—majority rule, of course—are obscure. The justification or validity of "special" meetings, "adjourned" meetings, and votes on important matters when several members of the minority or majority were absent cannot be evaluated today.

The rancor and recrimination that dominated the meetings at this crucial period finally had to come to a head. The minutes of the meeting of June 12, 1822, record an attack by a committee representing the majority upon the minority that gives some clues to what motivated the thinking of the two groups. In the Minute Book only the first paragraph of this report together with its final conclusion and resolution calling for the discharge of Strickland, may be found. The bulk of the report, consisting of six sheets (twelve pages in all) is gone. Someone has carefully removed these sheets. However, the original rough draft of the report of this committee was found in the archives of the prison on April 2, 1953—over one hundred and thirty years after it was written—and in it we find some of the differences between the members.

The committee, consisting of Caleb Carmalt, Coleman Sellers, and Roberts Vaux, reviewed the proceedings from the time that the architect was first considered and the plan was initiated. They pointed out that Haviland's principle of radiating cell ranges had been considered much more practicable than Strickland's circular blocks so far as initial cost, cost of supervision, and the location of facilities such as keepers' quarters, kitchen, and other housekeeping services were concerned. They verified this from statements made by the superintendent and engineer of the Pittsburgh prison who, by this time, expressed disappointment in the construction of their institution and endorsed the plan of radiating ranges as more practicable.

In caustic language, the committee tore to shreds the minority's complaints regarding the legality of certain meetings. Point by point they shattered the claims of particular minority members which were made from time to time outside the meetings as well as objections placed in the minutes.

Scorn was also shown to one member of the minority who objected because "it [the plan] was drawn and designed by a foreigner [Haviland] who was not entitled to preferment over native merit." "John Haviland," the committee replied, "was a citizen of the Commonwealth and was entitled to the rights and benefits of other citizens." They complained that one of the minority, who was seemingly a lawyer, "openly and publicly avows his determination not to render his professional services so far as to give this Commission advice and council." But "they [sic] give services and advice to William Strickland or anyone else gratuitously against the regular organized body of which they [sic] are integrant and constituent members" and "such a practice is at least calculated to destroy all confidence in the professional opinions they [sic] may give on matters connected with the duties of this Commission." [11]

The committee continued by revealing the flaws in Strickland's plan for both the interior of the prison and the front building. They claimed he had submitted revised calculations both at Pittsburgh and at Philadelphia and added: "What reliance can we place upon his estimates after these recalculations?" They accused the members of the minority of watchful waiting to adopt their own plans when members of the majority were absent. This is stated in the following words: "While . . . for successive weeks not one member of the Friends of Strickland were absent thereby plainly evincing that the opportunity was watched by them to dictate to, overrule, and defeat the objects of the majority." This following point in the committee's report is evidence of the bitterness engendered in the Commission: "But while in the adoption of this measure malignity of heart and corruption of principle—have been imputed to the members [of the majority] while their integrity has been impeached and their personal safety threatened and the most degrading insults have been cast upon them. . . ."

An even more serious charge of bribery may be gleaned from this amazing report, a charge by the committee that one of

[11] Thomas Bradford, a member of the minority, was the only lawyer on the Commission.

the minority refused to endorse the premium of $100 to the successful architect even though he earlier had voted in favor of offering such an award:

We will not ascribe such a change of sentiment to the operations of an external influence which has been carried to such an extent as to attempt practicing upon individuals with offers of a pecuniary recompense for thwarting and counteracting the deliberations of this body—the committee are not disposed even to insinuate that William Strickland or any of his friends would attempt such an act nor are they freely prepared to believe that such an attempt would be made without being treated with indignant and unmingled scorn.

The committee also manifested resentment at being charged with "stealing the minute books—insinuations of mutilating the order book" and feared that committee members were to be victims of "further attacks of the same character."

The next attack deals primarily with Strickland's attitudes as set forth in his letter of May 28, 1822, in which he considered his appointment of May 7 as valid, and to defend which he might institute legal proceedings. The committee wrote as follows:

We have no doubt that [the parts of his letter] are strictly and exactly such as more than one of the members would . . . have dictated and wished. We will not presume that they have done so but the Board, it appears, are not the authority to decide upon the binding nature of the obligation we have entered into—although they have already passed a resolution that it is neither binding or obligatory— This defiance of the authority of the body of the committee can be considered in no other light than as a plain decisive threat accordant of the sentiments so often expressed by his friends in the Board, that a suit in law will be instituted against the Commonwealth . . . the committee while they are prepared to anticipate and treat this menace with the contempt it merits can hardly believe that the folly and infatuation of his friends will lead him to this extremity because if the circumstances communicated to him by the committee of the 24th ultimo. have not been of sufficient weight to induce him to abandon an unauthorized contract, there are other ways that could easily be pointed out to settle such controversies.

The committee based its repudiation of Strickland on the fact that, during his alleged appointment, he refused to accept any responsibility for the execution of another's plan. The report stated:

If we can understand the plain self-evident and legitimate meaning of words—Strickland declares his appointment to be valid—that his appointment has divested us of all authority to establish plans—regulate, control—superintend the erection of this prison any longer —we must be regulated, controlled and governed in the whole of this process by William Strickland or else a forfeiture of the claim we could justly and legally have upon him to whom all our duties are now transferred—in case of an ill-managed, extravagant, injudicious waste of the public funds, or any other absurd and ridiculous folly in the execution of the work is a consequence.

The committee closed its attack on the minority with these words:

Whether the members who have been called the majority will feel themselves willing any longer to submit to the sacrifice of that feeling which every man who is not callous and insensible must suffer at finding all their operations thwarted, all their labors counteracted and all their decisions protested against by an organized, systematic and regular opposition is for them to decide; had such proceedings been anticipated, the practice of offering repeated substitutes, of protesting against every measure of any importance whereby the reasoning of one side only is placed upon the minutes, and that in distorted shapes, unqualified assertions, bold and extravagant suppositions and solemn and eventful predictions—is calculated and intended to influence and prejudice the minds of the government, members of the legislature, and their fellow citizens against them personally, while every unfair argument, every personal reproach and every impeachment of motive is calculated to destroy, if it has not already destroyed, all personal friendships, all liberal generous feeling toward each other, all manly and dignified interchange of sentiment and opinion and finally to defeat the intention of the framers of the law or at least retard its operation for a number of years.

The committee's resolution was "that any further communication with William Strickland is unnecessary—that the superintendent and clerk be informed that he has no authority over them nor any superintendence of the Building and that the clerk be directed to return him all his plans and drawings as well of the prison as of the front Building and outer wall and inform him that this Board do not recognize nor consider him as their architect."

No action was taken on this committee's report. Despite the strong language, so obviously reflecting the will of the majority, it failed to stem the minority's opposition. As a result of the controversy and bitterness, Roberts Vaux and Coleman Sellers absented themselves from subsequent meetings and Vaux even sent in his resignation to Governor Hiester, which the executive refused to accept. The minority, headed by Thomas Bradford, capitalized on this action by Vaux and insisted that he had divorced himself from the Commission when he wrote his letter of resignation. We may surmise that behind-the-scenes forces prevailed upon the majority to maintain their favored position regarding Strickland and Haviland.

During this period of turmoil, a committee composed of Thomas Sparks and Coleman Sellers had been appointed to proceed to Harrisburg to lay before the governor the plans for the new prison, together with the Minute Books. A member of the minority, Daniel H. Miller, had also been appointed to serve but refused to go to the state capital. Because Governor Hiester subscribed to the Haviland plan, as the letter below indicates, the minority again protested. It was their contention that the committee was illegal since the members had been appointed at a meeting when a part of the minority was absent and also because Miller had not accepted his assignment. Nonetheless, the committee was declared legal by the majority and eventually their travel expenses were duly paid over the protests of the minority. Governor Hiester's letter approving Haviland's plan is as follows:

Reading, August 22, 1822

Gentlemen:

You called upon me a few days since as a Committee of the Board of Commissioners for the erection of a state penitentiary . . . with a plan of a Building and a copy of several resolutions respecting it, adopted by the Board on the 14th and 24th of May last.

Having considered the same, it appears that proper attention has been paid to economy, security, convenience and the object of Solitary confinement, I can therefore feel no difficulty in giving my approbation to the plan proposed by the majority of the Board and do herewith approve of the plan of a Front Building drawn and designed by John Haviland and recommended by John Bacon and Daniel H. Miller in their report of August 28 last and adopted by the Board of Commissioners on the 14th of May together with the plan of the front walls and towers drawn in the said design and also adopted by the Board. I also approve of the alteration in regard to the arrangement of the cells proposed in the resolution adopted by the Board on the 24th of May last in the following words:

Resolved that the plan of the Pittsburgh prison be so altered that the plan of a prison drawn and designed by John Haviland so far as relates to the arrangement of the cells upon radiating lines instead of arranging them on the periphery of a circle be adopted.

I remain, Gentlemen, with much respect, your obedient,

Joseph Hiester

This official approbation by the governor—necessary according to the law—certainly enhanced the position of the Haviland group, although candor would insist that similar resolutions could have been laid before the governor showing definitely that William Strickland had for a considerable time been favored as superintendent if not architect.

Finally, after considerable but futile maneuvering to stem the advantage held by the majority, the resolution dated June 22 calling for the dismissal of William Strickland was passed at the meeting held September 17. Thus a year and a half had elapsed from the Commission's initial meeting in April, 1821, before Haviland was actually installed as official architect of the new Eastern Penitentiary.

It is significant that this final action was taken by the seven majority members, that is, the Haviland group, at a meeting where not one member of the Strickland, or minority group, was present.

The next difficult and embarrassing problem relative to this controversy, that of compensating Strickland for his services during the first months of the building operations, was forced upon the Commission. At its meeting, May 4, 1824, fully two years after the unsuccessful architect was repudiated, satisfactory settlement was made. This transaction itself was lengthy and fraught with feeling. A committee was appointed to ascertain what would be a "just and equitable compensation," and, in December, 1822, gave this report:

That they have been informed from respectable sources that from early in May until some time in June, Mr. Strickland attended three times a week and after that time was absent about a month; he attended again on the 12th of July and continued to attend three times a week for some time but how long your Committee have not ascertained. During the time Mr. Strickland attended, the Superintendent (Jacob Souder) consulted with him about the work. The latter part of his time he met the Building Commission every Monday afternoon and he went to the Falls of Schuylkill and Crum Creek to obtain stone for the work and gave the levels along the walls several times. Your Committee are of the opinion that Two Hundred Dollars would be a just and equitable compensation for the services rendered as far as they have come to their knowledge.

Signed December 10, 1822

Wm. Davidson [12]
Samuel R. Wood

However, Strickland submitted a bill for $499.31 dated November 12, 1822, and on May 11, 1824, the claim was adjusted in the following manner:

The Committee report that they have had a conversation with Mr. Strickland on the subject. They proposed to him that he should deduct from the amount of his bill for the month he was absent, to wit, $112.50 and the Committee recommend that $386.81 should be paid. Mr. Strickland very frankly acquiesced in the proposition and the Committee accordingly advise that an order be drawn in his favour for the above sum.

Signed

Wm. Davidson
Michael Baker [13]

[12] Davidson had been appointed to take the place on the Commission of Peter Miercken who died in July, 1822. Davidson was a Haviland supporter.

[13] Appointed in the place of George N. Baker who had previously resigned.

One other action that dealt with this interesting controversy had been taken some months previously. The awarding of the hundred-dollar premium to the successful architect was necessary. This matter was disposed of on October 30, 1822. The resolution reads:

That the premium of $100 offered by the Board by a resolution adopted May 1, 1821, be and the same is hereby awarded to John Haviland as the architect whose plan was adopted by this Board on the 24th of May, 1822 and approved by the Governor on the 22nd. of August last—and that an order be drawn on the Treasurer in Favour of John Haviland for the amount of the Premium offered.

This resolution was adopted at an adjourned meeting, at which were present six members of the Haviland majority group: Bacon, Carmalt, Davidson, Sparks, Vaux, and Wood (Coleman Sellers absent).

It was mentioned earlier that six sheets of the Minute Book are missing: the six that recorded the report of the majority group of the Commission. An explanation for the deletion of this report may be found in the proceedings. At the meeting of November 12, 1822 (five months after the report was submitted), Thomas Bradford, a member of the minority, made the following motion, seconded by Daniel R. Miller, also a member of the minority:

Resolved, That so much of the report of Caleb Carmalt, Coleman Sellers and Roberts Vaux made June 12, 1822 as contains personal reflections on the conduct or language of any of the members of the Board be expunged from the minutes, as the said reflections are made contrary to the Rule of the regulations of the Board passed August 7, 1821.

This rule stated, among other things, that the president was not permitted to have placed in the record anything stated in a meeting that cast reflection on any of the members.

This resolution of Bradford's was passed, and it is quite possible that the secretary was instructed to delete the pages. Fortunately, the report of the committee was found so that details concerning this bitter conflict are now revealed.

OTHER ITEMS OF CONCERN TO THE COMMISSION

The Building Commissioners were plagued with many other matters, none of them quite as bitterly debated as those already described. These questions dealt with wages, building materials, the sale of several parcels of ground in Philadelphia and owned by the Commonwealth, the grading of the city's streets contiguous to the new penitentiary, and, later, the difficult problems of heating and supplying water for the new prison.

Laborers' wages in those days were 87½ cents per day; stone masons received $1.50 per day. Later the pay of the masons was raised to $1.75. Although men usually worked from "sunrise to sundown," when spring arrived they insisted that their working day be cut to 12 hours per day, that is, from 6 A.M. to 6 P.M. It was also customary for contractors to furnish the workers with whiskey, so we find occasional notations in the minutes of payments for "whiskey for the workmen." Several attempts were made by persons to erect a "public house" near the site of the prison, but the Commission always fought these moves. However, one Thomas McGuire succeeded in setting up a tavern directly across from the new structure. To cope with this reality the Commission laid down the following on February 5, 1822:

The Board deem it highly expedient that every inducement be held to encourage sobriety on the part of the workmen engaged in the erection of the new penitentiary and in order that temptations and inducements to intoxication should be as far removed as possible from the vicinity of same, resolve that this Board will discontinue the employment of any person known to be subject to intoxication.

There were other important matters to be acted upon. While each contractor was obliged to obtain surety that he would fulfill his obligations promptly, there were several instances when certain materials were not available, especially building stone and wrought iron. The architect was obliged to scour the countryside for stone, most of which came from the Falls of Schuylkill and Crum Creek. There was at least one time when Haviland was authorized to go to New York to purchase iron because the foundries near Philadelphia could not furnish it in the quantities needed.

On occasion the Commission had difficulties with the auditor-general of the Commonwealth. There was a tendency for this gentleman to question the payment of such items as "carriage hire" and "refreshments" for visiting notables. The Commission submitted a bill for $37.29 for entertaining General LaFayette and Governors De Witt Clinton of New York, Geddes of South Carolina, and Shulze of Pennsylvania. Wrote the Commissioners in April of 1826:

It cannot for a moment be supposed that [the legislature] will refuse to allow the Commissioners, who receive no compensation for their services, the means of conveyance once a week to the work to perform the duties devolving on them, and by their presence and supervision insure to the Commonwealth economy, fidelity and dispatch from those employed to conduct the work or that the Commonwealth by their legislature would deny to the Commissioners the paltry sum charged for refreshments under the "peculiar circumstance" of the case.

There appear in the minutes a few instances that prove extravagance, or at least injudicious contracting. One has to do with the excessive cost of the wall of the prison; the other deals with the installation of 13 mantles or fireplaces in the front building by the architect. These two items are worthy of recording.

The report of the committee, discussed earlier in this chapter, indicates that certain members of the minority made ill-advised contracts for the laying of the wall:

The committee have no hesitation in acknowledging that they think the expense so much complained of in the erection of the outer wall is perfectly justifiable—it is a matter about which they believe there can be one sentiment—but why connect this in their protests [that is, of the minority] with the front Building. The reason of its being so expensive is a reason, and a measure exclusively their own, and one upon which their lips ought to be hermetically sealed. The friends of William Strickland, with one exception, are the men who ought to bear this consensus of censure to be placed anywhere. In all the estimates of the cost of this wall the laying of this stone is calculated at $1.20 per perch. Why is this extraordinary charge made? Because the work has been agreed to be done by the day; when the whole could have been accomplished and proposals were prepared to offer to this Board if they had concluded to do it by the perch at little more than half that expense and the friends of William Strickland who voted for this alarming inroad upon the appropriation are the men who cry aloud against the extravagance, the expenditure, the shameful waste of the public money. Let the responsibility rest where it belongs and we have no objection to bear our share if any censure is involved in it.[14]

The marble mantels set up in the front building precipitated a conflict. At a meeting held July 13, 1827, it was resolved to have the mantels that had been installed in the front building taken down. However, Haviland apparently explained the manner in which they were constructed and was willing to accept some responsibility for the cost since he contended that it was merely a misunderstanding.

Roberts Vaux, at a meeting held November 13, prophetically made this motion:

There has no doubt been a misunderstanding and [we] agree that in as much as the lapse of centuries may not witness the demolition of the work now under their charge and believing that every thing connected with it ought to be of the most durable character they feel themselves justified in recommending that the resolution of July 13 be rescinded and that a proposition made by the architect be acceded to, *viz.*, that the mantles should remain and that a bill now presented amounting to $512 be paid, he agreeing to pay the difference which is $208.

These fireplaces with their ornate marble mantels had an important functional value in those days. Why their installation was questioned is difficult to understand, although it is possible that Haviland considered beauty as important as function. These fireplaces graced the several rooms in the administrative "front" building until 1953 when they were all removed during the building's thorough renovation.

[14] From the report of Caleb Carmalt, Coleman Sellers, and Roberts Vaux, June 11, 1822.

☰ 3
The Early Days of Cherry Hill

LAYING OF THE CORNERSTONE

It was on May 22, 1823, that the cornerstone of the "Prison at Philadelphia" was laid. It is doubtful that many of the citizens of Pennsylvania were aware of the significance of the ceremony, but to the penal reformers residing in the city of Philadelphia it was a most important event. At last the dream of a quarter of a century was on the threshold of realization. The huge pile of masonry covering some ten acres of what had only recently been a cherry orchard was to become the apotheosis of a concept of penal treatment which was to stir the entire world.

The ceremonies were presided over by Roberts Vaux (1786–1836), noted Philadelphia Quaker philanthropist, who played an important part in the negotiations which led to the creation of this unusual institution for criminals. In the preceding chapter we discussed his important role as a member of the Building Commission.

Roberts Vaux was a modest man whose entire adult life was devoted to charity and public works. In his early life the loss of a sister had affected him so deeply that he had vowed to devote the remainder of his life to the benefit of humanity as a memorial to her. There was scarcely a civic, social, or educational organization in Philadelphia to which he did not belong. He gave generously of his means as well as of his time and mature judgment. It can be said of him that he ranks among the first of Philadelphia's long list of distinguished citizens.[1] His son Richard also played a very important part in the later affairs of the Eastern Penitentiary.

At six o'clock in the evening, a small group of interested

[1] See Negley K. Teeters, *They Were In Prison* (Philadelphia, 1937), pp. 152–60, for an account of the activities of Roberts Vaux as well as a short biographical sketch.

persons assembled to hear Roberts Vaux, who had at the last minute been asked to substitute for Thomas Sparks, president of the Commission, speak at the dedicatory services. Commissioners under whom the penitentiary was being erected were present. So was John Haviland, the architect, and Jacob Souder, the master of masonry, as well as a number of workmen who were engaged in erecting this prison.

Roberts Vaux's remarks were sober and brief. He stated that the occasion was calculated to awaken reflections at once "painful and gratifying." Painful because such was the erring character of man; his ungovernable passions and propensities to evil made it necessary for society to provide means for the punishment of those who transgressed its laws. Gratifying because a correct view of human nature, coupled with the indispensable exercise of Christian benevolence, had led to the amelioration of punishments. Vaux continued that justice was mixed with mercy, and while the community designed to teach offenders that the way of the transgressor is hard, it wisely and compassionately sought to secure and reform the criminal by the strictest solitary confinement.

Vaux congratulated his fellow citizens that Pennsylvania was the first state to abolish the cruel and vindictive penalties in vogue in European countries. These, he stated, rather than preventing crime merely familiarized the mind with cruelty and hardened the hearts of those who suffered such penalties as well as those who witnessed them. The substitution in Pennsylvania of milder correctives had, he said, excited the notice and respect of nations abroad, as well as of the other states in this country. Vaux concluded with these words: "It only remains for us to express our desire that this institution may truly answer the important purposes for which it is founded." [2]

The cornerstone contains a metal plate bearing the following inscription:

[2] Digested from an account of the ceremony by a "bystander" and published by Poulson's *American Daily Advertiser*, Saturday morning, May 24, 1823. One of the mysteries of old Cherry Hill is the whereabouts of the cornerstone. It has never been identified and it is not known whether it is in the wall or in the front building, part of which has been covered up by a dirt embankment.

Penitentiary
For the Eastern District of the State of Pennsylvania
Founded
Agreeably to an Act of Assembly passed on the 20th day of March,
in the year of our Lord one thousand eight hundred and twenty-one
Joseph Hiester, *Governor*
Arthur Gregg, *Secretary of the Commonwealth*
under the direction of . . .

Then follow the names of the members of the Building Commission, together with the names of John Haviland and Jacob
Souder.

SITE AND ARCHITECTURE OF THE NEW PRISON

The Building Commissioners gave considerable thought to
selecting the site for the new prison and finally settled on a
tract of land consisting of "ten acres, nineteen perches" situated about two miles northwest of Center Square, now known
as City Hall. This was one of 16 tracts that had been offered
for sale in response to bids. The land, which was owned by
Benjamin and Joseph Warner, commanded the crest of a slight
hill there known locally as Bush Hill. A street was cut through,
even at that early date, known as Francis Lane. This thorough-
fare was later designated as Coates Street and is now known
as Fairmount Avenue. Contemporary accounts refer to the
prison as situated on "one of the most elevated, airy and healthy
sites in the vicinity of Philadelphia." [3]

The Warner brothers refused the Commission's first offer of
$11,000 but later agreed to sell for $11,500 provided they could
salvage "the trees, shrubbery and fences; two small hay houses
or stables and the hay barrack; the mantel and fire places in the
mansion house; the copper boiler and stone troughs in the
milk house, and the crops in the ground." [4] The Commission

[3] In the records of the Building Commission appears this description of the
Warner site: "Eleven acres—two dwelling houses in Francis Street, first street
above Callowhill, running from Ridge Road to Schuylkill—north and south
lines 627 feet, east and west lines 750 feet. Two sides bounded by Public
Roads. Price $15,000." The Warners also offered an adjoining site, just west of
the above.

[4] Richard Vaux, *A Brief Sketch of the Origin and History of the State Penitentiary for the Eastern District of Pennsylvania* (Philadelphia, 1872), p. 54.

agreed to these provisions. Later a small additional tract adjoining the Warner site was purchased from James Harrison for $1,500.

The philosophy underlying this new prison called for a bold and unique architectural plan. As was pointed out in the first chapter, the Philadelphia reformers were frustrated by the arrangements of the Walnut Street Jail and were convinced that only in a judiciously designed prison could their cherished system of prison discipline be realized. It was because of this that the members of the Building Commission exercised such great care in selecting the plans for the prison.

The architect, John Haviland, was born on December 15, 1792, at Gundenheim Manor, Somersetshire, England. He was the son of James Haviland and Ann Cobley, daughter of the Reverend Benjamin Cobley of Ide, County Devon, and the rector of Dodbrook. A sister of his mother married Count Morduinoff, Minister of Marines under Czar Alexander I of Russia. Morduinoff was a close friend of John Howard, the great English prison visitor, and was present at the reformer's bedside when he died in the Crimea in 1790.

The young Haviland studied architecture in London under James Elmes. Later he visited St. Petersburg where he talked with Morduinoff and a Sir George von Sonntag, a former Philadelphian, and by them was probably encouraged to emigrate to America.[5] This he did in 1816, and settled in Philadelphia where he associated himself with Hugh Bridport in the architectural-consultant business.[6]

It is generally held that Haviland's interest in prison architecture stemmed from his association with Count Morduinoff, the friend of John Howard. This is substantiated by the following:

The memory of this honorable friendship was reverently cherished by the survivor [Haviland] who loved to dwell upon the discoveries and designs of the great Englishman [Howard]; and we cannot doubt

[5] See Norman B. Johnston, "Pioneers in Criminology—John Haviland," *Journal of Criminal Law and Criminology,* Vol. 45, No. 5 (1955), pp. 509–19.

[6] The Philadelphia Directory for 1818 lists the firm as "Haviland & Bridport, architectural and miscellaneous drawing academy, Southwest corner Chestnut and 7th."

that the young Haviland became auditor of previous reminiscences. It is certain that the friend who shared the last sympathetic throb of the heart of Howard was he whose hand was extended to guide toward our country the architect under whose directing skill was to arise the most complete embodiment which the world has seen of Howard's reform.[7]

Testimony of Haviland's versatility as well as of his energy may be shown by the Philadelphia edifices he was commissioned to erect during the period he was engaged on the construction of the Eastern Penitentiary of Pennsylvania: St. Andrews Episcopal Church, begun in 1822; the Philadelphia Deaf and Dumb Asylum, Broad and Pine, 1824–25; the Franklin Institute, Chestnut Street between 6th and 7th, 1825; and The Arcade, 1827.

Haviland married the sister of General von Sonntag. He died of apoplexy on March 28, 1852, and is buried in the crypt of St. Andrews Church, Philadelphia. He had two sons: Edward, who first studied law but later became an architect, designed several Pennsylvania county jails that have been attributed by some to his father; and John von Sonntag, who was admitted to practice law in 1846 but soon afterward left for England to live.

Before discussing the Haviland plan, a word about the man's influence on prison architecture is important. Prison architects of that day reflected the social thinking regarding the criminal and slavishly followed the architecture of the congregate jails of England. Haviland was obliged to create a new architecture to conform with the philosophy of separate confinement and implement it with the prevailing concepts of security and deterrence. While he may have transferred the idea of the medieval fortress to prison planning,[8] it must be stated that grim, forbidding prison plants were thought to be necessary. Certainly the Auburn and Sing Sing prisons were just as forbidding as the Philadelphia prison, as were also the Pennsyl-

[7] Sketch of Haviland in *Journal of Prison Discipline and Philanthropy*, Vol. I, No. 3 (1852), pp. 92–107.

[8] Harry Elmer Barnes, *Evolution of Penology in Pennsylvania* (Indianapolis, 1926), p. 143.

vania penitentiary being erected at Pittsburgh and the earlier prison at Charlestown, Massachusetts, built in 1806 by Charles Bulfinch. Then too, Haviland was impressed by these words of the Building Commission: "The exterior of a solitary prison should exhibit as much as possible great strength and convey to the mind a cheerless blank indicative of the misery that awaits the unhappy being who enters within its walls." [9]

Architects both here and abroad have paid tribute to Haviland's genius in combining function and beauty. The late Fiske Kimball, director of the Philadelphia Art Museum, stated that Haviland had given his prison "an imprint of artistic form;" he praised especially the front of the institution.[10] Equally complimentary was the modern prison architect Alfred Hopkins, who praised the builder of Cherry Hill for his design of the wall and the administration building. However, he deplored the fact that with Haviland "progress in prison architecture stopped." [11]

The interior of the prison has also been admired by many visitors, especially by those from abroad, who are impressed by the graceful lines of the blocks and the cells. Joseph Jackson, in his *Early Philadelphia Architects and Engineers*, quoted an unnamed architect of international reputation as saying the prison was the "most artistic [building] in the city" of Philadelphia.[12]

Albert Ten Eyck Gardner, archivist of the Metropolitan Museum of Art, writes along the same lines.

The idea that a prison building could have the qualities of a work of art is a somewhat arresting paradox. However, without pressing the point too far we may say that this prison comes nearer to being a work of art than any other building of its kind, and makes the examination of its unusual structure worth while and the story of its creator, John Haviland, worth retelling.[13]

[9] Minutes of the Commission, I, 115. For more discussion of this question, see Norman B. Johnston, "Pioneers in Criminology," p. 517.
[10] Kimball, *American Architecture* (Indianapolis, 1928), p. 116.
[11] Hopkins, *Prisons and Prison Building* (New York, 1930), pp. 44–45.
[12] Privately printed (Philadelphia, 1923), p. 155.
[13] Gardner, "A Philadelphia Masterpiece: Haviland's Prison," *The Metropolitan Museum of Art Bulletin*, XIV (1955), pp. 103–8. See also, Wayne Andrews, *Architecture, Ambitions and Americans* (New York, 1955), pp. 134–36.

Certainly Haviland's reputation was enhanced by his plan of the Philadelphia prison. A few years later when it was found necessary to rebuild the Western State Penitentiary at Pittsburgh his plan was adopted. In addition he designed the state prisons of New Jersey and Rhode Island as well as some county jails in Pennsylvania. All of them followed the massive lines of Cherry Hill. He also designed the first Tombs prison in New York city, which Charles Dickens referred to as a "dismal-fronted pile of bastard Egyptian, like an enchanter's palace in a melodrama."

How far the architectural plan of the Eastern Penitentiary was a product of Haviland's originality or imagination has long been a debatable question.[14] He was undoubtedly familiar with the various types of prison architecture then prevailing in Europe. There was first the Hospice of San Michele at Rome, part of which was designed for wayward boys. It was built in 1704 by the architect Carlo Fontano at the request of Pope Clement XI.[15] This establishment, so monastic in design and purpose, featured outside cell construction. In this style of prison design, each block had a corridor with cells on either side, the doors opening into the corridor and window slits piercing the outer wall of each cell. Haviland used outside cell construction at Philadelphia, but his original plan, as we shall note later, did not provide doors opening into the corridors.

Second, there was the prison at Ghent in Belgium, designed and administered by the "father of penitentiary science," Jean Jacques Philippe Vilain (1712–77). This structure, known as a *maison de force,* or rasp house, had been erected in 1771 for the detention of beggars and "sturdy rogues"—a house of correction. It was planned with eight radiating wings, each of which was a double-tiered cell block. All eight joined in a central *grande cour,* or central rotunda. The cells were placed back to back, thus forming inside cell construction. Frederick H. Wines, a student of penology, wrote in 1895 that this "stellar" idea of the Ghent prison may have influenced Havi-

---

[14] Barnes, *Evolution of Penology,* p. 142.   [15] See p. 12.

land in designing the Philadelphia prison.[16] It is possible, too, that the outside cell construction of the Hospice of San Michele may have impressed Haviland.

But there is much more reason to believe that the radiating principle was borrowed by Haviland from prisons and mental hospitals constructed during the decade of 1790–99 in England and Scotland. Perhaps the first of these were designed by the English architect William Blackburn. They were characterized by a central supervisory facility from which radiated four cell blocks or wings.[17] William Crawford, the English commissioner who visited this country in 1833 to study the penitentiary movement, tends to support the thesis that Haviland knew of this architectural style when he says, "There is no ground for claiming any originality for the American innovation of Haviland's . . . the radiating plan had long been adopted in the construction of the best prisons in England." He mentions as an example the Liverpool Borough Gaol erected in 1790.[18] All of these structures, however, were jails and houses of correction, not penitentiaries.

There has come to light a portion of a diary of a Philadelphia Quaker, Joshua Gilpin, written in 1799, which describes a radial prison located in Manchester, England, and erected in 1790. The diary is accompanied by a crude drawing that shows the keeper's center observatory, octagonal in shape (as later at Cherry Hill) with four radiating wings. The chapel occupies the second floor of the observatory. There is a close similarity between the main front building of the Manchester prison and the one Haviland designed for the prison at Philadelphia.

We know also that Haviland in 1819 designed a plan for a prison to be erected in Philadelphia County and it followed the scheme of having a central rotunda and four radiating cell blocks. This prison was never built, but the plan indicates that the architect had the radial plan in mind for some time.[19]

[16] Wines, *Punishment and Reformation* (New York, 1895), p. 135.

[17] For a discussion of these establishments, see Johnston, "Pioneers in Criminology," pp. 513–14.

[18] Crawford, *Report on the Penitentiaries* (London, 1834), p. 14 and n. 10.

[19] Negley K. Teeters, *The Cradle of the Penitentiary* (Philadelphia, 1955), pp. 141–42.

Haviland was no innovator. His prison plan shows no originality in its various parts. He may have borrowed his radial design from the English architect Blackburn, his outside cell construction from the San Michele prison at Rome, and his central rotunda or *grande cour* from Vilain's prison at Ghent. Even his exercise yards suggest the influence of William Strickland, his rival, since that architect had provided a small yard for each cell at the Western Penitentiary at Pittsburgh. But it was a sign of genius to combine judiciously all of the practical and successful features of these earlier institutions into one structure. This Haviland accomplished and in doing it he added a touch of beauty by molding graceful lines into imposing stone masses.

WALL AND FRONT BUILDING AT CHERRY HILL

While the mode of discipline of the new prison was one designed to strike terror in the heart of the prisoner—although the full effects of such loneliness seem never to have been fully realized by the philanthropists of Philadelphia—the outer great wall surrounding the enclosure, together with the central towers fronting on Francis Street (Fairmount Avenue) and midway between the two east and west towers, were likewise intended to deter. Haviland must have enjoyed a grim sense of satisfaction when he labored over the plans for the massive front building and its forbidding towers.

A contemporary enthusiast of the separate system, George Washington Smith (1800–76), described the institution as the most extensive building in the United States. He stated that "large sums of money have been expended for the purpose of giving an unusual degree of solidity and durability to every part of the immense structure." With keen admiration he explained: "This Penitentiary is the only edifice in this country which is calculated to convey to our citizens the external appearance of those magnificent and picturesque castles of the Middle Ages, which contribute so eminently to embellish the scenery of Europe."

The best method of describing the walls and façade of the

institution is to employ the language of the contemporaries. The front of the building is composed of large blocks of hewn and squared granite; the wall, 30 feet high and built of Falls of Schuylkill stone, is 12 feet thick at the base, and diminishes to the top, where it is two and three-quarters feet thick. At each corner of the wall is a tower for the purpose of overlooking the establishment; three towers, described below, are situated near the entrance gate.[20]

The façade is 670 feet in length and rests on a terrace which, because of the unevenness of the ground, varies from three to nine feet in height. There is a basement running the entire length of this front.

The front or main building is 200 feet in length and consists of two massive towers 50 feet high. These are crowned by "projecting embattled parapets, supported by pointed arches and rest on corbels or brackets." The narrow, pointed windows in these towers contribute to their picturesque effect. The space between the towers, known technically as a curtain, is 41 feet high and is finished with a parapet and embrasures.

The great gateway in the center was a conspicuous feature of the prison. It was 27 feet high and 15 feet wide. This gate was described by a contemporary writer in this fashion: "It is filled by a massive wrought iron portcullis and double oaken doors studded with projecting iron rivets, the whole weighing several tons; nevertheless they can be opened with the greatest facility." The gate was demolished in 1938 and replaced by a modern iron gate operated by electricity. The oaken planks were burned in the prison enclosure and the hundreds of large handwrought rivets distributed among the officials and staff members as souvenirs.

On each side of the main entrance, which George W. Smith referred to as "the most imposing in the United States," are enormous solid buttresses diminishing in offsets and terminating in pinnacles. A lofty octagonal tower, containing an alarm bell and clock in the early days, surmounts this entrance. On

[20] From George Washington Smith, *A Defense of the System of Solitary Confinement of Prisoners* (Philadelphia, 1829, republished 1833).

each side of the main building are screen wing walls pierced by small, blank, pointed windows and surmounted by a parapet.

The wing walls form a central passageway or foyer leading to the inside yard. On either side of this passage are two apartments consisting of basement and first and second floors, each with several rooms. In one basement, on the right or eastern side were, when the prison was designed, quarters for washing and ironing. Today this area contains the prison's arsenal, a guards' dressing room, toilet facilities for visitors, and a visiting gallery. On the left or western side of the basement were, at the time of the prison's opening, the kitchen and a bakery. Today the space is used as a guards' dressing room and as dining facilities for staff members.

On the first or ground floor were originally quarters for the keepers and store rooms. Today, on the right we find offices of the steward, accountant, and personnel staff; on the left are the physician's office, warden's office, and Board of Trustees' room. On the second floor, when the prison was opened, the space was used as the warden's living quarters, the office of the Board of Inspectors, an infirmary, and a hospital. Today, on the right we find the telephone exchange, office of the Director of Classification, and general offices; on the left, inmates' accounts office and quarters for the resident physician.

The Reverend Louis Dwight was much disturbed when he saw that the second floor of the front building was to be used both as the warden's home and a hospital. In his report for 1828 he wrote:

The usual and most convenient approach to and egress from the family rooms of the keeper, is through a narrow, inconvenient, winding stairway leading from the arched way to those rooms. By these arrangements the family of the keeper or warden, is literally subjected to imprisonment; surrounded by impervious walls and immovable grates, and can only enjoy the unobstructed light of heaven, by groping their way through a passage, better fitted for an entrance into a subterranean catacomb than to the residence of a civilized and christian family. Yet all this is a trifling matter, when compared to the horrors of a hospital within the walls of a family dwelling, where the shrieks of the insane and the groans of the dying are mingled, with the yells and curses of abandoned and profligate female convicts in adjacent apartments.[21]

In the central tower over the entrance was the apothecary's shop. Immediately inside the enclosure on either side of the main entrance were gardens, one "appropriated to the warden and one to the domestics." The space used for the warden's garden has long since been utilized for segregated exercise yards for those undergoing discipline or those who are considered too dangerous to mingle with the other inmates.

THE PRISON INTERIOR

Beyond the front or main building, the present-day visitor is confronted by buildings and cell blocks which were erected many years after the institution was opened. In due time, however, he reaches the octagonal central rotunda from which the original cell blocks radiate.

As Haviland designed the center building, the basement formed a general guard house while the ground floor provided accommodations for the under keeper and the watchmen.[22] Outside the second floor room of this building, which for many years served as the prison library, was a platform designed for the purpose of keeping watch over the entire prison. A bell was hung in the observatory roof to serve as an alarm and for purposes of general utility.

Richard Vaux writing in 1872 described this building as follows:

The center building is 40 feet in diameter. It is of an octagonal shape and each corridor opens into it. A good idea may be had of its form

[21] Boston Prison Discipline Society, *Third Annual Report* (Boston, 1828), pp. 41 f.

[22] "Originally the central rotunda was to house cells, a laundry, bake house, and below these a series of dungeons each with a private entrance from the floor above and a fireplace." Quoted by Norman Johnston, "Pioneers in Criminology," p. 514, and taken from Haviland's papers (ms. 1, dated July 2, 1821). These papers, loaned to the library of the University of Pennsylvania, are the property of the Somerset (England) Archeological and Natural History Society, The Castle, Taunton.

by likening it to the hub of a wheel from which the spokes, representing the corridors, radiate. It is two stories high. On the top is a lantern and lookout. In the lantern or cupola are eight reflectors, 20 inches in diameter, silver-plated, and by the use of gas [not available in 1829] the light is thrown at night into all parts of the ground. It

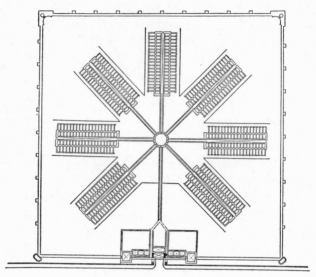

FIG. 1. HAVILAND'S ORIGINAL NUMBER OF CELL BLOCKS
EACH WITH 36 CELLS

is deemed one of the best protections. The height of these reflectors from the ground is about 50 feet. The center building stands in the exact center of the whole plot of ground.[23]

The rotunda or center building is the real hub and nerve center of the prison. In the early days the warden spent much of his time there, and today it serves as a post for the captain and his custodial officers. In the cupola perched high atop of the center building today may be seen the lonely watchman who is constantly on the alert. He carefully surveys the entire grounds, aided, of course, by the guards stationed in each of the four corner towers. These towers were not manned in the early days when each inmate was locked securely in his cell. Today the

[23] Vaux, *Brief Sketch of the Origin and History*, p. 65.

cupola guard realizes that much of the security of the institution rests on his vigilance.

The seven cell blocks that radiate from this common center represent the original prison. In later years, with the gradual addition of several more blocks, a clever system of mirrors was installed so that one guard standing in the center of the rotunda may see throughout all the corridors. Pictures of the cell blocks as early as 1897 show these mirrors. At that time there were 11 blocks.

The original of Haviland's plan of the prison has never been found, but we have an idea of what he had in mind from a pamphlet which he published in 1824. He planned to include in each cell block 36 rooms or cells, 12 x 8 x 10 feet, with exercise yards joined to each, 18 feet long.[24] This plan was to conform to the act of March 20, 1821, that specified the erection of 250 cells. But when the first three cell blocks were built they actually contained 38 cells each. Ten years later when the prison was partially completed, an act dated March 28, 1831, empowered the Board of Inspectors to increase the number of cells to 400. By this time three blocks were completed. To provide for the extra cells the Board decided to construct the remaining four blocks in two stories. Their discussion considered the possibility of erecting "two storied buildings, in the form of streets, with a trap-door and a yard on top," but this idea was abandoned.

Blocks 4, 5, 6, and 7 are all of two stories. Charles Dickens wrote in his *American Notes,* that the prisoners housed in the second floor galleries of these blocks, which, of course, had no exercise yards, were provided with two cells each to compensate for their restriction. William Crawford, the English commissioner who visited the prison in 1833, wrote that these prisoners were "not allowed to go out at any time into the open air." It does not seem possible, however, that no provision was made for exercising the prisoners in these upper galleries. With the use of the mask they could be and probably were exercised in the prison yard between the cell blocks.

[24] For an idea of what the original sketch was like, see cut, p. 66.

The construction of the last four blocks with their two stories created the opening wedge that gradually resulted in the eventual downfall of the separate system at Cherry Hill. As early as 1834 when the first investigation of the prison was initiated, testimony demonstrated that prisoners in their yards

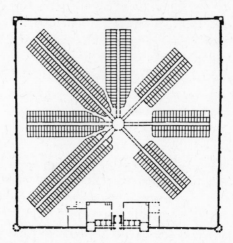

FIG. 2. A TRUE PLAN OF THE ORIGINAL PRISON DRAWN BY BLOUET AND DEMETZ IN 1837 (SEE PAGE 242).

on the ground floor were able to talk easily with those housed above despite the vigilance of the watchmen.

A number of ground plans, engravings, and cuts have been made of the Cherry Hill prison through the early years by various individuals. Many discrepancies appear so far as the size of the blocks and number of cells are concerned, especially involving the first three blocks. We have attempted in Appendix IV (pages 242–3) to resolve these variations.

A major expansion program was developed between 1877 and 1879 when Blocks 8, 9, and 10 were constructed.[25] In 1894 Block 11 was built. Block 12, three stories high, was erected between 1908 and 1911 by means of prison labor. A small block, consisting of eight cells, was built later for purposes of segregation. This is known as Klondike and is labeled Block 13. In 1926 Block 14 was built for the incoming prisoners. This

[25] See Fig. 7 showing the prison as it appeared at that time.

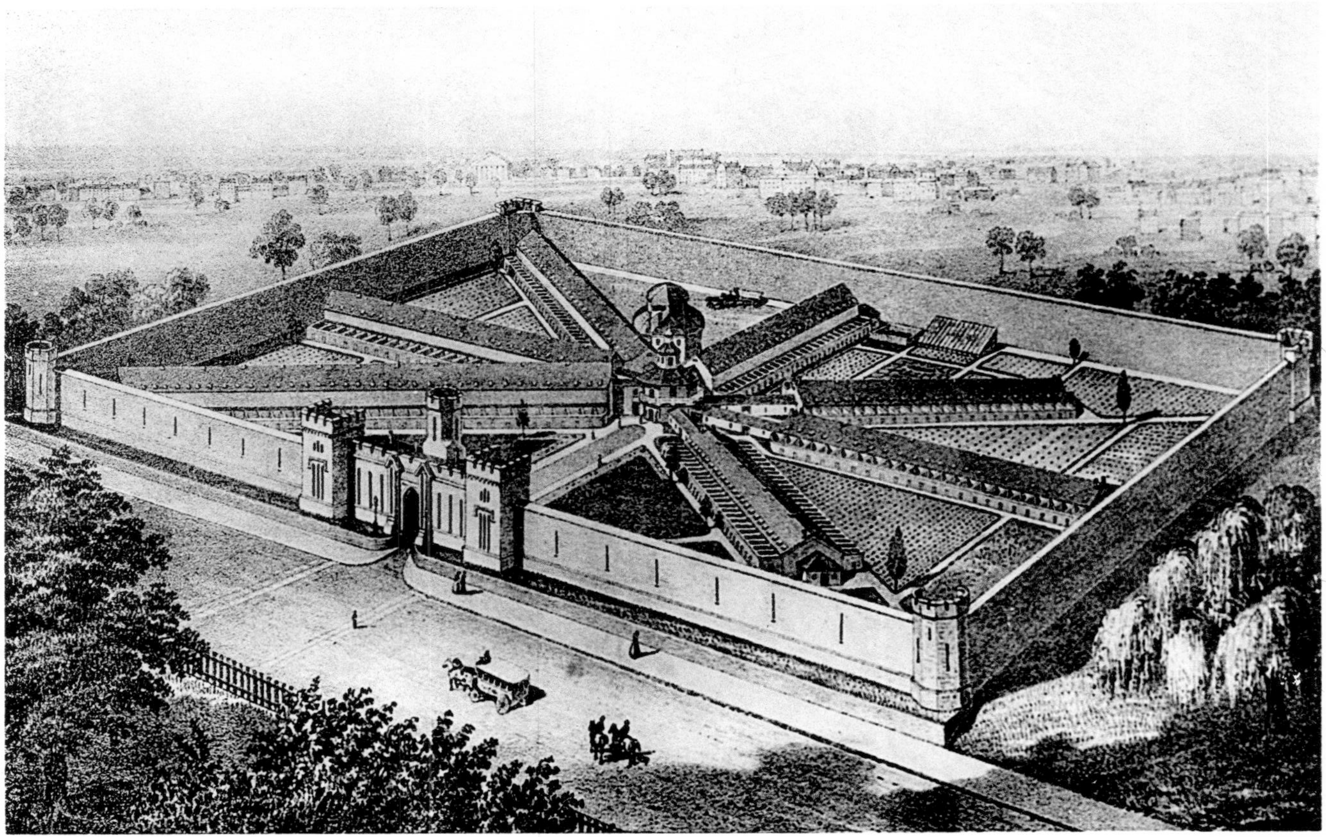

FIG. 3. TRADITIONAL ENGRAVING OF CHERRY HILL

FIG. 4. JOHN HAVILAND
    Painting by John Neagle

FIG. 5. ROBERTS VAUX

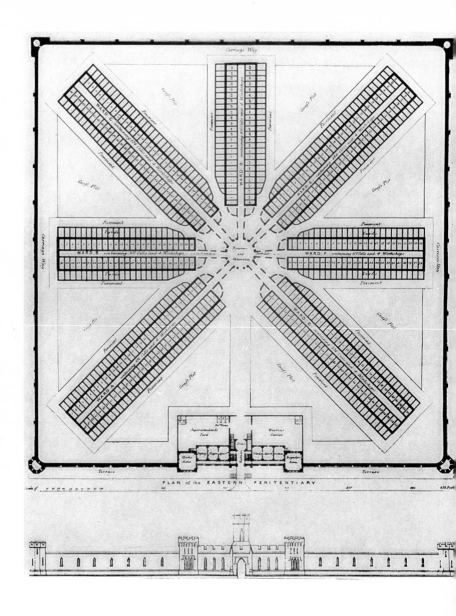

FIG. 6. PRISON PLAN BY WILLIAM CRAWFORD, ENGLISH COMMISSIONER

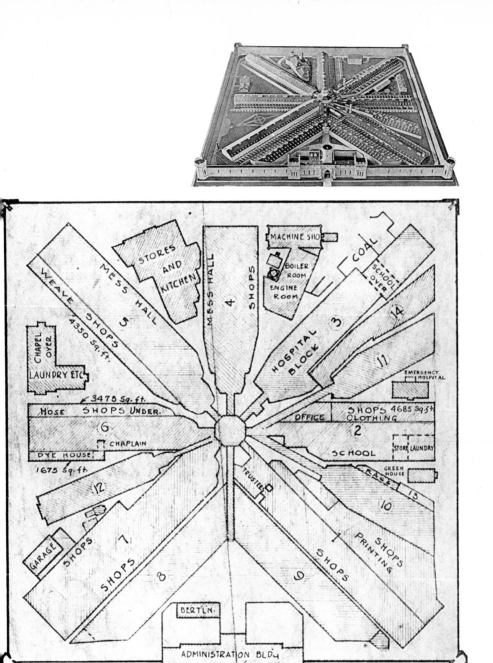

FIG. 7. MODEL OF PRISON FOLLOWING 1877
FIG. 8. A DRAWING OF THE PRISON DONE IN 1936 SHOWING ARRANGEMENT
OF THE CELL BLOCKS

FIG. 9. CHERRY HILL, THE PRISON AT PHILADELPHIA
From an oil painting hanging in the board room at the prison

FIG. 10. THE PRISON AS IT APPEARS TODAY

Courtesy, 111th Fighter Bomber Wing, Pennsylvania Air National Guard

FIG. 11. EASTERN PENITENTIARY
Note exercise yards

FIG. 12. THE PRISON CENTER

is the quarantine or reception block in which each new prisoner is housed until he is studied and his case disposed of by the diagnostic clinic. Today we see Cherry Hill cluttered with 14 cell blocks containing approximately 900 cells in an area designed for seven cell blocks to house 400 prisoners.[26] A new maximum-security block is at present under construction.

Since this famous prison was dedicated to the principle of separate confinement with labor, the cells were designed by Haviland with judicious care so that a maximum amount of room was available. It is doubtful that any American prison was originally planned with such commodious cell space. At the time the prison was first used, the only opening to the cell was through the exercise yard; there was none from the corridor. There were two doors covering one doorway leading from the yard into the cell. An inner lattice door was provided to admit air and sunlight as well as to secure the inmate when he was not exercising. An outer door of heavy planking which served to confine the prisoner in his cell closed over the lattice door. These doors were in the rear of the cell. Ventilation and sunlight were provided in each cell by a convex reflector piercing the "barrelled ceiling," thus forming a window eight inches in diameter and called by the architect a deadeye. If an unruly prisoner had to be disciplined, his cell could be easily darkened by placing a cask over the deadeye. Records show that this was done on occasion.

Much of the ironwork for the prison was forged at the Hopewell Furnace near Birdsboro, Pennsylvania. This colonial furnace, now a National Historic Site, has many of the old record books still intact. These records show that castings for door frames, racks, and "peepholes," aggregating about 57 tons, were purchased by the prison authorities from this famous furnace.[27]

The unusual arrangement of the cell doors, positioned in the

[26] Specific data on the cell blocks erected prior to 1925 may be found in Barnes, *Evolution of Penology*, pp. 201–5; see also, Vaux, *Brief Sketch of the Origin and History*, pp. 70–71. For a recent photograph of the prison see Fig. 10.

[27] Stated in a letter dated November 30, 1949, from Mr. Dennis C. Kurjack, at that time historian of the Hopewell Village National Historic Site, Birdsboro, Pennsylvania.

rear rather than in the front of the cell, proved awkward and impracticable. The overseers whose job it was to instruct the inmates in their labor were forced to enter the cells from the rear yard which, in inclement weather at least, was a nuisance. Then too, religious services, which were advocated by the founders of the institution to an almost fanatical degree, were seriously hampered since the ministers were obliged to call on each prisoner one at a time to impart the gospel. It was soon realized that if there were doors to the cells opening onto the corridors, the minister could preach his sermons at the head of the cell block nearest the central rotunda and all the prisoners could hear his voice at one time. Such doors were accordingly installed in 1831.[28]

Another novel arrangement was devised by Haviland for feeding the prisoner in his cell. In the front of each cell, facing the corridor, the stone construction was broken by a "feeding drawer and peep hole." The drawer was made of cast iron, and when closed it projected into the cell to form a table, which was used by the inmate for eating his meals. This device was so cleverly constructed that when the guard or keeper inserted food or any other object into the cell the inmate could not see him. The keeper, however, could peep through the aperture and see the inmate. When the corridor doors were installed, other arrangements for serving meals in the cells had to be provided.

On Block 3 today there are seven cells that do not have doors leading from the corridor. Apparently, quite early in the history of the prison some cells were expanded or enlarged by tearing out the partition between two of them. Thus when the doors were installed only one door was needed for the two cells. The other half of the enlarged cell still retains the small peep holes.[29]

The stone walls of the cells were whitewashed. The floors were also of stone, but later, to guard against the dampness, plank floors were laid down over the stone. This made the cells

[28] *Fourth Annual Report of the Inspectors*, December 31, 1832, pp. 12–13.
[29] See Fig. 13.

more comfortable, especially in winter. Each cell was furnished originally with an iron bedstead. Later these were replaced with wooden beds. The bed was so constructed that the inmate could rear it against the wall when it was not in use and fasten it with a staple, thus providing more room in the cell.

Other furnishings in the cell included a clothes rail, a stool, a tin cup, a wash basin, a "victuals" pan, a mirror, scrubbing and sweeping brushes, a sheet, blanket, and straw mattress. Each cell was also equipped with a crude form of flush toilet. In addition, a work bench was provided to keep the prisoner busy at his appointed task. The occupations, most of which were adapted to the small confines of the cells, were shoemaking, spinning, weaving, dyeing, dressing yarn, blacksmithing, carpentering, sewing, wheelwrighting, washing, wood turning, brush making, tin working, shuttle making, and last making.

METHODS OF HEATING AND SUPPLYING WATER

Two problems confronted the early management: one was the heating system and the other was the water supply. After prisoners were sent to the institution, the warden was obliged to install "warming stoves" in each cell. He stated in his first report that the hot air furnaces specified in Haviland's plan had not been installed so he had to purchase "six small stoves." However, he found them "troublesome, expensive and dirty." He further added that he had made arrangements to purchase an air heater sufficient to warm 20 cells.

A hot air system was eventually installed but certain defects were encountered, each of which had to be overcome by experimental modifications. The stoves, or cockles, in which the air was heated and conveyed to the cells were located in a "subterranean chamber." The temperature of the cells was rarely more than 60 degrees. While there were no records kept of the temperature (at least none have been found), we note that one source of information [30] refers favorably to the heating apparatus and consequent comfort of the cells in the Pentonville Prison outside London, which was copied after the Penn-

[30] *Journal of Prison Discipline and Philanthropy*, Vol. I, No. 4 (1845), p. 347.

sylvania System and erected on plans similar to those of Cherry Hill. The *Journal* article included a record of the day-by-day temperature of the Pentonville cells for February 1844 and 1845, and on not one day did it exceed 56 degrees. In fact, on many days it was as low as 49 and on a few days 47 degrees.

We are therefore entitled to believe that the prisoners were none too warm at Cherry Hill. Many complaints about the cold were raised in the monthly meetings of the Philadelphia Prison Society. In one instance (March 13, 1849), it was reported that "there was much suffering among the prisoners during the late severe weather, so that many were obliged to wrap themselves in their bed blankets and pace their cells to keep from more severe suffering."

The management at Cherry Hill was troubled by another defect of the heating and plumbing systems: they provided means of communication between the prisoners. One of the criticisms leveled at this prison by those not friendly to the system was that it was impossible to eliminate communication between the inmates. Dr. Robert A. Given, prison physician from 1844 to 1851, stated in his report for 1850: "I have heard various estimates of the amount of intercourse afforded to our prisoners, but they were all very much exaggerated. My own observation and the opinion of our most intelligent officers satisfy me that the average daily conversation of each prisoner does not exceed, if indeed it equals, ten minutes." It is quite certain that prisoners were able to communicate by means of tapping on pipes, floors, and walls. The records show many instances of punishments for the violation of the rule against this practice.

Because the elevation of the prison was approximately the same as the city reservoir at Fair Mount on the Schuylkill River, it was difficult to get an adequate water supply. Enough water was pumped to "carry off and cleanse the pipes of the prisoners' water closets," but the "reaction of the contaminated air after the water is discharged from the pipes causes the cistern to be impregnated more or less with it." Consequently there was no water for drinking purposes. A large well was dug in the prison yard. In the early days a horse working two hours each day pumped enough water into supply tanks to serve the institution for drinking and bathing. Later a six-horse-power steam engine supplanted the horse. The well, reservoir, and heating buildings were of stone and stood between Blocks 4 and 5. They may be seen in the early pictures of the prison. Not until 1854 was city water piped into the institution.

From the very opening of the institution, the sanitary conditions were deplorable and caused deep concern to the management. Dr. Given, a most conscientious and capable man, said: "I have known the clothes of persons walking through the corridors to become so saturated with the odor [from the unflushed toilets] that it was perceptible to others even after a walk of some miles in the open air." When Dr. Given retired in 1851, he was happy to report some improvement in the plumbing of the cell blocks.

COST OF THE EASTERN STATE PENITENTIARY

The amount of money that has been poured into the prison at Philadelphia during its existence of over 125 years could probably be ascertained by perusing the records of appropriations. It has been estimated that over $3,000,000 have been spent on the structure to date.

The cost of the site, legal fees, and clearing the land amounted to $13,115.52 according to the records of the Building Commission. The total outlay of money used in erecting the original seven cell blocks together with the wall and front building amounted to $772,600. Part of that sum, $99,476.60, came from the sale of certain city lots and the site of old Walnut Street Jail, all of which properties belonged to the Commonwealth.

When the Building Commissioners finished their business and turned their books over to the Board of Inspectors of the prison (the last meeting was held December 27, 1833), they recorded the following as receipts and expenditures, the latter of which paid for the wall, front building, and the first three ranges of cells:

RECEIPTS

Amount of monies received from the state treasury	$337,124.09
From the sale of lots in the City of Philadelphia	14,094.00
Sale of "old materials"	1,107.97
	$352,326.06

EXPENDITURES

Cost of site, including recording of deeds	$ 13,115.52
Amount expended on the work	334,447.19
Furnishing of cells for reception of prisoners & for office and house furniture	1,528.86
Leaving a balance of	3,234.49
	$352,326.06

During the investigation of the management of the prison in 1834, which we shall discuss in the next chapter, the charge was made that serious fraud had been perpetrated in the construction of the institution. Whether this charge was true or not, it is certain that Cherry Hill prison was an expensive and even extravagant structure for that era. William Crawford, the British commissioner, stated that much money was unwisely spent "on decorations." It was the most elaborate prison plant that had ever been built. Visitors from far and near came to Philadelphia to see it, and all were impressed by its massive wall and front building as well as by the judicious arrangement of the cell blocks.

McElwee's Report stated that 311 cells were built in 1834 with funds appropriated amounting to $772,600. Taking this over-all cost—for wall, front building, and cells—and dividing it by the number of cells, this would amount to $2,500 per cell. But the record shows the actual cost of the cells alone was $400 each in the one-story blocks and $300 each in the two-story blocks.[31] The records of the Building Commission show that the center building, including the reservoir, cost $3,660 and that the cell blocks, with 38 cells, cost $24,042 each.

It would be extremely difficult today to make precise charges regarding extravagance or fraud in the construction of this prison. Subsequent experience with prison construction leads

[31] *McElwee's Report* (Philadelphia, 1835), p. 199.

to the conclusion that the Cherry Hill prison was no more expensive to build than some modern penal establishments. But its cost was perhaps out of line for those days.[32]

RECEPTION OF PRISONERS

The reception of the prisoner at the Eastern Penitentiary in its early days was not much different from that of today. The same preparations for his sojourn in the institution were as necessary then as now. The same data were desired for his personal record except that in modern times more details regarding his early life, family, and interests are assembled. The prison staff is more specialized today with its psychologist, psychiatrist, social worker, educational director, and others interested in understanding the prisoner. In the early days no specialists other than the medical doctor were available. There was a chaplain, but he served in a volunteer capacity until 1838 when a salaried "moral instructor" was appointed.

We get our description of the preparation of the prisoner from *McElwee's Report.* He writes that the prisoner upon arrival was first examined by the warden. Then he was taken to a "preparing room," where he was "divested of his usual garments, his hair closely trimmed and where he [underwent] the process of ablution." Certain physical data were recorded such as color of skin, hair, and eyes; scars or physical blemishes; height; and length of foot. He was then given a "uniform and a hood was drawn down over his eyes and was conducted to his cell."

The first "preparing room" was, in reality, a small building in the front yard consisting of three rooms, in the first of which the prisoner undressed "and had his hair cut short," in the second "his person was cleansed in a warm bath," and in the third he was "clothed in the prison uniform."

Richard Vaux recorded that a new "preparing room" was built in 1871. It was located on the western side of the main

[32] Costs of some modern prisons: the Graterford Annex of the Eastern State Penitentiary, Pennsylvania, built from 1926–29, $7,770,000; the Jackson, Michigan, prison, $8,000,000; the Attica, New York, prison, built in 1933, $10,000,000; and the Green Haven, New York, prison, built in 1942, $7,790,000.

entrance at a short distance beyond the inside main gate. He
stated that it was "so secure that no combination of prisoners
to escape can be successful" and since "they are unknown to
the prison authorities [as to their record]" exceptional caution
had to be taken. He further said that "in passing from the front
to the center building and thence to their cells, they wear a
cap which prevents recognition in the day-time and secures
them from acquiring any topographical knowledge of the
ground plan of the penitentiary." [33]

Upon entering the cell the prisoner's hood was removed and
he was "interrogated as to his former life." Then one of the
"functionaries of the establishment uttered an address in which
the consequences of his crime were portrayed, the design of
his punishment manifested, and the rules of the prison amply
delineated." He was then "left to the salutary admonition of a
reproving conscience and the reflections which solitude usually
produces." *McElwee's Report* continues:

They reject, from sad experience, the daydreams of the sages who,
amidst the very bosom of society, have prated about the charms of
loneliness. Existence has no charms unless witnessed by, or enjoyed
with, our fellow men. The convicts feel it so. Ennui seizes them,
every hour is irksome, and they supplicate for the means of employment with the most abject humility. They consider labour as a favor,
not as a punishment, and they receive it as such. They are also furnished a Bible, some religious tracts, and occasionally other works,
calculated to imbue their minds with moral and religious ideas.[34]

The report of the inspectors, submitted January 16, 1833,
is especially interesting as an indication of the actual working
of the reformative principle of the system as it appeared to the
administrators:

We mark, generally, that at first the prisoner indulges in morose or
vindictive feelings, and is guilty of turbulent and malicious conduct;
but after a few weeks he adopts a more subdued tone, becomes reasonable, and his countenance indicates a more amiable state of mind;
is disposed to talk of his past life as one of misery and folly; begins

[33] Richard Vaux, *Brief Sketch of the Origin and History*, p. 69.
[34] *McElwee's Report*, p. 13.

to think that the barrier between him and a good reputation is not impossible; and that there are those in the community, whose prejudices against the condemned are not so strong as to induce the withholding a friendly countenance to his attempts at restoration. In many, the retrospect of life becomes a horrible and loathsome subject of reflection—the sense of shame and feelings of remorse drives them to some source of consolation, and the ordinary means of stifling an actively reproving conscience being denied by reason of their solitariness, the comforts of the Bible and the peace of religion are eagerly sought for.[35]

The prisoner's clothes were made of coarse cotton cloth. The winter uniform was described as a "roundabout, a vest, and a pair of pantaloons, made of cassinet, or sometimes very thick roundabouts, lined all through." Stockings were of wool to be changed every two weeks. The inmate was shod in a pair of "stout shoes." A cap finished his wardrobe. For summer wear the materials were of lighter weight. Certainly there was no attempt to humiliate the prisoner with a garish or degrading type of uniform as was done, for instance, in the early Massachusetts prison where, in 1812, red and blue uniforms were issued, and later, ones of red, black, blue, and yellow stripes. The only clue regarding colors at Cherry Hill was "such as are deemed suitable and convenient."

The food given the prisoners compared favorably in quality, quantity, and variety with other prisons of the day. The diet furnished the inmates of the Walnut Street Jail served as a pattern. For breakfast, it consisted of one pint of coffee or cocoa "made from the cocoa nut." For dinner, three-fourths of a pound of beef without bone or one-half pound of pork, one pint of soup, and as many potatoes as the prisoner wished. Occasionally boiled rice was served instead of potatoes. For supper, Indian mush was the main dish. One-half gallon of molasses was the lot of the inmate per month. Salt was given when asked for and vinegar as a favor. Turnips and cabbage "in the form of crout" were sometimes distributed. The daily ration of bread per inmate was one pound. The traditional

[35] *Journal of the Senate of Pennsylvania, 1832–33,* II, 509.

Christmas dinner consisted of a pound of pork, potatoes, and an apple. In later days it became a tradition to serve each inmate a "Dutch cake" on Christmas Day.

The prisoners were, of course, fed in their cells. The food was taken to them from the kitchen, which was in the front building, "in three little wagons" named by the prisoner waiter, one William Parker, Washington, Franklin, and Lafayette— "one for potatoes, one for beef, and one for soup." [36]

EFFORTS TO KEEP PRISONERS APART

If a prison operating on the principle of separate confinement was to be successful, it was necessary to keep its inmates apart. In European prisons where the Pennsylvania System was adopted, great use was made of the mask or hood which each convict pulled down over his face when he left his cell. Inmates were taken in small groups to the chapel or to work or exercise with masks over their faces.

But in Cherry Hill there was little necessity for using the mask since the inmate rarely left his cell. There are no references made to the mask in the annual reports of the inspectors and very few in the wardens' journals. McElwee, on a few occasions, alludes to its use, and Charles Dickens in his *American Notes* comments on it as follows:

Over the head and face of every prisoner who comes into this melancholy house, a black hood is drawn; and in his dark shroud, an emblem of the curtain dropped between him and the living world, he is led to his cell from which he never again comes forth, until his whole term of imprisonment has expired.

Warden Nimrod Strickland made the following entry in his Journal on September 3, 1855: "The new order of the Board requiring the yard and shop men, in passing from and returning to their cells, to wear hood-caps, with eye holes, was put into practice this morning." This would seem to indicate that the rule requiring the mask had not been strictly enforced.

The mask was used in the institution even as late as Warden Cassidy's administration (1881–1900), although during most of

[36] *McElwee's Report,* p. 208.

that time two men were placed in one cell together. In Warden Joseph Byers's Journal for March, 1904, appears the final entry regarding the mask: "All hoods, except when requested by the prisoner, discontinued."

Prisoners were given an opportunity to exercise in their individual yards one hour daily in two half-hour shifts. In order to make supervision easier, prisoners with alternate numbers were exercised at a time. Thus prisoners 1, 3, 5, . . . 11 were out of their cells at the same time, and prisoners 2, 4, 6, . . . 12 exercised later. A keeper patrolled the walls while another surveyed the entire establishment from the observatory tower over the center building. Every effort was made to restrain the exercising prisoners from conversing or from throwing notes over the walls. However, it was impossible for the guard in the tower to see into all the yards. This was obviously a defect in the planning by the architect.

The Reverend Louis Dwight, speculating on the problem of inspecting the inmates of this prison, stated that the walls of the yards were not prepared for keepers to walk on them and that in no place in the institution was there an inspection post that could survey the yards if certain inmates chose not to be seen. He added that it would take a guard for every five feet of wall to prevent any conversation between the prisoners during their exercise.

There is evidence that some of the inmates were permitted to keep small pets such as birds and rabbits in their cells and yards. Later records indicate that prisoners were also permitted to use their yards for the cultivation of vegetables and flowers. From a Philadelphia Prison Society report we find this panegyric regarding this yard privilege:

To many of the prisoners the privilege of cultivating fruits and flowers is a source of much satisfaction and may be of some useful reflection, leading their attention to the beneficent provision made by the Creator of all, to supply legitimate wants to his creatures. Who will affirm that the beauty and aroma of the unfolding flower, the delicious and healthful food afforded by the full-grown fruit, may not, in the stillness with which their cultivator is surrounded, appeal to his heart with an efficacy unattainable by the logic or the eloquence of Man, and soften and contrite it; implanting therein strong and enduring feelings of gratitude and contrition, with earnest and perhaps controlling desires for amendment of life? [37]

Two of these exercise yards still exist. Vestiges of most of them remain, but only as they form a part of the several buildings adapted for use as dining room, print shop, and other services. This was done by knocking out the stone walls between the yards and then covering the space with a roof.

Nothing appears in the first annual reports of the inspectors or of the warden indicating just how the prisoners were bathed or how frequently. But in a later report, the sixteenth, dated March, 1845, we get some notion from the following:

The daily escape-steam from the steam engine is passed into a tank containing about eighty hogsheads of water, which thereby is maintained at a temperature of about 90 degrees; ten separate cells, each having a bath, receive the prisoners that are brought separately by their overseers, and are allowed fifteen minutes for bathing; soap, fresh water, and a dry towel are furnished each. By this means 40 can be bathed per hour without any infringement of the separate system,—an officer walking in front of the grated doors of the bathing cells effectually preventing any possibility of communication. [38]

The report states that these baths were given weekly, but in the minutes of the Philadelphia Prison Society for 1845 it was recorded that the prisoners were bathed once every 20 days. The physician at the time, Dr. Robert A. Given, speaks of "the weekly use, by the prisoner, of the warm baths, now in operation." [39] Warden George Thompson in 1844 recorded the following relative to bathing, apparently during the summer months: "George Smith of the Prison Society was here to superintend the bathing of the prisoners in 3rd. and 4th. Blocks in the evening, in the pond erected between these blocks. Expressed

[37] *Acting Committee Minutes,* April 11, 1861.

[38] Quoted in the *Journal of Prison Discipline and Philanthropy,* Vol. I, No. 2 (1845), p. 173.

[39] Dr. Franklin Bache, first physician, resigned in 1835 and was succeeded by Dr. William Darrach, who served until 1843. He was succeeded by Dr. Edward Hartshorne who served only one year. Dr. Given served from 1844 to 1851.

satisfaction that this important matter could be effected without difficulty by increasing the number of ponds between each two blocks." The next year Warden Thomas Scattergood recorded that he had completed bathing the prisoners and hoped that by keeping at the work each prisoner would be bathed once each two weeks.

In 1845, Warden Thompson reported that he was employing, separately, some of the invalid prisoners in the cultivation of the large yards between the blocks. These inmates were under the supervision of "a careful officer, skilled in horticulture who takes special care that no two should approach or recognize each other; the yards being divided by the buildings makes this task easy, and the prisoner being aware that the privilege so highly valued would be lost by violating the rule, has no inducement thereto."

Six gardens were cultivated, and between 400 and 500 bushels of tomatoes "were one of the many descriptions of vegetables furnished." In addition these gardens provided, "under the physician's orders, separate employment for twelve invalids half a day each" demonstrating that the "plan was not only humane, but important in a pecuniary point of view—both in restoring health, and making those productive who were formerly the contrary." [40]

Also in 1845 Warden Thompson described the religious services in one block of 100 inmates. No mention was made of a curtain or of the use of the mask. But the outer wooden doors were apparently open and the inmates were in their individual cells. The Reverend Mr. Crawford instructed the inmates in singing and the warden remarked that "during the exercise there has been no attempt at communication." He adds: "I confidently assert this, as, if such attempts were made, detection would be almost certain. Two officers with woolen socks are passing constantly in front of the cells during service."

The inability to recognize each other or to have communication with their fellows undoubtedly struck terror in the minds

[40] From the inspectors' *Sixteenth Annual Report,* quoted in *Journal of Prison Discipline and Philanthropy,* Vol. I, No. 4 (1845), p. 379.

of those who were sent to Cherry Hill. The congregate nature
of the Walnut Street Jail, especially in its last days, presented a
sharp contrast to the new dispensation in the Eastern Penitentiary. A letter, purported to have been written by a prisoner
in the Walnut Street Jail to his mother, which "fell accidentally"
into the hands of Warden Wood gives credence to the fear
held by the inmates of that institution.

Walnut Street Jail, Philadelphia

Dear Mother:

The law has passed that all crimes now committed shall be sentenced to that terrible prison (the Eastern, or Bush Hill Penitentiary). The unfortunate being who is sent there will be immured
in a solitary cell, there to exist in seclusion and misery until his sentence expires, or death ends his sufferings. This prison will be done
away with in a year from March next; most of the men that shall
be in this house at the time, will be sent to Bush Hill.

Therefore, my beloved and excellent mother, commence now, and
let nothing deter you from persevering, until you obtain for me a
pardon.[41]

When the state prisoners of the Walnut Street Jail were to
be transferred to Cherry Hill, the warden of the prison and the
Board of Inspectors of the jail cooperated in handling this difficult job. The jail inspectors asked for help from the sheriff of
the county but were refused unless he could be given complete
charge of the operation. The Board next turned to the mayor
of the city and to Colonel Miller of the United States Marines.
Both of these gentlemen offered their assistance. Colonel Miller
supplied the necessary handcuffs and a detachment of 30
marines, the mayor a sufficient number of police officers.[42]

On October 5, 1835, 59 men and 10 women were transferred
to the Cherry Hill prison. Warden Wood's Journal records their
reception:

Arose early and had all our arrangements made to receive the
prisoners from Walnut Street. Soon after 8 o'clock they arrived in

[41] *Fourth Annual Report,* Board of Inspectors, Eastern Penitentiary, 1833,
p. 4.
[42] Minutes of the Board of Inspectors, Walnut Street Jail, see meetings of
October 3 and 4, 1835.

omnibus and carriages to the number of 54 white and black men—they returned and brought us 5 more men and 10 women, four white and six black. They were attended by several of the Inspectors of the Walnut Street Prison and a strong body of police officers. The men were all brought handcuffed two and two together. I placed them in two rooms on their arrival and then took them out in pairs and had their irons taken off and escorted each man by two persons, to the wash houses. Of these we had four—the regular one, the Dyehouse, and the two wash houses. Each working place had five men, two sets to convey the prisoners. By these arrangements we got the men all washed and in their cells by 10 o'clock.

The women required more time as they were all passed through the regular reception house. The men all came in their convict suits. I went into each room and addressed them and they behaved without exception well. The negro men sang one or two hymns together which I did not prevent. I went into 25 cells after dinner and took a description of them and was surprised at the very subdued appearance and uniform good conduct. The most of them expressed a determination to do and behave well and several asked for work. I believe the quiet and systematic mode we adopted throughout had a favorable effect and the mode of hooding them has a subduing one; not a man refused to have it put on; No. 499 (Levi Jones) was represented as a most outrageous fellow. I had him put into a dark cell at once as he was brought from the cells in Walnut Street as he had threatened some of the keepers. After dinner I had a talk with him. He appeared as humble and subdued as any of them and promised that he would do all in his power to please us and behave well. I took him at his word and placed him in his cell in the proper order.

Without an untoward incident, Walnut Street Jail was abandoned by its inmates and soon became merely an historic memory in the annals of Pennsylvania penology.

THE FIRST PRISONERS

The first prisoner to arrive at the Cherry Hill prison was a Negro named Charles Williams. The records describe him as "farmer, light black; black eyes; curly black hair; 5′ 7½″; foot, 11″; flat nose, scar on bridge of nose, broad mouth, scar from dirk on thigh; can read." He was sentenced to imprisonment for

two years on October 22, 1829, by the Court of Oyer and
Terminer of Delaware County for burglary. On July 31, 1829, at
10 P.M. he broke into the house of Nathan Lukens (Dowling
House) in Upper Darby and stole: "1 silver watch, value $20;
1 gold seal, value $3; 1 gold key, value $2." [43]

Williams entered the Eastern Penitentiary three days after
he was sentenced. He was born in Harrisburg, Pennsylvania,
and was eighteen years old when admitted. His duties in the
prison, according to *McElwee's Report,* included working in
the yard, cleaning, taking care of the horses, and attending the
mortar and stone carriers. In 1831, the two French commissioners De Beaumont and De Tocqueville visited the prison and
talked with this first prisoner, disclosing that he was a shoemaker
and that he made as many as ten pairs of shoes per week. They
wrote of him:

This man works with ardor. His mind seems tranquil; his disposition excellent. He considers his being brought to the Penitentiary as
a signal benefit of Providence. His thoughts are in general religious.
He read to us in the Gospel the parable of the Good Shepherd, the
meaning of which touched him deeply; one who was born of a de-
graded and depressed race, and had never experienced any thing
but indifference and harshness.

Warden Wood, in his Journal, wrote of this first prisoner:

October 25: Recd. this day Charles Williams a coloured man
Convicted in Delaware County of Burglary and sentenced to Two
Years. No physician having been appointed by the Board, James
Coxe, M.D. was called to make the examination required by law.
The weather being damp the Warden thought best as there was no
way to warm the Cells, to place the prisoner in one of the Rooms of
the Infirmary.[44]

October 26: Visited No. 1 who complained of a cough occasioned
he said by being left in a damp room in Chester Prison.

October 28: No. 1 expressed a wish to be allowed to go to work.

Williams was released on October 22, 1831.

[43] This information has not been verified and comes from one of the former
employees of the prison, Mr. Tom Collins.
[44] Williams was placed in a room in the central tower where he remained
until his removal to a cell on November 10.

Prisoner No. 2, John Smith, was 20 years of age, and was sentenced to one year from Chester County for horse stealing. He entered the prison November 7, 1829, and was discharged at the expiration of his sentence. Prisoner No. 3 was Richard Jones from Philadelphia County, aged 28. His crime was highway robbery and this was his third offense. Committed to the prison on November 21 of the same year, his sentence was 11 years, but despite this he was pardoned by the governor on July 6, 1832. Prisoner No. 4 was John Lavrow, 18 years old and a Philadelphian. He entered the prison on the same day as Jones. His offense was also highway robbery. Apparently Lavrow enjoyed special privileges in the prison; at least this may be surmised from the testimony brought out in the investigation of the management in 1834. One prisoner, William Parker, stated at that time: "I have seen No. 4 sitting in center house alongside William Baen [a keeper] reading newspapers. He was a white convict and had more privileges than any other prisoner —breathing the fresh air, walking about the yard on a Sabbath day particularly during divine services."

These four prisoners, together with six others, comprised the first group of inmates in the new prison.[45] They were the "guinea pigs" upon whom the advocates of the strange system of separate confinement were to experiment in their attempts to establish a new philosophy of penal discipline. Thousands more were to experience the rigors of this system before it was finally abandoned.

The first women sent to the prison were Amy Rogers, No. 73, and Henrietta Johnson, No. 74. Both were sentenced from Philadelphia courts for manslaughter. The former was sentenced to three years and the latter, who became a cook in the prison,

[45] No. 5, Howard Moore; No. 6, John Curran; No. 7, John Kiner; No. 8, John Stern; No. 9, Patrick Murray; No. 10, Ebenezer Lewis. John Curran, No. 6, was discharged in 1831 and became an employee of the institution. In fact, it was he who helped give Seneca Plimly the ice water ducking which became one of the scandals in the investigation of 1834. See *McElwee's Report*, p. 179; see also p. 101. Five of these first ten prisoners were convicted of horse stealing, with burglary, highway robbery, counterfeiting, and forgery making up the remainder of the offenses.

to six. They both entered the prison on April 30, 1831. It was the second offense for No. 73 and the third for No. 74. On December 10 of the same year two others, Ann Hinson, No. 100, and Eliza Anderson, No. 101, were sentenced by the Philadelphia courts for manslaughter. All four of the above were Negroes.

In 1836 there were so many females at Cherry Hill that it was deemed necessary to secure a matron for the women's block. Mrs. Harriet B. Hall, a "woman of christian character and discipline" was appointed by the inspectors who "felt confident that many of the unhappy females would be reclaimed from vice and wretchedness and restored to paths of virtue and true happiness." Women were committed to Eastern Penitentiary until 1922 when those remaining were transferred to the State Industrial Home for Women at Muncy or to county jails. During the early years the women were housed in the upper gallery of Block 7, but for many years prior to their eventual removal Block 2 was set aside for their incarceration.

EARLY WARDENS OF THE PRISON

It would seem that the first warden of the new prison had been groomed for the position. He was the astute Samuel R. Wood, a Quaker and a member of the Philadelphia Prison Society. He was also one of the inspectors of the Walnut Street Jail and a member of the Building Commission that supervised the building of Cherry Hill. In fact he was the secretary of this Commission during its 12 years of laborious work.

Samuel R. Wood was born August 25, 1776, in the quaint little hamlet of Blue Bell, Whitpain Township, Montgomery County, Pennsylvania, the son of John and Catherine Wood. There are few facts known about his life before he assumed charge of the new penitentiary. De Beaumont and De Tocqueville spoke very highly of Wood. They wrote that he was "a man of superior mind, who, influenced by religious sentiments, has abandoned his former career [sic] in order to devote himself entirely to the success of the establishment so useful to his community." [46]

[46] Quoted in *McElwee's Report*, p. 38.

A further word of testimony regarding this first warden came from the distinguished political scientist Dr. Francis Lieber, who translated the report of the commissioners mentioned above, *On the Penitentiary System.* Wrote Dr. Lieber: "I have never found a superintendent of any penitentiary of a more humane disposition, and clearer mind on all subjects of the penitentiary system than Mr. Wood; I must add here that I have received from no one more sound and practical knowledge of the penitentiary system, generally, than from Mr. Wood. I have for my part never become acquainted with a person whom I thought equally fitted for that station." [47]

Five years later when the warden's regime was under fire, the majority report of the legislative committee had the following to say about his attributes:

His mind seems to have been devoted with much earnestness to the cause of humanity, and the improvement for this purpose of what is now appropriately called the Pennsylvania Penitentiary System. Without any other compensation or reward than "the luxury of doing good," this gentleman devoted his time and means to this interesting, but to many, revolting subject. Not satisfied with the knowledge acquired in his own country, like the celebrated Howard, he visited the prisons of foreign countries, and there added to his already great experience. Such untiring singleness of purpose in the pursuit of knowledge for the alleviation of human misery, and the improvement of the moral condition of mankind, without any selfish motive to actuate it, is certainly indicative of a sound head and a pure heart.

This report continues by stating that the inspectors of the prison with great earnestness pressed upon Mr. Wood the acceptance of the situation of warden. . . . After some hesitation and reluctance he yielded to the importunity of the friends of humanity, who were anxious to place under his direction an institution which would carry into full effect, the great system so long urged by philanthropists and to which he himself had been so much devoted. [48]

A word of rebuttal to these encomiums must be appended here. The minority report of the investigating committee of the legislature elicits considerable feeling:

[47] *Ibid.*   [48] *Ibid.*, p. 37.

The biography of Mr. Wood is totally gratuitous. He did not, like
"the celebrated Howard, visit the prisons of foreign countries, without any other compensation or reward than the luxury of doing
good." He went to England for the purpose of improving himself in a
particular branch of his profession, and from thence to Russia with
Clymer's printing-press, not as a Howard. While in England he conversed with some of the benevolent Society of Friends from whom
he acquired some knowledge of the discipline of English prisons,
and on his return was appointed as an inspector of the Walnut Street
Prison, and was subsequently appointed Warden of the Eastern
Penitentiary. This is the sum and substance of the matter.[49]

Wood and William H. Hood, a former clerk at the Walnut
Street Jail and later a city alderman, were nominated for the
position as warden of the new prison. Wood was finally appointed at a salary of $1,500. Hood was appointed a member
of the Board of Inspectors in 1833.

Samuel R. Wood is supposed to have lived at one time at
244 Wood Street in Norristown, Pennsylvania, and to have had
a brother named Thomas. Samuel owned a farm at Plymouth
Meeting, a hamlet near Norristown, was in business, a stone and
lead mill with a Thomas Mervine on Ridge Road, about three-
quarters of a mile from the penitentiary, and was also in the
"mahogany business" with another partner named Jacob Zigler.

Wood resigned as warden in 1840. In his last report to the
inspectors he wrote: "I take leave of the institution with a hope
that it will prosper and with a firm and decided belief that so
long as the principles of our system are adhered to and carried
out, we shall find the Pennsylvania System effecting more practical good than any other yet adopted." He retired to a farm
near Catawissa, a small town in upstate Pennsylvania. We see
his name mentioned in the prison records of 1851 when he returned to Cherry Hill to make a settlement since certain irregularities were found in his accounts. These few facts concerning this early penal administrator are all that have been discovered to date.

Wood was succeeded by George Thompson whose term of

[49] *Ibid.*, p. 23.

office extended from 1840 to 1845. Thompson was an operator of a foundry known as the Mary Ann Furnace and Forge, located on Big Trough Creek, near Huntingdon, Pennsylvania, owned by one John Savage. Little is known of Thompson; his name is not recorded in any of the historical compilations of Huntingdon County.

The third warden was Thomas Scattergood, a Philadelphia Quaker. He was born January 22, 1803, the son of Joseph and Ann Rogers Scattergood. He was a tanner and railroad official and a member of the Philadelphhia Prison Society. He died October 15, 1883. His term as warden was from 1845 to 1850. That Warden Scattergood was a devout man may be gleaned from notations he made in his Journal. Here are some typical entries:

December 31, 1845: [The inmates had escaped an epidemic of smallpox that raged in the city.] To have been permitted thus far to have escaped the small pox . . . is certainly cause of thankfulness to that Being who regards all Mankind whether Bond or free as the peculiar objects of his Mercy and Love—In the earnest hope that the blessing of health may still be continued and the opening of the New Year may find us all sincerely desirous of promoting the best interests of the Institution we close our remarks for the year 1845.

January 1, 1846: The New Year—may its end find all engaged in the administration of the affairs of the Institution harmoniously labouring for its good.

December 31, 1846: In the retrospect there is much cause to be thankful to the giver of all good under a proper sense thereof, may grateful feelings be the clothing of our hearts, for the Blessing, and incite us to commence the New Year with sincere desires to perform the responsible duties devolving upon us with increased faithfulness.

January 1, 1849: The beginning of another year! May its end (if spared to see it) find us still more faithful in the performance of duty.

Devout though he was, Warden Scattergood was displeased at the sermon delivered to the prisoners on January 7, 1849, by one Mary Caley, "a female holding the station of a minister among those known as Hicksite Friends." Wrote the warden: "Her discourse was marked by an entire omission to direct the penitent to the Savior—so much so as to be the subject of general remark of those officers who heard it." Nonetheless, Mary Caley was back at her post in the prison on February 4.

Scattergood was succeeded by John S. Halloway who had been a clerk under Warden Wood. The son of Jacob Halloway, one-time principal keeper of the Walnut Street Jail, he served as warden at two different times: 1850–54 and 1856–70. Judge Nimrod Strickland from West Chester was warden between Halloway's two terms. Halloway was succeeded in 1870 by Dr. Edward Townsend, a Philadelphia dentist. Townsend served until 1881 when he was succeeded by Michael Cassidy, the first "career" warden. Cassidy had started in the prison as an overseer in 1861. His term as warden extended until 1900. Others who followed Cassidy for brief terms were Daniel Bussinger, 1900–1904; Joseph Byers, 1904–05; Charles Church, 1905–08; and Robert J. McKenty, 1909–23.

Upon his appointment as warden of the new prison, Samuel Wood called upon William Blundin, an employee of his in the stone mill and who lived in Norristown, to be gatekeeper. Blundin and his wife lived in the prison, and the fact that this woman had free run of the establishment brought her into the investigation of the prison administration in 1834. Warden Wood was a bachelor and her name was linked with his in the charges.[50]

The principal keeper of the establishment on its opening was William Griffith. Those in charge of instructing the prisoners in their handcraft work were called overseers. The custodial personnel were referred to as keepers.

The Philadelphia Prison Society was, in a sense, the "watchdog" of the regime at the new prison. Its members were ever mindful of their responsibility to the citizens of the Commonwealth and discussed the management of the prison at many of their meetings. However, two charges may be made against them. First, they were themselves so devout that they often failed to impute wrong intent in others, especially if such persons were clothed with authority. Second, they were naive to

[50] *Ibid.,* pp. 256–57.

the point of gullibility. Both the wily convicts and the astute administrators could easily hoodwink them. When the convicts simulated religion and posed as repentant, the Philadelphia reformers tended to believe them. In addition, they condoned "with regret" such punishments as the dark cell and the water douche or shower bath.

We do not know what the members of the Philadelphia Prison Society thought of the startling revelations brought out against Warden Wood and his staff during the 1834 investigation for nothing was set down in the minutes of the Society relative to this investigation. From the time the prison was opened until the investigation, not one word appears against the management of the prison involving punishments, escapes, violations of the separate system, or of irregularities in the financial operations of the institution. Surely they should have known of the rumors that were current at the time. This is one aspect of the Society that cannot readily be explained.

The first recorded complaints in the minutes of the Society appear years after the investigation: February 11, 1842, "some of the cells appeared to be neglected;" February 10, 1843, "several prisoners were out of their cells and might communicate with each other and some of the prisoners complained that their cells were too cold and a few that their food was not clean." Other recorded comments indicate that during September, 1843, the Society approved the "shower bath" [douche] as a form of punishment; on May 9, 1845, it was reported "that the old floors were in bad condition;" and in June of the same year it was reported that on Sundays when the usual number of keepers was not present "much noise takes place in the three single blocks." On March 13, 1846, a rather lengthy report was submitted stating that the institution was cold and that the labor conditions in the prison were unsatisfactory.

Apologists of the separate system contended that early irregularities in the prison management were inevitable, and that the years between 1829 and 1849 were "experimental" years. This theme is expanded by Richard Vaux, who was for 40 years the president of the Board of Inspectors and wrote widely in defense of the system. He stated that the attention of the inspectors was directed to the construction of the buildings and to practical management without much regard to the workings of the system upon which the penitentiary was established.

An examination of the records shows that the administration of the prison was unable to carry out a strict philosophy of separate confinement even from the very beginning. Consistently throughout the prison's history from 1829 to 1913, when the Pennsylvania legislature, at the request of Governor John K. Tener repealed the law under which the system operated, violations of the principle of separation were numerous. Long before 1913 the system was hopelessly failing. The governor's message to the legislature read in part:

The congregate method should be made a part of our penal system; and hence I recommend the passage of an act providing that the inspectors, commissioners and managers of penitentiaries, jails, houses of correction and refuge and reformatories shall be authorized, in their discretion, to have the inmates of such institutions congregated for the purpose of worship, labor, learning and recreation.

Here is the official end of the separate system of penal discipline in Pennsylvania.[51]

[51] This recommendation became law, No. 395, *Laws of the General Assembly, Pennsylvania*, p. 708.

≡4

Investigations of Cherry Hill

THE INVESTIGATION OF 1834–35

FEW public institutions escape the embarrassment of an occasional official investigation, and the prison at Philadelphia was no exception. During the period of this study, 1829 to 1913, the management of the prison was subjected to three such probes. One occurred in 1834, only five years after its opening; the second in 1897; and the third in 1903. In all of these the management came through only slightly discredited.

Great hopes were entertained by Pennsylvania's enlightened citizens for the system of separate confinement inaugurated in the Philadelphia prison. Great things were expected of Samuel R. Wood as warden, not only by the governing board of the prison but by members of the legislature and students of penal administration in that era.

Unfortunately, within five years after the opening of the establishment Warden Wood and his administration were under a cloud of disapproval. Rumblings of discontent concerning the internal management of the institution were heard in the legislature. Serious apprehension "was excited in the minds of men friendly to the system that wealth and family connexions were about to sanctify fraud, immense and palpable peculation and cruelty [which] if suffered to be pursued with impunity, would jeopardize the successful development of the principles on which it was founded." [1]

The two penitentiaries operating within the confines of the Commonwealth were administered by law through boards of inspectors appointed by the judges of the Supreme Court of the Commonwealth. This was later changed by the act of May 10, 1909, when the governor was given the appointing power. The inspectors of the Philadelphia prison were given respon-

[1] *McElwee's Report* (Philadelphia, 1835), p. 3.

sibility not only of operating the prison within the framework of the law of 1829 but of employing all personnel, including the warden.

Until the creation of the Department of Public Welfare in 1921, only one attempt—and that a rather feeble one—had ever been made to provide a centralized and uniform administration of the penal, reformatory, and correctional institutions of the state. This occurred when an act was passed on April 24, 1869, to create a Board of Public Charities. According to the terms of this act the governor was empowered to appoint five commissioners to serve for a term of five years as a Board of Public Charities. The board members or their agent were required to visit at least once a year all the charitable and correctional institutions in the state. Although they could recommend changes, they had only supervisory powers and could never assume any administrative direction or coordination of the various institutions. Not until the creation of the Department of Welfare was there any integration of the various institutions or was the authority of the Boards of Inspectors challenged.[2]

The Board of Inspectors of the prison at Philadelphia operated the prison until 1954 when the act of July, 1953, passed by the legislature went into effect. This act made mandatory the coordination of all correctional institutions in the state and established the office of Commissioner of Correction. In 1955 Governor George Leader abolished the Board of Inspectors, or Trustees as they were called, of the prison.

When the first investigating committee made its charges against the administration in 1834, the Board of Inspectors was as much involved as was Warden Wood. The inspectors were responsible to the legislature and to the governor. Their annual reports to the legislature were to contain an over-all description of their stewardship, yet one of the charges brought out in the 1834 probe was that the Board concealed many items of management that would undoubtedly have placed it in a bad light with both the legislature and the public. At the very

[2] See Harry Elmer Barnes, *Evolution of Penology in Pennsylvania* (Indianapolis, 1926), pp. 194–95.

time the investigation was underway the inspectors made the following glowing report:

The Pennsylvania System is emphatically a mild and humane system. Let us look for a moment at the condition of the majority of those who become subject to its regulation. We find them living a hurried and thoughtless life of hourly excitement, and shuddering at the possibility of a pause which could let in (to them, the demon) reflection. We see them wanting the ordinary comforts of clothing and cleanliness, without home save that afforded by chance companionship. We find them in the brothel and the gin-shop, giving up to all manner of excesses, indulging in every extreme of vice, self-degraded and brutal. We see them corrupted and corrupting, initiating new candidates in the race of misery and dragging them in their own vortex to a death of infamy and horror.

Where do we place them and how do we treat them? They are taken to the bath and cleansed of outward pollution, they are new-clad in warm and comfortable garments, they are placed in an apartment infinitely superior to what they have been accustomed, they are given employment to enable them to live by their own industry, they are addressed in language of kindness, interest is shown in their present and future welfare, they are advised and urged to think of their former course and to avoid it, they are lifted gently from their state of humiliation; self-degradation is removed, and self-esteem is induced. Pride of character and manliness is inculcated, and they go out of prison unknown as convicts, determined to wrestle for a living in the path of honesty and virtue. Is not that humane? [3]

Legislative investigations come and go. Some result in far-reaching reforms, some merely give lip service to improvements, and some end in a complete whitewash. Still others manage to whitewash and at the same time suggest the necessity of reform. The investigation of Cherry Hill in 1834 gave the prison administration a clean bill of health with a few mild reprimands and suggestions for reform. The committee appointed by the legislature was divided into two hostile camps, the minority consisting of one man, Thomas B. McElwee of Bedford County. McElwee assailed the majority findings and to him we are indebted for the publication of the proceedings.

[3] *Journal of the Senate of Pennsylvania* (1834–35), pp. 467 f.

The tone of *McElwee's Report* is bitter. From the evidence revealed, either the charges against the management were true or else there was wholesale perjury. We therefore conclude that the administration of the prison was at best decidedly lax and confused.

Warden Wood, on hearing that McElwee was about to publish the proceedings of the committee, announced apprehensively to the Board of Inspectors "that part of the testimony that could give an unfavorable impression relative to the management and discipline of this institution and aid in any prejudice and excitement against us" was about to be published. The Board had previously cleared Wood of alleged immoral and criminal offenses, a charge brought against him by some of his underofficers, but decided to do nothing to prevent publication.

The official investigation "for the purpose of examining into the Economy and Management" of the prison began when a joint committee was appointed from the Senate and House in the early part of December, 1834. However, the preliminaries for the inquiry were begun nearly a year before when hints that affairs were not well came from some disgruntled employees of the prison. Judge Charles Coxe, president of the Board of Inspectors, took down their testimony but from all we can learn no action was taken by the inspectors.

Since nothing came of these informal charges, several men "well-known and respectable" carried the story to the attorney-general, George M. Dallas, urging him to ask the governor to order a thorough investigation. Dallas immediately communicated with Judge Coxe asking for the testimony of the employees. On March 8, 1834, Judge Coxe sent Dallas the testimony of some 16 witnesses who had preferred charges against the management. This action had the sanction of the entire Board of Inspectors. After carefully perusing these charges, Attorney-General Dallas wrote to Governor George Wolf on November 26,

I believe it is my duty to submit the subject to you, that, if deemed necessary, measures may be taken alike to preserve this valuable in-

stitution in the esteem of our fellow citizens, to remove all doubts
as to its system of discipline and general management, and, if abuses
really exist, to reform them before much mischief shall have been
produced.[4]

Before discussing the charges let us see how Warden Wood
reacted to this preliminary inquiry. As early as December 3,
1833, he wrote to his superiors,

I have been surrounded by spies who, while they were shewing
respect and civility to me, have been closely watching for years all
my movements, in order if possible at their own time to pervert the
same to my injury; the Secretary handed me the evidence . . . and
I see little else than suspicious surmises, reports of low dirty bar
room village scandal . . . and not a single fact.[5]

About the same time the warden found to his consternation
that some of his overseers were "Deists," while one was "a
strong sectarian who was busy inculcating among the prisoners
his own notions." Throughout the subsequent hearings some
of these alleged "Deists" were not permitted to testify. Each
witness was scrupulously examined as to his religious views,
and if he expressed any religious unorthodoxy, he was excused
or his testimony was discounted.

After it became inevitable that the legislative committee was
to make a thorough investigation of the management of the
prison, Warden Wood wrote in his Journal for Christmas Day,
1834, "At home all day & a gloomy one. Never knew what
trouble was before. The Board of Inspectors met and remained
in session until 10 o'clock."

The charges were serious. They embraced a variety of loose
practices which, if true, would be inimical to efficiency in any
institution and would tend to break down the morale of employees possessing any degree of integrity. That some of the
charges were based upon unimpeachable evidence is undoubtedly true; that some were exaggerated may also be true; and
that some grew out of a misunderstanding of the purpose of
such an institution as the Eastern Penitentiary is quite obvious.

[4] *McElwee's Report*, p. 114.
[5] In a letter from Wood to the Board, in Journal of the Board of Inspectors.

Certainly the mass of evidence and testimony paraded before
the committee during the five weeks' hearing—December 16,
1834, to January 22, 1835—was variously interpreted by the
members sitting in judgment. Accordingly, a majority and a
minority report were prepared. An enumeration of the charges
is as follows:

1. Practices and manners among the officers, agents and females,
licentious and immoral . . . generally known to and participated
in by the Warden and his deputies.

2. Embezzlement and misapplication of the public provisions and
public property, and of the public labor, to the private and unauthorized use and advantage of various persons connected with the
institution, and of others unconnected with it . . . as also to the use
and advantage of the Warden, for the improving and working of a
farm and factory belonging in whole or in part to the said Warden.

3. Cruel and unusual punishment inflicted by order of the Warden
upon refractory convicts; exemplified in the two following cases:
the case of one convict, who, in the depth of winter, was tied up
against the wall attached to his cell by the wrists, while buckets of
extremely cold water were thrown upon him from a height, which
partly froze on his head and person, and he was shortly after discharged as incurably insane: and the other case of one, in whose
mouth an iron bar or gag was so forcibly fastened, that his blood
collected and suffused up in his brain and he suddenly died under
the treatment.

4. Known practices and habits inconsistent with the object and
principles of a penitentiary and its system, subversive of its order,
regularity and security; such as the giving of large entertainments
within the prison, by the Warden, carousing and dancing late at
night in the apartments of [the deputy and his wife], within the
walls, frequent intoxication, habitual intercourse with lewd and
depraved persons, and irregular hours also on the part of the wife
[of the deputy] and with the knowledge and connivance of the
Warden.

5. A frequent and illegal practice in the treatment of convicts
by the Warden, of departing from, and in effect disregarding the
sentences of the courts of justice; relaxing their severity, commuting
their inflictions, or evading their real meaning; thus substituting his

individual caprice or discretion for the decisions of the law, and defeating the regularity and precision which ought to characterize the penitentiary system.[6]

Elaborating upon these charges it was testified that prisoners were allowed out of their cells on numerous occasions to wait on table in the various apartments of the administrative staff; that immoral conduct was practiced between the deputy's wife, Mrs. Blundin, and employees; and that work earning large sums of money was completed by prisoners for private gain or personal use rather than for the state.

Subsequently the investigation disclosed that severe punishments were administered in certain refractory cases. It was proved beyond question that iron gags, strait jackets, the practice of ducking, the "mad or tranquilizing chair," severe deprivation of food, and minor other punishments were imposed, in some cases with severe results.

The charge dealing with severe and unusual punishment, while not the most significant of the over-all indictment, was certainly the most sensational. It is worth examining first since it demonstrates how easy it is for prison administrators, when fear and vacillating policies characterize a penal establishment, to resort to cruelty.

The system of separate confinement lends itself easily to certain types of punishment. If an inmate in his cell refuses to work, his food may be stopped or he may be placed on a restricted diet, or his tools, books, or any other article he may prize may be withdrawn for a period of time. Complete idleness is one of the most effective punishments in a prison, and coupled with lack of companionship it becomes even more intense.

This type of punishment was resorted to on numerous occasions in the early history of Cherry Hill. For example, William Griffith, the principal keeper, was having trouble with No. 50, William Napier, a notorious robber. Napier was born in County Down, Ireland, and at the time of his conviction was 36 years

[6] *McElwee's Report,* p. 34.

of age. He had for many years been a "man-of-war's man," over six feet tall and "robust and athletic." He possessed "a remarkable fierce and stubborn temper."

Careless in his work Napier would frequently spoil it and, capitalizing on the fact that he was blind in one eye, would often complain that his good eye was sore and ask to be placed on the sick list. Griffith, detecting the sham, removed his tools and books and restricted his visits to a minimum. Before a week had elapsed Napier began to grow uneasy. He paced his cell continuously and begged for work. He admitted that he had "been playing old soldier." Nevertheless, his pleas went unanswered. He would exclaim to the keepers, "Give me back my work or I'll go crazy" or "For God's sake give me a book or I shall die." At the expiration of three weeks his work was returned to him and he became "unusually diligent" and never gave any further trouble.

There is plenty of evidence to support the charge that other punishments were inflicted on certain prisoners during the first five years of Wood's wardenship. There was first the dark cell. This form of punishment can be labeled excessive although it may work little hardship if the cell is normally comfortable and the prisoner is given adequate food and exercise. Evidence at the investigation showed that often a prisoner was placed in an unheated cell with no bedding except perhaps a blanket and with little food—often only bread and water—provided infrequently. One instance that came before the committee was the case of a "yellow boy" from Delaware County, No. 132, by the name of Charles Warrick. He was only 16 years old when he was sentenced to five years for arson. His offense in prison was "cutting up some upper leather of shoes." The report reads,

One convict was kept in this situation [the dark cell] for forty-two days; on the evening of that day one of the keepers was attracted to the cell of this miserable wretch by repeated knockings at his wicket; on looking in at the cell, the convict exhibited every symptom of delirium produced by starvation; he was on his knees, his eyes rolling in phrensy, and his frame reduced to a skeleton by the severity of his punishment. On the keeper inquiring why he had knocked, the miserable boy held out his little tin cup in his hand and exclaimed, "my father told me to knock to get a little mush."

The keeper in violation of discipline gave him some bread, and next morning reported his case to the physician who entered in his Journal, "No. 132, weak from starvation." Notwithstanding this entry, the prisoner was not released, and on the second day after, the keeper again reported the case to the physician who entered in his Journal after having examined the prisoner's health, "suffering from starvation." He was then released by order of the warden in so emaciated a state that he had to be supported from the dungeon to his cell by two men.

A second type of severe physical punishment was the shower bath, or water douche. This was at the time widely used in American prisons. It had several variations, but the most usual was to pour water on a victim from a considerable height. The severity of the punishment varied with the temperature of the water or of the atmosphere and with the number of pails thrown. The case alluded to in the investigation was that of one Seneca Plimly, No. 75, who was 19 years old when he entered the prison on May 14, 1831. His home was Bradford County, and he had been convicted of horsestealing. The prison records refer to him as an "idiot," but it is also listed that he could read and write. He was pardoned by the governor on February 10, 1832.

When Plimly was subjected to the water douche "the weather was extremely cold, he was in a state of nudity, and icicles formed on his hair, and his person was encrusted with ice."

Another punishment was to be placed in the "mad or tranquilizing chair," which had been invented by Dr. Benjamin Rush for the purpose of subduing excitable mental cases in the Pennsylvania Hospital. Known usually as the "Mad Chair" or "Composing Chair," it was a large box-like affair, constructed of heavy planking to resemble a chair. The prisoner was placed in the contraption, his arms fastened above the elbow by straps to the back. Another strap was passed about his body through holes in the chair and fastened behind. Handcuffs were placed on his hands. Other straps were passed about his ankles and firmly fastened to the lower part of the chair. The victim had no resting place for his feet. It was impossible for him to move any part of his body or his limbs. The pain was intense, yet it is recorded that while in the chair some prisoners were severely beaten. When released the prisoner's legs and arms were usually badly swollen.

Other punishments were the strait jacket and the iron gag. The former was frequently used throughout the nineteenth century in both prisons and insane hospitals. It consisted of a piece of sack or bagging cloth of several thicknesses, with holes for the admission of the hands. In the back were eyelets through which a strong cord was laced back and forth. The collar was fitted about the neck of the victim and the cord drawn up tight in the back. Often persons were laced so tightly in this contrivance that their necks and faces were black with congealed blood. Dr. Franklin Bache, the prison physician, approved of its use to subdue unruly or emotionally disturbed prisoners. Dr. Bache (1792–1864) was the great-grandson of Benjamin Franklin.

The iron gag is thus described by the investigating committee of the Eastern Penitentiary:

This was a rough iron instrument resembling the stiff bit of a blind bridle, having an iron palet in the center, about an inch square, and chains at each end to pass around the neck and fasten behind. This instrument was placed in the prisoner's mouth, the iron palet over the tongue, the bit forced back as far as possible, the chains brought round the jaws to the back of the neck; the end of one chain was passed through the ring in the end of the other chain drawn tight to the "fourth link" and fastened with a lock; his hands were then forced into leather gloves in which were iron staples and crossed behind his back; leather straps were passed through the staples, and from thence round the chains of the gag between his neck and the chains; the straps were drawn tight, the hands forced up toward the head, and the pressure consequently acting on the chains which press on the jaws and jugular vein, producing excruciating pain, and a hazardous suffusion of blood to the head.[7]

It was while fastened in this device that one convict, No. 102, Matthew Maccumsey, died June 27, 1833. He was un-

[7] *Ibid.*, p. 18.

doubtedly an obstreperous prisoner and had been "gagged" on numerous occasions. At the time he came to the prison from Lancaster County he was 42 years of age. He was sentenced to 12 years for murder. The prison physician's verdict of death was "apoplexy." Commenting on the prisoner's death, Dr. Bache stated in his report: "This prisoner was received into the penitentiary in an imperfect state of health, the consequences of habitual intemperance. During the whole period of his confinement, he frequently exhibited symptoms indicative of a radically diseased and shattered constitution." [8] He stated at the hearing that a moderate use of the gag was one certain means of restraining a prisoner who insisted on communicating with his fellows, but he deplored its use when it was drawn to the last link.

Warden Wood's Journal has the following entries with reference to this episode:

June 27, 1833: No. 102 Maccumsey having on several occasions got the man next him [unidentified] talking and being detected in the act last evening, I ordered the straight [sic] jacket on No. — and the gag on No. 102. This I saw put on about 8 o'clock. About 9 o'clock I was informed by Wm. Griffiths that they had found him in a lifeless state. I immediately went to him and found him warm but with no pulse. We tried to bleed him and used ammonia and many other things but life was extinct. Dr. Bache was to see him but could do nothing.

June 28: Dr. Bache made a post mortem examination on No. 102 and found that he had died of apoplexy and gave a certificate accordingly.

The presence of Mrs. Blundin, wife of the underkeeper, inside the walls of the prison was considered a mistake, according to the majority report. It was admitted that she caused considerable irritation among the employees. There was evidence that she disported herself in a highhanded and even a profligate manner. Testimony was brought that she drank to excess, was coarse and even lewd in her speech, immoral in her relations with men, indiscreet with the warden and the prison clerk,

[8] *Fifth Annual Report*, Board of Inspectors, December 21, 1833.

John Halloway, and systematically spirited out supplies to her relatives. These supplies consisted of lard, meat, potatoes, lamp oil, tea, and other items of value.

Another charge against Mrs. Blundin was that she held "carousing parties" late at night in her quarters in the front building. Some of these parties were referred to as "quilting parties" but most of them were described as revelries. The minority looked askance on these parties. It protested in highly · moral tones as follows:

What! dancing and revelry and drunkenness within the very walls of a Penitentiary, in the hearing of the robber, the incendiary, and the murderer; in the very face of the wretched prisoner, who is cut off from all joys, from liberty, from intercourse with his fellow men, and this too with the knowledge, assent, and approval of the Warden! and "not a subject of much importance."

Contrast the prisoner in his gloomy cell, pondering over his crimes, his wretchedness, his utter desolation, probably repentant, humble and submissive, mourning over his loneliness; with the boisterous inebriated crew, whose licentious mirth assails his palsied ear as if to taunt his wretchedness and triumph in his sufferings. He listens to the indistinct note of the music: "Like warbled strains that sink remote" and his heart is pained. He hears the chorus of many voices, the joyous burst of mirth and glee and he thinks they come from hearts innocent and spotless, such as his was in boyhood. Memory recalls the scenes of other days, of the friends of his youth, of "The Mother that wept over his childhood." He feels that others can banish care and sorrow, but he is wedded to the worm that never dies. It was cruelty, rank cruelty, in the committee to say that such conduct was "not a subject of much importance."

A quilting frolic, a riotous assemblage of Bacchanalians and Cyprians within the very walls of an institution consecrated by the laws to the suppression of crime and the punishment of the criminal, and yet the committee say it "was not a subject of much importance." [9]

Mrs. Blundin often called upon prisoners to open oysters, cook terrapin, wash clothes stained with ointment to cure "the venereal," and, in short, to obey her commands or gratify her whims at any hour of the day or night. Former prisoners

[9] *McElwee's Report,* p. 131.

and discharged employees testified that on many occasions the warden was ignorant of what was going on and claimed they were afraid to tell him of the gross irregularities they witnessed. Even the majority report was obliged to make the following statement:

We consider it unfortunate that Mrs. Blundin was ever permitted to reside within the walls of the penitentiary; and perhaps to this circumstance most of the mischiefs complained of may be traced. . . . No evidence was given to show practices and manners licentious and immoral on the part of Mr. Wood, nor of any such on the part of Mrs. Blundin . . . in his presence and with his knowledge. Of John Halloway, the clerk of the institution, evidence was given of improper language having been used in his presence, but not by him. It may be too, that indiscretion may have betrayed this gentleman into a greater degree of familiarity with this woman than a delicate sense of propriety would justify.[10]

The minority report was not so restrained on these points. It contended that both Wood and Halloway had amorous relations with the woman. Mrs. Blundin was discharged from whatever duties she had assumed and was asked to leave the institution. This order was in June, 1834, before the public hearings began. No charges were made against her husband, who apparently dispatched his duties conscientiously and sympathetically, although he participated in the punishment of prisoners, including the gagging of Maccumsey. However, no prisoners cast any aspersion on him during the hearings.

The charge that provisions and public property as well as convict labor were diverted to private use seems, from the testimony, to have been true. We have already referred to the pilfering by Mrs. Blundin. Isaac Cox, prison carpenter and free laborer, listed many items that went into the hands of the warden and some of the inspectors. Mr. Wood was in partnership with other men, and many items taken from the prison and work finished by the inmates found their way to Wood's mahogany and stone mills. Cox stated that John Bacon, one of the inspectors, received "folding-doors, and side-doors for his parlour

10 *Ibid.*, pp. 38–39,

. . . washboards and mouldings, pilasters around the doors"
for his home; a "frame building was framed for Mr. Wood"; "a
table, step-ladder, and a chicken-coop, an ironing-board, a large
chest, a chopping-board, and a refrigerator" for Judge Coxe,
president of the Board; and a refrigerator went to Mr. Hood,
another inspector. Three kegs of nails were sent to the warden's
farm. Cox made a wagon for Inspector Bacon worth at least
$100 for which Bacon paid $40. The testimony shows considerable confusion regarding compensation for work done and for
articles taken by Wood and the inspectors. It is impossible to
know whether there was outright pilfering of state property
or merely great laxity in bookkeeping.

The majority report passed over this charge rather lightly but
did recommend that in the future no work should be done for
the wardens or the inspectors. It further prohibited any employee, including the warden, to engage in any outside business
while in the employ of the state.

As for the charge of permitting prisoners out of their cells,
there was plenty of evidence that several were employed around
the establishment at various tasks, were able to see one another,
and on occasions to converse together. Cooks in the front building, those engaged in household duties for the warden and the
Blundins, went about their duties unmasked. Men helping the
free workmen in the prison yard were able to converse.

Judge Coxe, president of the Board, deplored the fact that inmates could communicate one with the other since he admitted
that the practice defeated the purpose of the separate system.
His only defense was that he thought that Warden Wood was
a man of integrity and had a definite conviction concerning the
original premises of the Pennsylvania System. It is of some importance to note from Judge Coxe's testimony that he thought
the warden should be given a free hand in developing the system. He referred the committee to the statement of the inspectors in their second annual report in reference to Mr. Wood:

Among the living, the warden is one of its earliest, and most intelligent advocates and one of its most practical friends. In the opinion
of this board, a better opportunity can never occur of testing the

excellency of the penitentiary system of solitary confinement at labour, and, that for its present prosperous state, this institution is mainly indebted to its warden.

That Judge Coxe stood alone among the Board in accepting the original charges against the warden and his management is indicated by the fact that he resigned his post. His letter, in advance of the investigation, dated February 1, 1834, states: "Satisfied that abuses exist . . . to an alarming extent, and that all efforts on my part . . . to remove them have been fruitless I can no longer allow my name to be used to authenticate acts of the Board nor consent to preside over its deliberations."

The majority report agreed with Judge Coxe and others who were friends of the system as it was interpreted in Pennsylvania that any communication was a violation of that system and that every effort should be made in the future to prohibit the practice. Of course, it was almost impossible for such a system to endure without violations. Communication through privy pipes could not be eliminated. All through the later 1840s there was much evidence that inmates were able to communicate with one another. Yet this cherished system could not be maintained unless there was no possibility for prisoners to communicate with and thus contaminate one another. There is evidence that as the years went by many compromises were made by later wardens with the strict and meticulous observance of the philosophy of separate confinement. The investigation of 1834 was but the first proof that the prohibition of communication between prison inmates is practically impossible.

THE INVESTIGATION OF 1897

The charges which prompted the legislature to appoint a joint investigation committee in April, 1897, were preferred by a distinguished Philadelphian, the Honorable James Gay Gordon, a jurist of long standing. The grand jury of April of that year had reported to Judge Gordon's court that many of the cells of the prison were in a filthy condition, that the diet was of inferior grade, and that there existed an attitude of indifference if not cruelty toward some of the inmates, especially those who were insane. The inspectors of the institution immediately appealed to the legislature to make a thorough investigation of the charges, denying that any of them were true.

Our knowledge of this investigation comes primarily from the typed proceedings of the hearings of the committee which met at the prison throughout the months of May and June.[11]

The reports show that Judge Gordon, under oath, charged the authorities of the Eastern Penitentiary of neglect and wanton cruelty, of beatings and maimings, and of making false reports to the governor and legislature concerning the number of insane prisoners in the institution. He specifically charged that a convict died in the Norristown State Hospital for the Insane of wounds inflicted on him at the prison on the night of his removal from that institution, that is, he was murdered at the Eastern Penitentiary. He further charged that certain inmates had been clubbed by overseers and that at least one had been tied to a heating pipe in his cell and consequently received severe burns on his arms.

The Norristown Hospital case did not actually involve the prison except for the charge that the inmate (who had been pronounced insane and recommended for removal to the hospital) had been severely beaten at the prison the evening he was transferred. It was established by testimony that he died a few days later. The superintendent of the hospital testified that the man had been received in good physical condition, showing no signs of the beating, and had actually died from mistreatment at the hands of an attendent in the hospital. Later the attendant was indicted and tried for murder but was acquitted.

The investigating committee interrogated the warden and each member of the Board of Inspectors at some length. They all denied the charges made by Judge Gordon. They stoutly maintained that no clubbings were ever inflicted except when the overseers were attacked by prisoners or when inmates re-

[11] The record consists of twelve sheafs of typed testimony and may be found in the State Record Office at Harrisburg.

belled against removal from one cell to another. Various overseers were also questioned but all denied cruelties. The officials
also denied that the food was inadequate or that the cells
were filthy.

The investigation brought out the difference in the approach
toward the disposition of the criminally insane. It is obvious
from the testimony that the prison management strongly believed that those who were insane when brought to the prison
or who developed mental diseases after their incarceration
could be treated adequately in the institution. It was advocated
that a special cell block be set aside for such use. Judge Gordon
and others maintained that the criminally insane should be
handled in the state mental hospitals. At this time there was
some agitation throughout the state for the creation of a special
institution for the criminally insane.

There were differences of opinion between Warden Cassidy
and the prison physician regarding the sanity of some of the inmates; however, the physician's diagnoses were always accepted.
The warden insisted that many inmates feigned insanity, which
he called malingering. His attitude justified the overseers in
wielding the club with less restraint than the situations war-
ranted.

The Philadelphia jurist, under the rules of the committee,
was not able to substantiate his charges against the management. He asked for immunity toward some of his witnesses who
were prisoners at the time. This was denied. He asked for permission to interrogate his witnesses himself. This, too, was denied. The judge bitterly assailed the committee for not permitting him to examine his own witnesses. He protested against
the rules drawn up by the committee.

The committee concluded its hearings by extending the
prison management a clean bill of health. But no person today
could read the testimony without believing that severe beatings
of inmates had occurred, despite the fact that the warden justified such punishment in the name of discipline. Judge Gordon
was obliged to submit to a scathing denunciation by the committee, who wrote, among other things,

A judge who descends from his seat on the bench to make sworn charges of such gravity against public officials should substantiate them. The mere statement of the fact that such charges emanated from a judge on the bench, and that after having been given the fullest opportunity to prove them fails utterly, carries with it a more severe criticism of his conduct than can any language of this Committee. Moreover, the officious hunting from cell to cell to elicit complaints from irresponsible criminals undergoing their sentences, is an abuse of the privilege of a prison visitor and a distinct offense against the interests of the Commonwealth; because it cannot fail to excite false hopes and insubordination among the convicts, which are injurious to them and subversive of all the objects for which prisons are maintained.[12]

An impartial reading of the testimony would clearly indicate that some inmates were brutally beaten and that many more insane prisoners were in the establishment than were reported by the management. The courageous jurist did not deserve the rebuke of the committee. Judge Gordon was an important citizen of Philadelphia, a distinguished jurist for many years, and a man of unblemished integrity. He was convinced that charges of cruelty made to him by inmates were true, but under the rules of the committee he could not substantiate them.

Warden Cassidy's testimony reveals the status of discipline as well as the philosophy of the institution which at the time was changing from the separate system to the congregate system. While the warden referred to his system as the individual-treatment system, a large number of cells contained two occupants and some of the larger ones held as many as five. He contended that he strove to separate the hardened offender from the novice so contamination would be reduced to a minimum. He was doubtlessly sincere since he was still convinced of the advantages of the separate system. But in practice, due to the shortage of cell space, he was obliged to make concessions to the prevailing and more popular congregate system.

Cassidy was a career warden of the old school. His death in 1900 marks the end of an era in penal treatment in Pennsylvania.

[12] The report of the committee may be found in *Journal of the Senate of Pennsylvania*, II (1897), 2298–2305.

THE INVESTIGATION OF 1903

In the Seventy-fourth Annual Report of the Eastern Penitentiary (1904) may be found information revealing that another
investigation of irregularities within the prison was being considered.

On August 5 last a committee was appointed by the President of
the Board of Inspectors to examine into the alleged trading and
improper furnishing of articles to convicts by a watchman of the
institution. The scope of the examination was extended to cover the
entire accounts of the institution and its methods; this examination
was made by a public accountant and was thorough and exhaustive.
As a result of the irregularities and derelictions of duty presented
to your Board, several of the officers were dismissed.[13]

From the Journal of the Board of Inspectors it appears that
a thorough investigation of the internal management of the
prison was conducted by the Board of Public Charities which
made its report to the inspectors on January 3, 1903. Briefly,
the committee found the following irregularities:

1. Furnishing of prison food to officers and employees.
2. Lack of supervision over the storekeeper and other employees.
3. Laxity in the supervision of funds of the caning and chair
   factory; the overseer of this department was a son of the chief
   overseer.
4. Favoritism in diet and favors to particular prisoners by
   certain officers.
5. Aid by one of the inspectors to a prisoner in the transmission
   of a large sum of money from the prison in an irregular way.
6. Purchase of food in which an inspector had an interest and
   procurement of fire insurance for the prison from a company
   in which this inspector was an officer.
7. Failure of the warden to keep proper accounts of old iron,
   brass, etc.
8. Procurement of food by officers.
9. Use of prisoners as servants in the families of the warden and
   chief overseer.

[13] Seventy-fourth Annual *Report*, 1904, p. 6.

As a result of this bill of particulars, two of the members of the Board resigned. Warden Daniel W. Bussinger also resigned and the Board appointed the moral instructor, the Reverend Joseph Welch acting warden. Several officers were dismissed. Apparently there was a tightening up of administrative practices, since the management carried on without criticism for some years.

≡ 5
Charles Dickens and His Cherry Hill Prisoners

WHEN the novelist Charles Dickens made his initial visit to America in 1842, he had already produced some of his most lasting works. At the age of 30, when he landed in this country, he had to his credit the well-known classics *Pickwick Papers* (1836–37), *Oliver Twist* (1838), *Nicholas Nickelby* (1839), and *The Old Curiosity Shop* (1841).

To entertain such a distinguished guest was a real privilege. He was royally received by Americans everywhere. He seemed pleased with his reception and wherever he went thoughtfully complimented the people and their institutions. But what he wrote about this country in his *American Notes,* published later that same year, shocked the sensibilities of the entire nation to such a degree that it took years for the wounds to heal.

No doubt in many instances he wrote the truth, but some claimed that he took advantage of his reputation to toy with strict veracity to an alarming degree. Certainly the diatribe he hurled at the penitentiary in Philadelphia did not pass unchallenged. The friends of the separate system of prison discipline rallied to its defense heroically, calling in experts whose opinions were far more authoritative than those of the British author.

It was on March 8, 1842, that Dickens made his pilgrimage to the Philadelphia prison. He signed the register of visitors in a bold hand underlined with flourishes. His signature may be seen today in the visitors' book.

The warden's Journal records that "Mr. Dickens of England visited here today and ate lunch at the prison with a few gentlemen," probably some of the prison's inspectors. He was within the walls only about two hours. The warden at the time was George Thompson. The author was accompanied through the institution by Matthew Bevan, chairman of the Board, and

Richard Vaux, newly appointed member. Dickens was quoted as saying: "The Falls of Niagara and your Penitentiary are two objects I might almost say I most wish to see in America."

Every courtesy was extended the novelist. He was taken from block to block and from cell to cell. He spoke to many prisoners in their separate cells. As he left the prison he said, "Never before have I seen a public institution in which the relations of father and family were so well exemplified as this." Richard Vaux stated years later that "not one word of criticism or of objection was then or there made [by Dickens]. He did not even express a doubt of the success of separate confinement as a system of penal discipline." [1]

Nevertheless, what Dickens saw in the prison gave him enough ammunition, aided by his fertile imagination, to indict separate confinement and the Pennsylvania System of prison discipline in such terms of vituperation that the members of the Philadelphia Prison Society were compelled to repair the damage he had wrought throughout the world.

The novelist's denunciation of Cherry Hill and its system began with these words: "The system here is rigid, strict and hopeless solitary confinement," and "I believe it, in its effects, to be cruel and wrong."

The system may have been rigid and strict but it was not one of "solitary confinement." Dickens was either not astute enough or unwilling to distinguish between the strict solitary confinement that had been advocated by some of the original supporters of the Pennsylvania System and the final system that was adopted, which permitted labor in the cells, books, visitors from the community, and exercise in the adjoining yards. It may have been severe but it was not as bad as the novelist painted it. His next remark is worthy of inclusion.

In its intention, I am well convinced that it is kind, humane and meant for reformation; but I am persuaded that those who devised the system and those benevolent gentlemen who carry it into execution, do not know what it is that they are doing. I believe that very

[1] This and the above quotes are from Richard Vaux, *A Brief Sketch of the Origin and History of the State Penitentiary for the Eastern District of Pennsylvania* (Philadelphia, 1872), p. 111.

few men are capable of estimating the immense amount of torture and agony which this dreadful punishment, prolonged for years, inflicts upon its sufferers. . . . I hold this slow and daily tampering with the mysteries of the brain to be immeasureably worse than any torture of the body; and because its ghastly signs and tokens are not so palpable to the eye and sense of touch as scars upon the flesh; because its wounds are not on the surface, and it extorts few cries that human ears can hear; therefore I denounce it as a secret punishment which slumbering humanity is not roused up to stay.

The rejoinder to Dickens's attack may be found in the *Journal of Prison Discipline and Philanthropy,* official publication of the Philadelphia Prison Society, for January, 1861. It was made at the request of the Society by William Peter, distinguished consul-general of Great Britain, who was stationed in Philadelphia during the visit of Mr. Dickens. Mr. Peter visited the prison to make his investigation of Dickens's charges some time in early 1844.[2]

With the aid of clues from both Dickens's and Peter's accounts, together with an examination of the warden's Journal, it has been possible to identify the prisoners interviewed by the novelist. Two of these, the German known to Dickens's devotees as the "Dutchman," and the "poet . . . who wrote verses about ships and the 'maddening wine-cup' and his friends at home," have become classics. The other cases have not been referred to by those writing on the Dickens episode.

In presenting the cases here, first will appear the account by Dickens, then the prison record and, in some instances, comment by the moral instructor or the warden, and finally what William Peter had to say.

THE CASE OF WILLIAM WHITLEY

Dickens

The first man I saw was seated at his loom, at work. He had been there six years, and was to remain, I think, three more. He had been convicted as a receiver of stolen goods, but even after his long im-

---

[2] See Negley K. Teeters, *They Were In Prison* (Philadelphia, 1937), pp. 229 f. For another criticism of Dickens's account of his visit to the prison, see Joseph Adshead, *Prisons and Prisoners* (London, 1845), especially his section on "The Fictions of Dickens."

prisonment denied his guilt, and said he had been hardly dealt by. It was his second offense.

He stopped his work when we went in, took off his spectacles and answered freely to every thing that was said to him but always with a strange kind of pause first, and in a low, thoughtful voice. He wore a paper cap of his own making, and was pleased to have it noticed and commended. He had very ingeniously manufactured a Dutch clock from some disregarded odds and ends; and his vinegar-bottle served for the pendulum. Seeing me interested in his contrivance, he looked up at it with a great deal of pride, and said that he had been thinking of improving it, and that he hoped the hammer and a little piece of broken glass beside it "would play music before long." He had extracted some colours from the yarn with which he worked, and painted a few poor figures on the wall. One of a female over the door, he called *The Lady of the Lake.*

He smiled as I looked at these contrivances to while away the time; but, when I looked from them to him, I saw that his lip trembled, and could have counted the beating of his heart. I forget how it came about, but some allusion was made to his having a wife. He shook his head at the word, turned aside, and covered his face with his hands.

"But you are resigned now!" said one of the gentlemen after a short pause, during which he had resumed his former manner. He answered with a sigh, that seemed quite reckless in its hopelessness, "Oh yes, oh yes! I am resigned to it." "And are a better man, you think?" "Well, I hope so: I'm sure I may be." "And time goes pretty quickly?" "Time is very long, gentlemen, within these four walls!"

He gazed about him—Heaven only knows how wearily!—as he said these words; and in the act of doing so, fell into a strange stare as if he had forgotten something. A moment afterwards he sighed heavily, put on his spectacles, and went about his work again.

Record

William Whitley, No. 1066; entered prison February 19, 1839; 33 years old; from Dauphin County, Penna.; printer; dark complexion; gray eyes; black hair; 5' 6½"; foot, 10⅛"; small pox mark; larceny; four years; Quarter Sessions Court, Montgomery County; second offense here; time out and discharged February 19, 1843; good English, education; married. Says he has not drank [sic] but his appearance belies his statement.

His first offense: Entered prison April 22, 1835; No. 393; 28 years old; Dauphin County; printer; forgery; 7 years 6 months; Q.S. Court Lancaster County, Penna.; 1st. offense; discharged July 27, 1837; pardoned; expiration date of sentence, October 22, 1842; well educated, married, one child, never drank.

In 1839 the Reverend Thomas Larcombe, the institution's moral instructor, wrote concerning William Whitley: "Seems to have some right views of religion but no heart in it. Have good reason to hope that the Son has wrought his work in him. Alas! Alas!"

On Whitley's release, Warden Thompson wrote in his Journal: "This prisoner has never been punished or reprimanded during his entire incarceration."

William Peter

During his imprisonment he had been allowed to correspond to his wife—a most respectable woman—who supported herself and her children by needle-work, and whose letters to her husband were full of kind and excellent advice. On quitting prison he received $51 for extra work, and now earns a comfortable livelihood by his labours as a journeyman printer. As far as I am able to learn, he is none the worse for his imprisonment, either in body or mind, nay, as to the latter, much improved. He is in correspondence with the chaplain, and writes a very good letter.

THE CASE OF CHARLES LONGHAMER, BETTER KNOWN AS LANGENHEIMER

Dickens

In another cell, there was a German, sentenced to five years' imprisonment for larceny, two of which had expired. With colours he had procured (from scrap materials) he had painted every inch of his walls and ceiling quite beautifully. He had laid out the few feet of ground, behind, with exquisite neatness, and had made a little bed in the centre, that looked by the by like a grave. The taste and ingenuity he had displayed in everything were most extraordinary; and yet a more dejected, heart-broken, wretched creature, it would be difficult to imagine. I never saw such a picture of forlorn affliction and distress of mind. My heart bled for him; and when the tears ran down his cheeks, and he took one of the visitors aside, to ask with trembling hands nervously clutching to detain him, whether there was no hope of his dismal sentence being commuted, the spectacle was really too painful to witness. I never saw or heard of any kind of misery that impressed me more than the wretchedness of this man.

Record

Charles Longhamer, age 35, Saxony, Germany; paper stainer; never bound; swarthy complexion, blue eyes, dark hair, 5′ 5″; foot 10 inches; no marks; first conviction; parents dead; reads and writes German; sober, drank beer; wife and child; 30 cents.

Langenheimer was a troublemaker from the time he entered the prison. Four days after he arrived he attempted suicide. Warden Thompson noted in his Journal, "This morning at letting out time, Charles Langenheimer, No. 1274, attempted suicide with a shoe knife by stabbing himself in the abdomen and cutting the large vein and wounding the artery in his left arm. When found by the watchman he was insensible lying in a pool of blood." On June 25 he made a second attempt at suicide by "cutting himself in a number of places but not anywhere mortally."

The moral instructor reported as follows:

Called in to see him on Monday May 18, afternoon. Appeared somewhat excited but not more than enough to shew that he was a spirited, resolute kind of man. Denied his guilt and insisted that some other person, I think an Irishman who kept store, must have been guilty. Could not understand the drift of his conversation on account of his foreign or German accent and his quick manner of speaking. He seemed oppressed with the length of his sentence and spoke of it several times. Seemed to have no sense of religion. Was called in next morning and found him lying in his bed in the act of having a wound dressed, inflicted by himself, perhaps half an hour or an hour before, in an attempt to commit suicide. On further examination an incision was found in his upper arm which probably was inflicted before the wound in the upper part of his stomach. Since learned this was not so. Made a second attempt to commit suicide and makes great promises of reform. *Not much hope.*

On July 2 the warden wrote, "Removed 1274 from the infirmary to a cell and put him to work winding bobbins. Appeared rational but endeavored to conceal a nail. Begged hard for a knife to cut his bread with. Had his cell searched and everything removed by which he could injure himself."

On June 19, 1844, the warden wrote that this obdurate prisoner refused to work and was placed in the dark cell under "restraints as to his hands." He was released nine hours later on promise of good behavior.

Following is Langenheimer's long record at Cherry Hill:

Prison Number	Date of Entering	Offense	Sentenced	Release Date
1274	May 5, 1840	larceny	5 years	May 15, 1845

Details of offense: Charged with stealing $250 from the till of Daniel K. Grim; upon another bill was indicted for stealing $100 from the counting-house of William Potts & Son in Second Street above Race. Judges Barton, Conrad and Doran of Philadelphia Quarter Sessions Court sentenced defendant to two years on the first count and three years on the second count. [Philadelphia *Public Ledger,* May 16, 1840. Dickens interviewed the prisoner during this sentence.]

2912	June 25, 1852	counterfeiting	1 year	June 28, 1853

Details of offense: As Carl Morris, Langenheimer was convicted of passing a counterfeit note and sentenced to one year in the Eastern State Penitentiary June 28 by Judge Thompson. [From *Public Ledger,* June 30, 1852.]

3251	February 25, 1855	larceny	2 years	February 24, 1857

Details of offense: Charles Langenheimer, convicted of larceny, was sentenced by Judge Kelley to two years in the Eastern Penitentiary. [*Public Ledger,* February 26, 1855.]

4442	April 4, 1861	larceny	19 months	March 11, 1862
7153	March 12, 1872	larceny	2 years	January 12, 1874
8048	September 9, 1875	larceny	1 year	August 9, 1876
8777	April 5, 1877	larceny	1 year	April 4, 1878

Details of offense: Pleaded guilty to stealing a silver watch, property of T. S. Marshall. He took it from Marshall's vest which was hanging on the wall of a workshop at 36th and Filbert Streets. [*Public Ledger,* April 5, 1877.]

A–14	September 9, 1879	larceny	3 years	May 10, 1882

Details of offense: Charles Langenheimer pleaded guilty to the larceny of $10 from the safe of a store at Ninth St., near Girard Ave. This is the prisoner mentioned by Charles Dickens in his *American Notes.* [*Public Ledger,* April 11, 1879.]

A–1301	July 12, 1882	larceny	1 year	June 12, 1883

During the intervals when Langenheimer was not in the Cherry Hill prison at Philadelphia, he served five terms in other institutions: three in the County Prison at Philadelphia, one in the Baltimore penitentiary, and one in New York city. He appears on the prison records through the years as Longhamer, Langenheimer, Carl Morris, and William Morris.

William Peter

The German (who had ornamented his cell and laid out the few feet of ground behind with such ingenuity and neatness) came in May, 1840, and will leave in May, 1845. He had been convicted of two offenses for each of which he was condemned to two years and a half imprisonment. The sentence has been considered by some as too severe; but as for him being a "dejected, heart-broken, wretched creature"; as for his "forlorn affliction and distress of mind," I could discover no signs or symptoms of either. He was in excellent health and spirits as mortal need be, conversed freely about his situation, and expressed confident hopes, that he should, through the kindness and recommendations of the governor and others, be able to get into good employment as a paper-stainer, on the expiration of his term of imprisonment. He is an ingenious and clever fellow but a great hypocrite, and evidently saw Mr. Dickens' weak side—saw, "Drops of compassion trembling on his eyelids, ready to fall, as soon as he told his pitiful story."

I have heard Mr. Dickens accused of willful misrepresentation. Of that I most fully absolve him. I do not think that he would be guilty —knowingly guilty—of a falsehood for any consideration. But all things are not given to all men; and the very faculty which has enabled him to excel in one species of composition, almost incapacitates him for some others. His prison scenes are much akin to Stearne's. Still I believe that he never deceived another without having first deceived himself.

The finale to this story of Charles Langenheimer is as dramatic as Dickens's visit to the prison. It is found in the news story of the old derelict's petition to end his days in the grim Cherry Hill prison. The following newspaper clipping comes from the Philadelphia *Press*, March 21, 1884.[3]

This Is The Last of Me
The Dying Words of the Convict "Dickens' Dutchman."

Dickens' Dutchman is dead and buried. He has gone to join that innumerable caravan of which the man who made him famous long

---

[3] The writer is indebted to Mr. James Shields of Philadelphia who has long been interested in Dickens's visit to the Philadelphia prison.

since became a member. His feeble light flickered out before the sun was up on Friday morning last, and that same evening he was buried with the customary pomp of a pauper convict's funeral in the Potter's Field on old Lamb Tavern Road.

Charles Langheimer would probably never have been heard of outside of the police court had not the distinguished English novelist, while making his American tour, singled him out as an example of the evil effect of the system of solitary confinement. He was already quite an old jail bird when Dickens stumbled across him in the Eastern Penitentiary.

He was born in Saxony, Germany, in 1804 and was apprenticed to a mason under whose direction he learned five trades. He did not fancy pasting bricks together, so he forsook that occupation and took up the paint brush. He drifted to this country when 32 years of age, and immediately entered upon his long career of petty larceny. He had only one hobby—stealing. He did not steal to get rich, because the thefts of his lifetime, for which he recompensed the law with forty-three years' imprisonment, did not aggregate $1,000.

It was in the middle of May, 1840, when he first entered the portal of the Eastern Penitentiary. He was convicted of two cases of petty larceny and had been sentenced to undergo five years' imprisonment. No particular notice was taken of him, because it was not then known that he had determined within his bosom to make Cherry Hill his home for the rest of his natural life. He had served out two years of his term when Dickens, who was at that period in the height of his fame, a literary autocrat who was writing his "American Notes" in haste to repent them afterwards at his leisure, visited the penitentiary. Langheimer was a wily, consummate hypocrite. He understood Dickens' purpose in visiting the penitentiary, and was quick to seize the opportunity to intrude himself significantly upon his attention. Affecting an air of deepest misery, he crept with the feigned step of fear and palsy beneath the eyes of the novelist, bemoaning his wicked existence. Dickens' imagination was fired by this assumed misery, and he told a woeful tale of the life of a convict in solitary confinement in his "American Notes."

The book made Langheimer famous, and so many people from everywhere visited his cells that, after his first term had expired, he shortly managed to commit another larceny, and was again sentenced for two years. Thereafter, to the close of his life, he was not happy out of jail. He pined for the curious attention bestowed upon him by visitors, and boasted that he would die in prison.

On the 7th of July, 1882, he was passing the feed store of Laird & McGee, at Twenty-third and Spruce Streets. Noticing that the store contained no one, his old desire to steal took possession of him and he sneaked in and rifled the money drawer of $10. He was caught and tried, and sent to the penitentiary for one year. That was his last term. In July last his time expired, and he went to the home of his stepdaughter, Mrs. Peter McCoot, who lived in Richmond.

There he lived in obscurity, gradually declining in vitality until the 14th of February. On the evening of that day a feeble jerk was given at the huge bell that hangs inside the penitentiary door. The guard responded, and outside found a little old man with silver gray hair, cleanly dressed, begging to be allowed to go inside. It was Langheimer. He said he had come back to die. He was taken inside, and placed upon a cot. From that day his vitality ebbed away. Towards the last he lost consciousness, and forgot that he was Dickens' Dutchman. He died quickly. Only Overseer Wilkinson was with him. He threw up his thin white hands, and said, "This is the last of me." And so it was. In five minutes he was dead. A certificate of "exhausted vitality" was made out, and his body, after having been placed in a pine box, was put in Potter's Field. He was buried in the only suit of clothes he had in the world, and not even his name was put on the coffin lid.

Thus died Dickens's "Dutchman." He survived the great novelist by 14 years.

THE CASE OF ALFRED SHANK

Dickens

In the third cell, was a tall, strong black, a burglar, working at his proper trade of making screws and the like. His time was nearly out. He was not only a dexterous thief, but was notorious for his boldness and his hardihood, and for the number of his previous convictions. He entertained us with a long account of his achievements, which he narrated with such infinite relish, that he actually seemed to lick his lips as he told us racy anecdotes of stolen plate, and of old ladies whom he had watched as they sat at windows in silver spectacles (he had plainly had an eye to their metal even from the other side of the street) and had afterwards robbed. This fellow, upon the slightest encouragement, would have mingled with his professional recollections the most detestable cant; but I am very much mistaken if he could have surpassed the unmitigated hypocricy with which he declared that he blessed the day on which he came to that prison, and that he would never commit another robbery as long as he lived.

Record

Alfred Shank, No. 1565; entered prison July 18, 1842; 51 years of age (formerly known as John Burns); native state, New Jersey; blacksmith; Negro; eyes and hair black; 5' 6¼"; foot, 10¼"; lame in left foot, scar on left side, upper lip and left bridge of nose; burglary; 7 years, sentenced General Sessions Court, Philadelphia; third offense, second here [Three times convicted, twice to Walnut Street Jail, once in New Jersey]; expiration of sentence, July, 1849; reads and writes, sober, widower; died in prison November 3, 1845.

His first offense; entered prison, April 3, 1837; No. 733; under name, John Burns, born a slave; 46 years old; New Jersey burglary; five years; Court of Oyer and Terminer, Philadelphia; fourth offense, April 3, 1842; can read and write, sober.

Prison minister's entry, April 3, 1838: "No. 733, John Burns. Old convict, means now to abandon his old course. But has no present desire to love and serve God."

Later statement by moral instructor (July 8, 1842): "Left April 3 last, out three months and returned; profane and hardened. Says if he had kept away from D—— Wh——s he would not have been here now."

William Peter

The "black burglar" came in April, 1837, went out April, 1842—came in again on July 13 following. Just as Mr. Dickens described him, "a very dexterous thief." He had been convicted of stealing silver spoons and seems to glory in his crime, telling me that, though bred to the iron trade, he liked the silver trade much better—scorns to be thought a common thief, and calls himself a burglar by profession—has a mania for plunder that can never be cured. He is one of those who "laugh and grow fat" in spite of all punishment.

THE CASE OF THOMAS PARKS

Dickens

There was one man who was allowed, as an indulgence, to keep rabbits. His room having rather a close smell in consequence, they called to him at the door to come out into the passage. He complied, of course, and stood shading his haggard face in the unwonted sunlight of the great window, looking as wan and unearthly as if he had been summoned from the grave. He had a white rabbit in his breast; and when the little creature, getting down upon the ground, stole back into the cell, and he, being dismissed, crept timidly after it, I thought it would have been very hard to say in what respect the man was the nobler of the two.

Record

Thomas Parks, No. 195; entered prison November 9, 1833; native of Ireland; 35 years of age; laborer; light; gray hazel eyes; light brown hair; 5′ 9½″; on right arm in India ink a female figure and the letters, M.P.T.P.; left wrist broken; murder; twelve years; Oyer and Terminer Court, Philadelphia; first conviction; let out June 18, 1842; pardoned and discharged; reads and writes a little; married.

The prison minister wrote on November 9, 1833, "No. 195, Thomas Parks. Has some correct version of religious views, conducts well, feels very deeply for having been the instrument of his wife's death. Prays and reads Scriptures daily, yet is not divinely enlightened; hopes to meet with her in Heaven who was driven away in his wickedness."

William Peter

The man "allowed to keep rabbits" went out in good health in November, 1842 (eight months after Dickens' visit). He now resides in Canada and according to letters received from him by his countrymen, is doing well.

THE CASE OF JAMES WILLIAMSON

Dickens

There was an English thief, who had been there but a few days out of seven years; a villainous, low-browed, thin-lipped fellow, with a white face who had as yet no relish for visitors, and who, but for the additional penalty, would have gladly stabbed me with his shoemaker's knife.

Record

James Williamson, alias Northwood, No. 1469; entered prison December 9, 1841; born, London; forty-four years of age; gunstock maker; light; dark gray eyes; light hair; 5′ 4⅛″; small mole on each cheek; larceny; seven years (detained three years county prison);

General Sessions Court, Philadelphia; second offense; pardoned January 22, 1845; reads and writes; drinks some; married.

Previous record: No. 1168: James Webb, 42, born in London, gunstock maker, bound in service; 21; light complexion; dark eyes yet light hair; 5′ 4⅛″, foot, 9½″; a mole on each cheek, first conviction; parents dead—died about nine years ago; can read and write; drinks but seldom gets drunk; married and three children; cash, 90 cents; silver pencil; pen knife and gold ring.

The moral instructor stated of this Williamson alias Webb, No. 1168, "Dogged silence apparently indifferent and hardened and seems to be accustomed to prison. Was pardoned and discharged July 25, 1840. Gave information to Warden Wood in relation to counterfeiters and bank note plates, etc." Of No. 1469, Williamson, the chaplain wrote, "A hardened and hopeless thief and burglar by profession." The record states: "Pardoned a 2nd. time for police purposes January 21, 1845, 4 yrs. in prison. Robbed Bailey & Kitchen of something like $50,000 worth of silver and gold."

William Peter
The "English thief" looks good in health and is conducting himself well.

THE CASE OF JOHN BROWN

Dickens
There was a German who had entered the jail but yesterday and who stared from his bed when we looked in, and pleaded, in his broken English, very hard for work.

Record
John Brown, formerly F. W. Rosenberg, No. 1514; entered prison February 24, 1842; thirty-two years of age; born in Germany; shoemaker; swarthy; gray eyes; brown hair; 5′ 7¼″; foot, 10⅜″; burglary; five years; Oyer and Terminer, Montgomery County; third offense here; discharge date, February 24, 1847; reads and writes; drinks, single.

No. 704: John F. J. Rosenbaugh; Germany; no trade; never bound; light complexion; grey eyes; brown hair; 5′ 7¼″; 10⅜″; 1st conviction; reads and writes; parents alive; gets drunk; single.

No. 1062: Same as John F. J. Rosenburg, same as 704.

No. 1514: John Brown, formerly 1062 and 704. Sentenced February 24, 1842, burglary; five years. Received March 7. O. T. Montgomery Co.; Cash, $1.25, left for him by B. C. Watson.

The chaplain wrote of him at the time of his first conviction, "Professes to be converted. This young man appears to be constantly in a happy state of mind. Full of exulting gratitude to God; he certainly appears to rejoice in his confinement."

Two years later, he wrote, "This man professed conversion and seemed as happy as any creature could be when first in this place but returned in a few weeks, said it was impossible to get work, was turned out of every situation as all knew by his work that he had been in the penitentiary."

Of No. 1514 the moral instructor wrote, "Only 7 days discharged and convicted for five years. Was not sane when discharged. Is altogether hardened, wicked, and hopeless now. Time out; discharged; hopeless."

Mr. Peter did not comment on the case of John Brown.

THE CASE OF GEORGE RYNO

Dickens

There was a poet who, after doing two days' work in every four-and-twenty hours, one for himself and one for the prison, wrote verses about ships (he was by trade a mariner), and the "maddening wine-cup," and his friends at home.

Record

George Ryno, No. 1292; entered the prison July 10, 1840; native of New Jersey; thirty years old; sailor; swarthy complexion; hazel eyes; dark hair; 5' 9½"; foot, 9¾"; long scar on left cheek near mouth, letters G. R. tattooed on right arm; larceny; three years; General Sessions Philadelphia; second conviction; time expired July 10, 1843; discharged; reads and writes; drinks; single.

This prisoner wrote a kind of doggerel verse and gained the interest of some of the officials of the prison. They made it possible for him to have a collection of his verses printed under the pseudonym of Harry Hawser. The title of his book was *Buds and Flowers, of Leisure Hours.* Copies of it may be found in Philadelphia libraries today.

The moral instructor made the following entries regarding this prisoner:

Seems to be reckless and hardened. Little or no sense of shame. Parents respectable; has been 7 or 10 years at sea, most of the time in the Navy of U.S. Seems of a light trifling spirit. Disposed to smile at the introduction of any serious topic. Brother twice in this prison and died here. Father, since head keeper of Trenton prison and a cruel and bad man, said to be.

On the margin of his Journal he adds, "Parents living; Episcopal; no proper religious instruction; lived where liquor was sold; drank hard. Went to Sunday School."

William Peter
The Poet had been discarded by his father some years before for intemperate habits; he received on quitting the prison $30 for extra work, besides the $50 for the copyright of his book. He is now in respectable business, reconciled with his father, and respectably married (his wife knew of his imprisonment). He frequently visits the warden and is, to all appearances, well in mind, body, and circumstances.

But despite this favorable prognosis George Ryno returned to Cherry Hill. He was convicted of larceny and entered the prison as No. 2312 on January 27, 1848, sentenced from Philadelphia to two years and one month. The chaplain wrote of him at this time, "Evidently a painful struggle to the prisoner to meet me and to make his face as Brass, another hardening process; careless and hopeless." Ryno, listed at this time as "sailor and barber" was discharged February 27, 1850.

Many years later, William Tallack, secretary of the Howard Association of London, stated that this "poet" had written a pamphlet in defense of the separate system in which he stated that his imprisonment was "the happiest event of his life" since it "had dissolved improper connections, remodelled his tastes, improved his mind, and, he trusts, made better his heart." [4] We have no way of knowing just how Tallack came into contact with the "poet," nor do we have a copy of Ryno's "essay" in defense of the system.

[4] Tallack, *Penological and Preventive Principles* (London, 1896), p. 164.

THE CASE OF FRED FAUSTENBURG

Dickens

There was an accomplished surgeon who attended a fat old Negro whose leg had been taken off within the jail.[5]

Record

Fred F. Faustenburg, "the accomplished surgeon" No. 1290; entered the prison July 1840; thirty years of age; from Hanover, Germany; surgeon; swarthy complexion; hazel eyes; dark hair; 5′ 4⅞″; foot, 9½″; a scar at second joint of left thumb; larceny; 2 years, six months; General Sessions Court, Philadelphia; first offense; discharged, January 8, 1843; reads and writes; temperate drinker; single; cash. $5.45.

The Reverend Mr. Larcombe wrote of this prisoner, "Says he had collegiate education, was a Druggist, Surgeon and Physician. Seems deeply affected with his deplorable condition. Knows not how the temptation overcame him suddenly to steal a pair of gold spectacles; had $50 in his pocket and was in no immediate want. Discharged in good health and mind; promises reform; *no hope.*"

William Peter

The accomplished surgeon came in July 1840 and left in January 1843, in good health—he is now employed in a large apothecary's establishment in South America, and conducting himself with propriety. He has written to the chaplain, thanking him and the officers of the prison, for their kindness to him during his confinement.

THE CASE OF DAVID JOHNSON

Dickens

Sitting upon the stairs, engaged in some slight work, was a pretty colored boy. "Is there no refuge for young criminals in Philadelphia, then?" said I. "Yes, but only for white children." Noble aristocracy in crime.[6]

---

[5] The "fat old Negro" was James Reynolds, No. 1142. The moral instructor wrote of him: "Seems hardened and indisposed to have conversation of a serious kind; little desire for any. Leg amputated. This may spoil his trade in future, hope so! Age, 51; in for larceny."

[6] At the time of Dickens's visit the Philadelphia House of Refuge did not admit Negro children. In 1850 a department was erected for Negroes.

Record

David Johnson, No. 1453; thirteen years old; Negro; native of Brides-
burg, Pennsylvania; entered November 10, 1841; servant; black hair
and eyes; 4′ 5½″; foot, 9⅛″; scar on knuckle of each hand; arson;
two year sentence; General Sessions Court, Philadelphia; first offense; time out and discharged, November 10, 1843; cannot read or
write, parents living.

The moral instructor's statement was, "Parents living. Put out
at 11 years old; No religious instruction. Cause of crime (arson)
revenge. Shrewd, a strong disposition to steal and stole various
articles in prison."

William Peter

The pretty colored boy was quite ignorant and uninstructed when he
entered, but learned whilst in prison to read, write, and cipher; has
now a good place as servant to Mr. ——'s family, and behaves remarkably well.

THE CASE OF SAMUEL DAVIS

Dickens

There was a sailor who had been there upwards of eleven years,
and who in a few months' time would be free. Eleven years of solitary confinement!

"I am very glad to hear your time is nearly out." What does he say?
Nothing. Why does he stare at his hands, and pick the flesh upon his
fingers, and raise his eyes for an instant, every now and then to those
bare walls which have seen his head turn so grey? It is a way he
has sometimes.

Does he never look men in the face, and does he always pluck at
those hands of his, as though he were bent on parting skin and
bone? It is his humour; nothing more.

It is his humour, too, to say that he does not look forward to going
out; that he is not glad the time is drawing near; that he did look
forward to it once, but that was very long ago; that he has lost all
care for everything. It is his humour to be a helpless, crushed, and
broken man. And, Heaven be his witness that he has his humour
thoroughly gratified!

Record

Samuel Davis, No. 58; entered the prison December 14, 1830; aged forty; native of Camden, New Jersey; farmer; complexion, mulatto or half Indian; dark eyes, black curly hair; 5′ 3⅞″; foot, 10″; no marks, charge, rape; sentenced twelve years; convicted Oyer and Terminer Court, Bucks County; pardoned and discharged, November 2, 1842; first offense; release date, December 14, 1842; cannot read or write.

We read of this discharged prisoner from Warden Samuel Wood some five years after he had resigned his post and was living in Catawissa, a small town in upstate Pennsylvania. In a letter the warden sent to the Philadelphia Prison Society, dated March 18, 1845, he commented on the fictions of Charles Dickens. He wrote that he had recently had a visit from "the sailor," that is, Samuel Davis. He wrote,

Last spring this man came to my works. He said, "that hearing at Catawissa that I resided but four miles distant he thought he must come to see me." I was pleased that he did so; first, because he had been nearly nine years under my almost daily observation and care; secondly; he had been nearly twelve years in separate confinement; had seen fewer persons, and had less to amuse him, in the way of reading and writing, than most of the prisoners; and lastly, because he was one of the most prominent characters in Dickens' *Notes*. I had full opportunity and took much pains, to ascertain the real state of his mind; and, after the strictest scrutiny I could make, came to the conclusion, that his faculties were as sound as on the day he entered the prison.[7]

The prison minister made this comment on Samuel Davis as he contacted him in the institution on the day of his arrival, December 14, 1830: "Exceedingly excited, enraged at the judge and threatens revenge. Swore if knife or pistol could be had, would revenge his wrongs upon the prosecutor; also had sold himself to the Devil and wanted to rush on to Hell for revenge —did not wish to hear of religion."

William Peter

The sailor had been convicted of rape—he left with no appearance

[7] *Journal of Prison Discipline and Philanthropy*, Vol. I, No. 2 (1845), p. 204.

about him of the "helpless, crushed, and broken man," but in apparent health and spirits. His first request, on being liberated, was to have a "chew of tobacco." He is now in the employment of a farmer in the interior of the state, and said to be conducting himself well.

THE CASES OF THE THREE YOUNG WOMEN

Dickens

There were three young women in adjoining cells, all convicted at the same time of conspiracy to rob their prosecutor. In the silence and solitude of their lives, they had grown to be quite beautiful. Their looks were very sad, and might have moved the sternest visitor to tears, but not to that kind of sorrow which the contemplation of the men, awakens. One was a young girl; not twenty, as I recollect, whose snow-white room was hung with the work of some former prisoner, and upon whose downcast face the sun, in all its splendour, shown down through the high chink in the wall, where one narrow strip of bright blue sky was visible. She was very penitent and quiet; had come to be resigned, she said (and I believed her); and had a mind at peace. "In a word, you are happy here," said one of my companions. She struggled—she did struggle very hard—to answer, "Yes," but raising her eyes, and meeting that glimpse of freedom overhead, she burst into tears, and said: "She tried to be;" she uttered no complaint; "but it was natural that she should sometimes long to go out of that one cell; she could not help *that*," she sobbed, poor thing!

Record

The three young women in adjoining cells. All entered the prison November 2, 1839.

No. 1174: Louisa Harman; aged 19; native of Delaware; servant; black to mulatto; eyes and hair black; 5′ 1⅝″; foot, 9″; scar on right shoulder; offense, conspiracy; seven year sentence; Criminal Sessions, Philadelphia; first offense; pardoned and discharged May 27, 1844; time expired November 2, 1846; cannot read or write; single; left parents at 12 years of age.

No. 1175: Elizabeth Thompson; aged 22; native of Albany, New York; servant; was a slave and freed at 18; black hair and eyes; 5′ 5″; foot, 10″; no scars; conspiracy; seven years; reads and writes; sober; married with two children; discharged May 10, 1844; mother alive.

No. 1176: Ann Richards; 17 years old; New Jersey; servant; light mulatto; black hair and eyes; 4′ 10¾″; foot, 8½″; no scars; discharged May 20, 1844; cannot read or write; sober; single; mother died when she was 10, never knew her father.

The moral instructor wrote concerning these girls as follows:

1174: Louisa Harman. Nearly white; has little to say. Seems melancholy in the prospect of 7 years' imprisonment; no proper sense of her sin; says she was kept by Lewis Albright who took the money. Says she did not. She has lived two years in a house of ill fame. 1175: Elizabeth Thompson. Weeps very much; denies any participation in the crime; says she knew the two girls, particularly 1176. Says she was kept by L.A. and kept for such purposes (to ensnare and rob, I suppose). She had no business to be in such company but was accidentally there and not privy to their design to rob. Has a husband who left her; does not know where he is; has two children; wept when she mentioned them; lived with her mother opposite those girls. 1176: Ann Richards. This young creature is very light; also says Lewis Albright brought her from New York where she lived in a house of ill fame; had lived so one year; says she took the money like 1174 in feeling no compunction or fear of God but melancholy.

William Peter

The "three young women in adjoining cells" . . . have nothing "very sad" in their looks, or in any way calculated to move "the sternest visitor to tears." They have been a kind of decoy ducks for keepers of low brothels and were convicted of conspiracy to rob their prosecutor. They came to prison quite ignorant and untaught, but now read, write, cipher, and word remarkably well. One of them (she to whom Mr. Dickens particularly refers) told me that their imprisonment had been "a very good thing" for them all, and that she did not know what would have become of them had they not been sent there—that they have been very bad girls, and used to be drunk from morning to night —and indeed, "had no comfort or peace except when drunk." She hopes now that she shall be able to earn an honest livelihood. Her parents (who are respectable coloured people in another state, and from whom she ran away at fifteen) are now reconciled and have written to say that they will receive, and do what they can for her when she comes out of prison. She has become an excellent seamstress, and they are now all out of prison, in good service and said to be conducting themselves with propriety.

☰6
Prison Practices and Policies in Cherry Hill

INTRODUCTION

THE years between 1840 when the first warden resigned and the beginning of the twentieth century witnessed many changes in the social and economic life of the nation, and many of these made their impress on the prison. The influx of immigrants from Europe, the growing number of runaway slaves concentrating in the larger cities of the North, the great technological improvements in heating, communication, industrialization, and medical knowledge—all made it necessary for the administrations to change their policies. The repercussion of the War between the States, the consequent freeing of the slaves, and the disorganization of returned soldiers were reflected in the national crime rate. The ups and downs of prison population as well as the changes in vital statistics may be seen in the Cherry Hill reports for this period. While there were many Negroes in the Philadelphia prison prior to 1860, the number from this racial group climbed more rapidly during the last half of the century.

Prison policies and practices change slowly, but they do change, in large measure through necessity of events. As one reads the annual reports from 1829 to 1900, major changes are discernible along with ones of small moment. The old whale and lard lamps as well as candles were replaced by the installation of gas in 1856, and this in turn was supplanted by electricity in 1888. City water was brought into the prison in 1854, where up to that time the only water supply was from wells within the yard.

The city encroached heavily on the prison as new streets were laid out and residential homes erected. The pigs and cows that were kept within the confines of the high stone walls had to

be removed as the population of the prison increased, and even
the trees in the yard were cut down in 1854. In 1853 it was
found necessary to replace the worn-out shingle roofs of the
cell blocks with less combustible ones of slate. In 1857 the inspectors found to their dismay that the Bank of Pennsylvania
had closed its doors with a $7,200 deposit belonging to the
prison "gone," as they ruefully remarked, "into the abyss made
by the absence of that honor and integrity which should have
sustained the character of that institution."

In this chapter we shall describe the various practices of the
inspectors and wardens as they managed the prison down
through the years. In 1872, under the leadership and inspiration of Richard Vaux, president of the Board, complete statistical tables were compiled of data concerning the prisoners who
were confined in the prison from its opening date. Items covered were: number received each year, sex, age distribution,
nationality, marital status, educational and moral (temperance
and intemperance) habits, and types of crimes committed.
These data were compiled through 1874 cumulatively, but
from that date on, only on an annual basis.[1] By the close of the
year 1900 there had been received at the prison 20,454 prisoners.

In discussing prison practices it is easy to overlook their im-
pact upon the prisoner. The psychological effect on the individual of the admission procedure, the transition from a state
of freedom to one of restriction, the labor policy, and the rela-
tionships with physician, moral instructor, and the overseers
are difficult to appraise. There are no autobiographical data or
individual testimonials on which we can draw to weigh the
effects of the conventional practices that were set in motion by
the prison administration, but we do have some scattered bits
of information which suggest that the former inmates of Cherry
Hill reacted to prison life much as do the present ones. We find
such information in the reports of the moral instructor, the
physician, and the warden, as well as in the reports of the

[1] For such data see *Forty-fifth Annual Report*, 1875.

visitors from the Philadelphia Prison Society, and even in letters written by prisoners and apprehended by the administration.

IDENTIFICATION AND CLASSIFICATION PROCEDURES

The law of April 23, 1829, which governed the discipline of the Eastern Penitentiary, prescribed (Article V) that the new prisoner should

be examined by the clerk and the warden, in the presence of as many overseers as can conveniently attend, in order to become acquainted with his or her person and countenance, and his or her name, height, age, place of nativity, trade, complexion, color of hair and eyes, length of feet, to be accurately measured and that these shall be entered in a book provided for that purpose together with such other natural or accidental marks, or peculiarity of feature or appearance, as may serve to identify him or her, and if the convict can write, his or her signature shall be written under the said description of his or her person.

It was further required by the law (Article VIII) that, upon discharge, the prisoner

shall take off his prison uniform, and have clothes which he or she brought to the prison restored to him or her, together with the other property, if any, that was taken from him or her. . . . It shall be the duty of the warden to obtain from him or her, as far as it is practicable, his or her former history; what means of literary, moral or religious instruction he or she has enjoyed; what early temptations to crime by wicked associations or otherwise he or she was exposed to; his or her general habits, predominant passions, and prevailing vices, and in what part of the country he or she purposes to fix his or her residence; all of which shall be entered in a book to be kept for that purpose, together with his or her name, age, and time of discharge. . . . If the inspectors and warden have been satisfied with the morality, industry, and order of his conduct, they shall furnish the discharged convict with four dollars, whereby the temptation immediately to commit offenses against society, before employment can be obtained, may be obviated.[2]

[2] Most of these data were carefully recorded and may be found in the State Record Office at Harrisburg, Pennsylvania.

Not all discharged prisoners merited the four dollars; in some instances the "reward" on leaving the prison was prorated on the basis of "merit."

Here are a few descriptions of prisoners as found in the warden's Journal.

No. 693. Robt. McClinton. Aged 24. Born Harrisburg, Pa. Laborer. Bound and served [apprenticeship] till 19. Mulatto—black eyes and hair. 5′ 8⅛″, foot 10¼″—scar on forehead. First conviction. Can spell. Parents dead. Got drunk every Saturday night. (25 cts., single).

No. 986. John Wilson, al. James Heath. Aged 29. Born in New York. Sail maker. Never bound. Went to sea at 15. Swarthy, light hazel eyes, brown hair. 5′ 8″, foot 10½″. On left arm two anchors, star and wreath in Indian ink. Father died two years ago. Reads and writes. Drinks. (25 cents).

No. 1339. Jane Evans. Aged 60. Born in Delaware. Servant. Bd. and stayed till her master died. Black woman. 5′ 3½″ high. Foot 9¾″ long. Small scar on left cheek near nose. First conviction. Parents dead—lost father when young. Cannot read or write. Drank and sometimes got out of the way a little. Single. Rec'd. Dec. 4 for arson. Two years, Philadelphia County.

This crude system of identification was in practice until the Bertillon method was installed in 1904 by Warden Joseph Byers. This system, developed by Alfonse Bertillon, the famous chief of the French *Service d'Identité Judiciare*, embraced all of the individual identifications earlier used but added many more. Some of these were: span of arms, sitting height, length and width of head, width of ears, length of various fingers, and, of course, any anomalies. Front and profile photographs were included, and Warden Byers also added the system of finger prints to his identification program.

During the decade of 1855 to 1865 the inspectors of the Eastern Penitentiary attempted to classify the prisoners along the lines suggested by the quasi-science—popular and respectable in those days—known as phrenology. These officials can be excused for making use of phrenology, since it had considerable scientific status during the first half of the nineteenth century.

A number of phrenological studies were made by prison administrators during the peak of its fad. M. B. Sampson's *Rationale of Crime* (1846), a book avowedly based on phrenology, was prefaced by Eliza Farnham, noted superintendent of the women's division of Sing Sing prison of New York.

Annual reports submitted by officials of Cherry Hill for this period show the tendency to place criminal behavior in phrenological categories, although the word was never used. The Reverend Thomas Larcombe listed the predominant passions as acquisitiveness, destructiveness, combativeness, and amativeness. In this last category he found the corresponding crimes to be rape, attempt to ravish, and licentiousness.

After the newly arrived inmate was questioned and measured he was given his prison clothes, and his civilian attire and usually meager personal property were packed away until the day of his release. He was then taken blindfolded to his cell, where he was informed of the rules of the institution and assigned to some form of labor. We do not have a copy of the rules that were in practice during the first years of the prison, but we have a set of regulations adopted December 5, 1840, which was addressed

To the Prisoner in His Cell

You are desired strictly to observe the following rules established by the inspectors for your government.

1st. You must keep your person, cell and utensils clean and in order.

2nd. You must obey promptly, all directions given to you, either by the Inspectors, Warden, or Overseers.

3rd. You must not make any unnecessary noise, either by singing, whistling, or in any other manner; but in all respects preserve becoming silence. You must not try to communicate with your fellow-prisoners in the adjoining cells, either from your own apartment, or during the time you are exercising in your yard.

4th. All surplus food must be placed in the vessel provided for that purpose; and all wastage of materials, or other dirt, must be carefully collected and handed out of the cell, when called for by the Overseer.

5th. You must apply yourself industriously, at whatever employment is assigned you; and when your task is finished, it is recommended that your time be devoted to the proper improvement of your mind, either in reading the books provided for the purpose, or in case you cannot read, in learning to do so.

6th. Should you have any complaint to make against the Overseer having charge of you, make it to the Warden or Inspector—if against the Warden, to the Inspector.

7th. Be at all times, in your intercourse with the officers of the Penitentiary, respectful and courteous, and never suffer yourself to be led astray from your duties, by angry or revengeful feelings.

8th. Observe the Sabbath; though you are separated from the world, the day is not the less holy.

The Inspectors desire to treat every prisoner under their charge with humanity and kindness; and they hope that in return, the prisoner will strictly conform to the rules adopted for his government.

At the same time rules were adopted for the staff of the institution, dealing with the duties of the overseers who served both as instructors and guards, the watchmen upon whose shoulders fell the responsibility of custody, and the front gate-keeper. They were as follows:

Rules
Overseers

The Overseers must be vigilant in the performance of their duties; have a strict oversight of the conduct of the prisoners, and see that they are industrious in the performance of their labor; and whenever they observe anything of a suspicious nature in the actions of a prisoner, they shall forthwith apprize the Warden of it, in order that requisite precautionary measures may be adopted; in all their intercourse with the prisoners, it is expected and enjoined upon them to preserve mild and conciliatory conduct toward them; to suppress every passion or resentment, and at all times and on all occasions, show entire self-possession, but resolutely, and with unflinching firmness of purpose, enforce the discipline of the Penitentiary.

The Overseers, as well as all others connected with the management of the Penitentiary, are positively forbidden the use of intoxicating liquors, profane language, or other immoral conduct, under the penalty of being forthwith discharged, at the option of the Warden or Inspectors.

The Overseers shall by turns, of two in number, lodge within the centre building, to be ready upon an emergency to give their advice or assistance to the watchmen.

The Overseers are especially directed to report any complaints, grievances or reasonable requests made by the prisoners, immediately to the Warden, who shall advise the visiting Inspectors thereof at their next succeeding visit.

Watchmen

The Watchmen shall be especially under the direction of the Warden, and shall enter upon and be relieved from the performance of their duties, at such hours as he may from time to time, prescribe.

One or more of them shall patrol the yard, carefully examining every portion of it in the course of their rounds; see that all is safe; and should necessity require it, they shall, upon any emergency, apprize the night overseers resting in the centre building.

For sleeping on their watch, or neglect of any prescribed duties, they shall be liable to immediate discharge from service.

Gatekeeper

The Gatekeeper shall diligently observe all persons who pass in or out of the Prison; and admit no stranger or person unconnected with the Prison, or the business thereof, without permission from one of the Inspectors or the Warden. All printed orders of admission shall be preserved by him, and returned to the Inspectors or Warden who may issue the same.

With the prison rules constantly before him, the prisoner was left to himself. But his every move was watched as he worked alone in his cell or took his daily exercise in his little yard, since he was the ward of the Commonwealth for the duration of his sentence. In his close confines he ate, slept, worked, pursued his education, and was afforded religious council.

By the end of the century a crude beginning of what is known in modern penology as classification can be detected. Cherry Hill prisoners were never divided into "grades" as was common in congregate prisons, where there was, for example, one grade for all new prisoners until they had demonstrated that they could behave themselves, after which they were eligible for a higher grade, or those under punishment were placed in a lower grade. By 1897 Warden Michael Cassidy had developed a kind of initial classification or quarantine system. He de-

scribed it for the joint legislative commission that investigated
the penitentiary in May and June of that year, as follows:

The prisoner is first taken to the bath room, all his clothes are taken
from him, and he is given a suit of clothes. A mask is put over his
face and he is brought up within the inside gate in the bath room.
Then he is brought here, to the office, and a descriptive list is taken,
in which any marks upon him, his height, habits and like matters
are noted. This includes anything that we know about him. That is
hunted up. Then he is taken to a room in one of the galleries that
is especially reserved for newcomers. He is placed there until he is
interviewed by the doctor, the moral instructor, the school teacher
and others. . . . After I get to know something about the man who
has just come in and after he has been in the specially reserved cell
for perhaps a week or ten days, then I determine where he is to go
and I locate him. . . . If he is a "crime class" man I do not hesitate
to put him with a "crime class" man. If he is here on a first conviction, I consider that fact. . . . But first convictions do not always
indicate anything to guide me. There are many first convictions
or where prisoners are very bad people. The point with me is to find
that the man is not a crime class man.

The annual reports of the early wardens give no clue as to
the methods of selecting the staff of the prison. The overseers
were probably picked because of their knowledge of the various trades set up in the institution, but the watchmen apparently needed no specific previous training. The early wardens
gave no thought to that which is today known as "in-service"
training; there were rules for both the watchmen and the overseers but no training on the job.

Warden Townsend in 1879 seemed to have been the first to
introduce some training for his staff. He wrote in his report for
that year, "At the close of the daily duties, a half hour is maintained [for training purposes] five evenings of each week. All
who attend appear interested, and none are absent except those
on night duty." [3] Some years later Warden Cassidy described
his system of staff training as follows:

One night in the week—every Monday night—all the officers assem-
ble, before they go away—in the office in which this committee is

[3] *Fifty-first Annual Report,* 1880, p. 46.

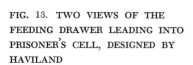

FIG. 13. TWO VIEWS OF THE
FEEDING DRAWER LEADING INTO
PRISONER'S CELL, DESIGNED BY
HAVILAND

FIG. 14. MEN WORKING IN CELLS
  After the 1860s separate confinement was no
  longer enforced

FIG. 15. MASK OR HOOD WORN IN EARLY DAYS

now sitting; and there the warden instructs them how to do, what they are to do and when to do it, and gives them any instructions that are necessary in respect to their duties or to the treatment of the prisoners. Any directions they then receive are received by them all at one time in the same way; and there is no after consideration given if they don't do what they are told to do, that they didn't know better that "I never was told that." They are told what they are to do. Every Monday night they meet and get the instructions.

Cassidy may have been an uneducated man, blunt and perhaps hard-bitten, but he had come up through the ranks and knew his duties and responsibilities. According to the penology of his day, he knew prison administration and he knew criminals.

THE SYSTEM OF PRISON LABOR

Productive labor had been one of the features of the successful program developed in the Walnut Street Jail following its renovation in 1790. Throughout the following years, the board of that prison continued to be impressed by the reformative value of hard, productive labor. Hence the Board of Inspectors of the Eastern Penitentiary took the same position as their predecessors.

As was stated earlier, some of the enthusiasts of the Pennsylvania System were opposed to the principle of furnishing work for the prisoners in the state's prisons. We noted, too, that no work had been provided for the prisoners sent to the Western Penitentiary when it was earlier opened at Pittsburgh. It was believed by many that solitude, unmitigated, should be the lot of the convicted criminal, but this position was overruled.

The question of providing labor was definitely settled by the act of April 23, 1829 (Section 2), which decreed that work should be given each prisoner in his cell.[4] Usually the prisoner was granted the "favor" of working after the first week. That some type of occupation was regarded as a privilege is demon-

---

[4] The labor controversy is ably handled in the *Journal of Prison Discipline and Philanthropy*, Vol. II, No. 2 (1846), pp. 120–21. See also Richard Vaux, *A Brief Sketch of the Origin and History of the State Penitentiary for the Eastern District of Philadelphia* (Philadelphia, 1872), p. 87.

strated by the fact that one of the penalties in the prison was the withdrawal of the offender's tools for a period of time.

For a short period following the opening of the prison in 1829, when the construction of the cell blocks occupied much of the attention of the administrative officers, some of the prisoners were employed on construction work. Few prisoners were allocated to labor in the cells, but if a new prisoner showed any skill in the building trades, such as bricklaying, iron working, smithing, or the like, he was immediately drafted to labor in the prison yard, alongside hired workmen.

But this practical procedure was admittedly temporary. The real system of prison labor at Cherry Hill had two fundamental objectives: training of the inmate in some skill by which he might conceivably make a living upon his release from prison, and producing products to be sold by the administration to help defray the cost of the institution.

In the early days of prison labor in this country the system most frequently used was the contract system and its variation, the "piece-price" system. The contract system simply involved the letting out of the prisoners' labor to contractors who furnished the machinery and the raw material and had the work supervised by men in their employ. In such a system, which was introduced and used effectively in the Auburn-type prisons and which spread throughout the entire system of prisons in this country, the prison management had nothing to do with the operations. The contract system was particularly vicious since it had within it the seeds of exploitation of the captive labor force.

Its variation, the "piece-price" system, was free of the undesirable features of the more widely used system. By means of "piece-price" the contractor might or might not furnish the raw material, and the prison furnished the equipment, machinery, and the prisoner manpower and also supervised the operation. The contractor purchased such of the finished product as passed his inspection. This was the method that was so successfully introduced in the Walnut Street Prison in 1790. Another form of this method is often referred to today as the "public account" system, in which no contractor is involved. It is the responsibility of the Board of the prison or its agent to market the prison-made product. It was this system that was introduced into the Philadelphia prison in 1829.

By law it was the duty of the inspectors and, through them, the warden, to purchase the raw materials and market the finished products, which were serious responsibilities to be added to the many duties of operating the institution. The first president of the Board of Inspectors, Judge Charles Coxe, wrote in his first report to the legislature, regarding labor,

When a convict arrives he is placed in his cell and left alone, without work and without any book. . . . But few hours elapse before he petitions for something to do, and for a Bible. . . . If a prisoner has a trade that can be pursued in his cell, he is put to work as a favor; as a reward for good behavior, and as a favor, a Bible is allowed him. If he has no trade, or one that cannot be pursued in his cell, he is allowed to choose one that can, and he is instructed by one of the overseers, all of whom are master workmen in the trades they respectively superintend and teach. Thus work, and moral and religious books, are regarded and received as favors, and are withheld as punishment.[5]

Since Warden Wood was a firm believer in labor for the prisoners, he proved diligent in supervising the program from its crude beginnings until the day he resigned. He was convinced that prisoners, with few exceptions, could earn their maintenance if the state would provide enough material and equipment. He made exceptions of those whose sentences were less than two years and those who were too feeble or infirm to work. In his second annual report (1831) he wrote,

. . . every prisoner, with four exceptions, who has been here even six months, is now earning his maintenance. These exceptions are, first, No. 19, who was brought here ill, and whose illness continued without cessation, until the time of his decease. Secondly, No. 8, who was an invalid at the time of his reception, and continues so. Thirdly, No. 34, who is upwards to sixty years of age, and infirm; and fourthly, No. 35, who is also infirm, and seventy-two years of age.

With the opening of the institution shoemaking was introduced, and the very first prisoner, Charles Williams, was set

[5] *First Annual Report*, 1830, p. 9.

to work making shoes. He had had no previous experience, but it was reported by Warden Wood that within four days he had made a pair of shoes that passed inspection. By 1831, Charles Williams was making as many as ten pairs of shoes daily.

Shoemaking was soon followed by weaving, and throughout the next 50 years these two basic trades continued to be taught in the prison. Shoes, brogans, and cloth were the main products sold to contractors. However, in many instances prisoners pursued carpentering, smithing, shuttle-making, and prison-maintenance work.

From October 25, 1829, to December 1, 1840, the inmates had met all of the expenses of maintenance, exclusive of the salaries of the officials, and a balance remained of $393. A balance over maintenance expenses was reported for 1831 and 1832, but a loss was declared to exist in 1833 and 1834. The deficit was attributed to a general business depression in the country and to the failure of the state to provide enough working capital to maintain prison industries on the highest level of efficiency.

The warden was hard pressed to find ready markets for the prisoners' products. He sold them wherever he could find a buyer, and there were even times when he shipped some of the goods to agents or "salesmen" in the western counties who "peddled" them throughout the frontier of Pennsylvania and Ohio. A few letters in the archives indicate that such methods were none too successful.

Despite periodic statistical reports submitted by the warden, it is difficult to ascertain just how profitable prison labor was at Cherry Hill. Not until the 1850s do we find adequate data concerning this basic phase of prison management.

In 1831 there were 87 prisoners in custody: 43 were engaged in weaving and dyeing; 18 in shoemaking; four were blacksmiths; three were doing carpentering; two were employed as carvers, two were locksmiths; two were engaged in woolpacking; and one each in carriage making, tailoring, cooking, and washing.

In view of the fact that reformation was always considered

a cardinal principle of the Pennsylvania System (after it was once settled by law), it was natural that the Board of Inspectors should especially stress the reformative value of industry. Harry Elmer Barnes in his *Evolution of Penology in Pennsylvania,* published in 1927, has presented the most adequate history of prison labor at Cherry Hill. The following analysis is taken from his work.

The inspectors looked at prison labor in two aspects. First, it was praised as a preventive agency designed to keep the mind of the prisoner occupied to the exclusion of all evil thoughts and reflections. Second, it was highly regarded as a positive factor, in that it aimed to provide the prisoner with a trade so that he might become a self-supporting individual upon obtaining his freedom.

The authorities not only stressed industry within the prison, but also urged with remarkable vigor and consistency for 50 years the necessity of a comprehensive system of vocational instruction for all youths of the Commonwealth, to the end that the alleged economic cause of crime might be uprooted at its source. The great emphasis placed on the reformatory value of industry and the slight emphasis placed on economic phases as a contribution to maintenance must not, however, be viewed as wholly the product of theoretical, ethical convictions.

It was rather, in part at least, a defense reaction which developed as a result of the generally unsatisfactory economic status of the industrial system of the Eastern Penitentiary in contradistinction, for example, to the contract system in operation at such places as Sing Sing and other Auburn-type prisons.

When, as was the case in a few brief periods, the industries of the Cherry Hill institution were in a relatively prosperous condition, the inspectors proudly referred to the fact and pointed to its reduction of maintenance charges. On the other hand, when, as was usually the case, the productivity of the establishment was relatively low, the authorities invariably found that great virtue resided in the reformatory aspects of prison industry and warmly congratulated themselves upon having escaped the dangerous exploitation that so engulfed the Auburn-type institutions, where material productivity and financial gain were the primary aim of prison discipline.

The inspectors of the prison denounced with religious fervor "associative" labor as practiced in practically every other prison and clung tenaciously to labor in the cells. They refused to see the inexorable trend toward workshops with power machinery which, it was claimed all too optimistically, permitted prisons to pay for themselves. Richard Vaux, especially, serving as spokesman for the Board, was disturbed with this trend and at the claims of wardens operating such prisons. In 1875, for example, he wrote in despair to Joseph R. Chandler, one of the editors of the *Journal of Prison Discipline and Philanthropy*,

My dear Chandler, you who hold so powerful a pen, won't you write on the subject—*Does It Pay?* I feel sure it can be demonstrated that it does not. There is not a prison in the United States which for a period of ten years has yearly made a profit by its associate labor, unless there are some exceptional circumstances which can explain the fact. . . . Will you not excite the members [of the Pennsylvania Prison Society] to earnest, active efforts on behalf of our grand system of Penal Discipline, that under the sanction and name of that Society some demonstration shall be made against the false doctrines, and heresy, and error, which is fast affecting public opinion in favor of the paying system of prison discipline? [6]

Warden Cassidy, some years later, denounced labor-saving machinery in these words:

You fill your prisons with the most improved machinery and work against the laboring man outside. The state has no right to interfere with him in his labor, nor to run all sorts of improved machinery against him. Let the man outside use the machinery and let the man inside use his hands. . . . The state has no right to make machines out of its prisoners. [7]

But whatever their dominant motive, one can scarcely fail to commend the attitude of the inspectors in assigning priority to vocational training and reformation over material productivity as the initial aims of prison industry. One cannot, however,

[6] *Journal*, N.S. 14 (1875), p. 63.
[7] *Warden Cassidy on Prisons and Convicts* (Philadelphia, 1897), p. 30.

agree that the methods pursued by these same authorities in attempting to achieve their end were always well-chosen or sagacious.

Only sketchy details of the prison's program of industry in the early days are known. No accurate and consistent data were included in the inspectors' reports until the law of May 31, 1844, compelled them to submit a complete statement of receipts and expenditures. Even after that date no comprehensive figures were given as to the number of prisoners employed in a given industry. From 1854 to 1871 regular reports were made of the employment of the prisoners received, but these reports were filled with tidbits of information on diverse matters and included little statistical information regarding employment. Following the creation of the Board of Public Charities in 1872 such essential information was provided.

As stated above, weaving and shoemaking were almost the sole industries at Cherry Hill, although a few prisoners were employed at picking oakum and wool. The latter are tasks of sheer drudgery, and were quite commonly found in the English workhouses of the eighteenth and nineteenth centuries. In picking oakum the prisoner literally picked the single strands of hemp from short pieces of tar-encrusted rope and placed them in a pile. These hairy strands were sold to chandlers for use in caulking ships.

In the physician's report for 1850 he condemned the industries of Cherry Hill—shoemaking, weaving, and oakum-picking —from a medical standpoint as being purely sedentary and thus "proverbially deleterious." This was the opinion of the prison's most active and outspoken physician, Dr. Robert A. Given. He went further in his report, recommending that the cells be enlarged by combining the exercise yards. In his opinion, the recreational value of the small yard space, much of which never had the direct rays of the sun and in consequence was always damp, was negligible. He advocated other facilities for exercise. In the enlarged cells, machines for making shoes could be installed and thus improve the health of those working at this task. At the same time he submitted this report he commented that fully a third of the inmates were completely idle or "engaged at that detestable wool and oakum picking."

In his report for 1861 Warden Halloway placed his finger on the main difficulty of depending on the prisoner's labor to support a penal institution. He wrote,

To one unacquainted with the character of prisoners and prison labor [it should be pointed out] that every branch of industry requires more or less time to acquire a knowledge of its mysteries; that four-fifths of all those who enter prison are such as have never followed any mechanical art as a settled means of living; that many of them have no capacity beyond that of mere day labor, with indolent, vagrant habits to overcome in not a few, and we shall cease to wonder that so small an amount is not readily realized.[8]

In 1850 the inspectors introduced chair-caning to supplant the picking of oakum. This became one of the most important of the prison's industries during the latter part of the century.

In the decade of the War between the States, hand weaving began to die out, due to the mechanical progress in this operation developed in outside manufacturing. Handlooms could not compete with power driven looms. Shoemaking supplanted weaving during the 1870s and was carried on quite extensively until the manufacture of hosiery was developed during the next decade.

By the close of the eighties, the great improvement of mechanical devices for the manufacture of shoes put an end to the extensive handcraft shoemaking in the cells of the prisoners. Cigar (seegar) making, carried on as early as the sixties, was pursued by about 90 inmates by 1876, but this disappeared by the turn of the century.

Opposition to prison labor by outside labor groups was voiced quite early in Pennsylvania. The first such protest is recorded in the Journal of the Board of Inspectors for August 19, 1835, when the warden reported: "Individuals have been endeavoring to produce excitement against prison labour. The Shoemaker Society states that no member of their society will work for any person who shall furnish the Eastern Penitentiary with work."

[8] *Thirty-third Annual Report*, 1862, p. 48.

He reported that over 100 workmen of the L. D. Alricks Co. had refused to continue their jobs because that firm supplied the prison with leather. However, no action was taken by the Board, so we have no way of knowing how this early protest of free laborers was resolved.

Following the industrial depression of 1893, restrictive laws were passed in Pennsylvania, largely instigated by the labor unions. The number of prison inmates working on productive jobs immediately declined until idle prisoners outnumbered those working. In 1897 the destructive Muelbronner Act was passed, which virtually brought an end to productive prison labor in the state. This act made it illegal for the state to employ more than five percent of its prison inmates in the manufacture of brooms, brushes, and hollow-ware or ten percent in the manufacture of any other kind of goods, or to use machinery operated by power to make products fabricated elsewhere in the state by free labor. The effects of this law prompted Warden Cassidy to state in his report for that year,

The industries formerly pursued have been practically abandoned: 1st. because the concentrated efforts of labor organizations have caused the legislature to pass laws which make the handling of prison made goods unprofitable; 2nd. because automatic machinery has been so perfected that the labor of hands is almost dispensed with; no thought or skill is required to look at a machine driven by artificial power and turning out four times the quantity of manufactured goods required to supply the market.[9]

In despair the inspectors turned to the expediency of permitting the prisoners with some degree of artistic skill to manufacture various types of fine hardware and woodwork. Resulting profits were turned over to the prisoners' welfare funds. It was not until 1915 that the present state-use law was passed which made it possible for tax-supported institutions and agencies to purchase what products they needed from the state's prisons. In Pennsylvania it has always been voluntary.

This, then, is the story of prison labor in the Cherry Hill penitentiary up to the turn of the century. In several respects it is still

[9] *Sixty-eighth Annual Report,* 1898, p. 124.

the story in that institution as well as in the vast majority of the state prisons throughout the country.

RELIGIOUS AND MORAL INSTRUCTION

Despite the fact that the Eastern Penitentiary of Pennsylvania was conceived and dedicated in a religious atmosphere, by a devout group of citizens deeply concerned with penal reform, the legislature was tardy in appropriating funds for religious and educational purposes. The law of 1829 provided for an unsalaried chaplain but the Board of Inspectors found it impossible to fill the post.

The law read: "They [the inspectors] shall attend to the religious instruction of the prisoners and procure a suitable person for this object, who shall be the religious instructor of the prisoners: *Provided,* their services shall be gratuitous" (Article I). In the *First Annual Report* of the inspectors we read,

The Inspectors are required to attend to the religious instruction of the prisoners, and to procure a suitable person for this object. . . . It is further provided that the services of this officer shall be gratuitous. The ministers of the gospel, who might have leisure or disposition to accept the appointment, are generally unable to perform such services without a suitable provision for themselves and their families. Had any candidate been presented to the board, under these circumstances, it is not probable a proper choice could have been made; but as no one has offered, the board has been unable to appoint any religious instructor, and the only instruction of that character afforded the convicts, has been derived from the imperfect efforts of the other officers of the institution.

Within the year, however, we find religious work gratuitously carried on in the prison by some Philadelphia ministers. The Reverend Charles Demmé of the German Lutheran Church took charge of this work, assisted by the Reverends Samuel W. Crawford and James Wilson of the Reformed Presbyterian and Associate Reformed Churches respectively. The Philadelphia Bible Society furnished the inmates with tracts and Bibles.

The inspectors continued their annual plea for a paid religious instructor, so on April 16, 1838, the legislature authorized the appointment of a "moral instructor" but made no provision for a salary. Nevertheless, the inspectors succeeded in securing the services of the Reverend Thomas Larcombe, a Baptist minister who was also employed as a teacher in the city's schools. His salary, apparently paid out of the institution's general funds at first, was $800. Larcombe was born in Philadelphia, May 12, 1791, ordained at Hopewell, New Jersey, in 1821, and held pastorates at Burlington and Bordentown, New Jersey, and at Colebrook, Connecticut, prior to returning to Philadelphia.

Larcombe was no sooner installed as prison chaplain than the legislature was besieged by petitions from citizens urging that that office be discontinued for fear of proselytizing. It is possibly because of this apprehension that the legislature had postponed the matter for so long.

George Combe, the noted Scotch phrenologist who visited Cherry Hill in January, 1839, wrote in his book *Notes on the U.S. of North America during a Phrenological Visit in 1839–40,*

No single circumstance in the history of Pennsylvania indicates the low state of general information among the people more strongly than the extraordinary fact that after erecting this penitentiary at great expense, the Legislature continues insensible to every entreaty of its legal guardians to be furnished with adequate means of moral and religious instruction of its prisoners.

Louis Dwight painted a gloomy picture of the well-intentioned efforts of the volunteer chaplain. In his report for 1836, two years prior to the employment of Larcombe, he visualized the procedure as follows:

But if there was a chaplain, he might stand in a long and lofty avenue, between the solitary cells, and the little feed-hole drawers, as they are called, might be set open, and a veil hung up between them, so that no one prisoner could look across the avenue and see another; and then, if thirty-six prisoners, being the number arranged on either side of one avenue, will put their heads close to the feed-hole drawers, and the chaplain will stand at the end of the avenue, and speak loud enough, and with a slow and distinct articulation, they can hear his voice, but they cannot see his face. This is the preached gospel as they have it in the New Penitentiary in Philadelphia.

Dwight questioned whether the legislature would ever support a chaplain "to preach in so much vacant space," and he seriously doubted that "any minister of Christ" would spend his strength "in such a place of preaching, with so few hearers." He was even more caustic about the development of a Sunday school for prison inmates.

Yet Warden Wood was quite impressed with the superior adaptability of the Cherry Hill arrangement for individual religious instruction.

In what manner can man be placed, where the words of the gospel would be more impressive than in their situation sitting alone, without seeing or being seen by any human being; nothing to distract their thought, or divert them, from the truths delivered to them; alone when they hear, and left alone when the minister has finished, to ponder and reflect.[10]

While this method of imparting the gospel may have appealed to Warden Wood, its use in the New Jersey prison at Trenton was condemned by officials as tending to intensify the soporific effect of the sermons and to encourage the natural impulse to phantasy.

Through the years the moral instructor was assisted by some of the city's clergymen. In addition to the Reverend Mr. Crawford, mentioned earlier, the Reverend Mr. Rafferty of the Catholic faith and Rabbi Michelbach participated. Members of a "benevolent group" of women visited the female block.[11]

The duties of Mr. Larcombe proved to be as difficult as Louis Dwight had predicted. The chaplain was obliged to pursue his spiritual counseling on an individual basis, passing from cell to cell. Thus the bulk of his time was absorbed in personal ministration rather than in group services. He taught basic subjects to the illiterate prisoners as well, for during the first decade religious and educational subjects went hand in hand. By 1845, when the population had increased, Mr. Larcombe was given an assistant in the person of one Mr. Williss, an overseer who served as a teacher. Later, in 1850, a Reverend George Neff was

---

[10] *Journal of the Senate, 1830–31,* II, 465.

[11] The Association of Women Friends. For information regarding this group, who visited females in the city's prisons, see Negley K. Teeters, *They Were in Prison* (Philadelphia, 1937), pp. 248–64.

employed as a part-time teacher. Neff was also in the employ of the Philadelphia Prison Society as an agent to assist discharged prisoners.

By 1854 Larcombe found his schoolteaching duties a bit onerous since they distracted from his first love, that of spiritual adviser. He wrote in his report for that year, "The Moral Instructor has ever regarded literary instruction to be highly important as subsidiary to moral and religious training but can never regard it as a substitute for that higher teaching which the Son of God ordained for the effectual recovery of men from vice and iniquity." It must have been satisfying to the chaplain when, in the same year, the inspectors appointed a full-time teacher in the person of Abram Boyer. The Reverend George Neff, part-time teacher, was released.

The Reverend Mr. Larcombe experienced some resistance to his spiritual activities from some of the overseers. Warden Thompson recorded in his Journal for February 8, 1841,

Dismissed James Tweed overseer for improper conduct, viz., 1st. threatening Mr. Larcombe with personal violence at the time he was executing his duties in visiting the prisoners; 2nd. calling him a liar— both of which charges he admitted in the presence of Mr. Halloway and myself—the only extenuation he alleged was that Mr. Larcombe gave the bible to one of his prisoners when he had deprived him of books to force him to perform his task, also that he conveyed an erroneous report to one of the Inspectors.

The chaplain soliloquized on overseers in the flyleaf of one of his journals (embracing the years 1845–50):

Difficulties of the moral instructor: Overseers conceive hostility against him for trivial causes or for none at all—sometimes for the obvious discharge of duty. They either speak to their prisoners against him or insinuate something to his disadvantage and their prisoners to court the good will of those who can make their situation pleasant or afflictive, misrepresent him or having their imagination imperfect they watch him closely and often wrongfully interpret his language.

The Baptist chaplain expressed some hostility to the Catholic faith:

No. 877. Thomas Foley, Ireland: An Irish Catholic. From the
Scriptures has obtained a knowledge of true religion and rejects the
Superstitions of Popery. Knows that without regeneration he cannot enter the Kingdom of Heaven. Convinced partially of conditions,
is not converted but will strive, etc.

No. 882. Patrick McGuken, Ireland: Seems hopelessly under influence of superstition. Is visited by the priest.

No. 885. Patrick Brady, Ireland: Seems divested to some degree
of the errors of Popery.

How much insight Larcombe possessed would be difficult to
state. Fortunately, he kept a Journal, part of which is available,
that records some significant data concerning the captive members of his flock and sometimes ends with a reflection. A few of
these taken from random are of interest.

No. 876. John Nugent, barber. Understands pretty well what is
required in order to Salvation, but seems not to feel; head very white
but not from age; June 1839 professed conversion; have found it in-
sincere as I supposed; pretends he only meant to try me. Incurable.

No. 878. James Loller, 33, Virginia mulatto; in the fulling mill,
very taciturn, no disposition to converse upon religious subjects, of
course indifferent to them.

No. 879. Henry Brown, 20, Lancaster County; Professed to be a
Catholic. Is very ignorant; does not believe the Bible; Mind changed
by reading Gleig's *History of the Bible;* seems not serious. Says his
mind has been anxious for three months past.

No. 883. James Aspey, 24, Ireland; very pious in his way; Visited
by a priest. Is doing penance.

Cryptic statements appear throughout his Journal such as,
"no hope"—such was the case for so many that he shortened
it to "n.h.;" "a brutal and hardened German infidel;" "has conducted better than before but hopeful;" "tenderer than any
other—wept when I spoke of his parents." Other notations of
interest are:

732. Stephen Serrett. Was in the infirmary suffering from "King's
Evil" [scrofula]; has felt sin like a heavy load but it has passed away
without a sense of pardon; continues to pray; hopes to reform.

731. John Morris. Professes the hope to enjoy acceptance with God

through Christ; professes a clean knowledge of religion and evinces a mild, resigned spirit, a simple child-like trust in the Lord Jesus.

1093. Henry Chapman, 12, black, Bucks County, arson, 2 years. A small boy—seems like a smart and intelligent child, affirms his innocence and declares the burning of a mere barrack of straw to have been occasioned accidentally by playing with Loco Foco matches.

874. Hiram Kelsey. A sort of wild man of the woods, has lived a semi-savage life in western wilds, no sense of religion.

872. Elizabeth Lemon, Mifflin County, perjury, one year. Has been living in prostitution two or three years during which produced repeated abortions. Had a pious mother who on her death bed and often before seriously admonished her of her course of levity and folly. Fear that Prostitution, the Penitentiary and the gallows would be her portion. Says she has seen nothing but sorrow in her sinful course. Weeps at the remembrance of her mother and her past life. Thus far desires to repent and turn to God. Not much stability of character.

898. John Davis says his name is Larkins. His cognomen among thieves is the Red Rover—an old convict and thief.

920. George Thomas. Does not read the Scriptures; has no wish to repent. Says he is a free man, obviously deranged. Tells me "go talk to the convicts about such damned stuff." (A dangerous fellow) [crossed out in ink].

Larcombe continued as chaplain until his death on October 1, 1861. He was succeeded by the Reverend C. M. Breaker, who died within three months of assuming his duties and who was, in turn, succeeded by the Reverend John Ruth who remained at the post for many years.

The chaplains of our early prisons believed criminals could be cured through religious conversion, and all of their activities were centered on personal salvation. In their annual reports they rejoiced over what they believed to be genuine repentance in the prisoners; they also sighed occasionally that their efforts went unrewarded. There is a singular monotony in their reports, but, judged at this distance, no one could accuse these men of God of shirking their responsibilities. Here is a typical report for the year 1846, signed by Larcombe:

While there has been no special religious influence pervading the Penitentiary, it gives me pleasure to state, that the continued use of the ordinary means has not been unrewarded. There have been repeated instances of favourable impression on the minds of individuals, which have the stamp of permanency. Two prisoners have exhibited, in sickness and death, the efficacious influence of an enlightened hope, which divested death of its sting, and the grave its terrors. In addition to these, I have received information of 21 Discharged Prisoners, during the past year, who are hopefully reformed. With 17 of them, I have had personal intercourse, and from 4, credible intelligence has been received.

The report of Mr. Ruth, Larcombe's successor, for the year 1868 is revealing so far as sustained diligence is concerned. It deals with both moral and secular instruction as shown in the accompanying table.

Moral instructor Ruth's data show that the individual prisoner, immured in his lonely cell, saw the chaplain personally only a little better than once per month, aside from listening to his sermons on Sunday. The inmate was better off so far as secular education was concerned, apparently having one individual lesson per week. Thus he had contacts with those institutional people concerned with "treatment" approximately five times per month.

Yet if we appraise the chaplain's labors we see that he visited approximately 600 prisoners about once a month which called for 20 to 25 visits a day, exclusive of Sunday. This totals about three visits per hour.

Other visitors were also concerned with the moral instruction of the prisoners in Cherry Hill. The members of the Philadelphia Prison Society, whose activities will be discussed below, accepted it as their solemn duty to visit the inmates.

EDUCATION

Formal education, as distinguished from vocational education, was started in a small way in American prisons as soon as they were built. Such education contemplated exclusively the three fundamentals of reading, writing, and ciphering. In general, the instruction was placed in the hands of the chaplain.

FIG. 16. MICHAEL CASSIDY, WARDEN, 1881-1900

FIG. 17. RICHARD VAUX

ACTIVITIES OF THE MORAL INSTRUCTOR, 1868, BY MONTHS

Months	Prison population	Visits for Moral Instructor [a]	Visits per prisoner (percent)	Prisoners receiving secular instruction	Percentage of population receiving secular instruction	Secular lessons per month	Secular lessons per prisoner (percent)	Total moral visits and secular lessons	Total per prisoner (percent)
January	592	615	1.06	165	27.87	682	4.13	1297	5.19
February	616	655	1.14	173	28.08	722	5.48	1397	6.62
March	611	635	1.03	163	26.68	803	4.92	1438	5.95
April	621	675	1.08	148	23.83	607	410	1282	5.18
May	638	656	1.02	160	25.07	622	3.89	1278	4.91
June	619	663	1.07	147	23.74	588	4.00	1251	5.07
July	604	631	1.04	147	24.33	480	3.37	1111	4.41
August	613	651	1.06	145	23.65	238	1.64	889	2.70
September	629	662	1.05	146	23.21	574	3.93	1236	4.98
October	696	635	1.06	138	23.15	587	4.26	1222	5.32
November	613	641	1.04	134	21.86	604	4.51	1245	5.55
December	630	670	1.06	143	22.69	612	4.28	1282	5.34

[a] Excludes Sabbath services.

The development of prison schools was painfully slow and the evolution of an educational system even more so.

Since the state of Pennsylvania was tardy in appointing a chaplain for the Cherry Hill institution, we find no record of teaching in the early years. This was not the case in the institutions patterned after the Auburn System, whose records show that the chaplains in these institutions were highly motivated in teaching the illiterate inmates to read. The objective was to make them proficient enough to read the Scriptures. Here is an example of what the Reverend Gerrish Barrett, chaplain in Sing Sing prison, reported on his efforts to teach an illiterate in 1829:

Feb. 22. Began the first verse of Genesis and learned 4 letters.
Feb. 23. Learned 5 letters more.
Feb. 24. Could say all the letters in the first line.
Feb. 25. Knew all the letters in the first verse.
Feb. 26. Knew all the letters in the two verses.
Feb. 27. Spelled all the words of one syllable.
Feb. 28. Partially learned the words "created" and "heaven."
Mar. 1. Besides learning "created" and "heaven" more perfectly, spelled the word "beginning" correctly.
Mar. 2. Read the first verse in the Bible for the first time.
Mar. 3. Read the first line in the second verse.
Mar. 4. Read all the second verse.
Mar. 5. Read correctly the third verse.
Mar. 6. The fourth verse.
Mar. 7. Five verses.
Mar. 10. Six verses.
Mar. 18. Read with ease the sixteenth verse.
Mar. 19. To the twentieth verse.
Mar. 22. To the twenty-third verse.
Mar. 29. Read correctly the first chapter of Genesis.[12]

The first warden at Cherry Hill was alert to the problem of illiteracy at an early date. In his fourth annual report in 1833, he stated that of the 142 prisoners received "only four had been well educated, and only about six more could read and write

[12] Orlando F. Lewis, *The Development of American Prisons and Prison Customs, 1776–1845* (Albany, 1922), p. 112.

tolerably." Yet there is no indication that any instruction was provided the prisoners, not even by the volunteer chaplains who visited the prison.

Illiteracy was high in those days because schooling was a private matter and was furnished only to the children whose parents could afford it. The public school was not generally accepted for some 20 years after the opening of the Philadelphia prison.

The inspectors of Cherry Hill in their report for 1839 stated that, aside from the chaplain's religious duties, he "visited the sick and instructed the ignorant." The warden had his explanation of the high rate of illiteracy in the Commonwealth at the time. It was due, he said, to the practice of hiring out children by their parents for "the purpose of obtaining their small earnings (very frequently to keep themselves in idleness and debauchery)." The warden did not state that the system of indenture flourished everywhere at that time and that the public school was nonexistent.

The philosophy of the prison inspectors toward education as well as religion, expressed in their report for 1842, was part of a plan to impress upon the inmate that he "should regard his cell as the beautiful gate of the Temple leading to a happy life and by a peaceful end, to Heaven." It was the hope of the inspectors that the injunction "return, repent and live" should "be heard in the prisoner's solitude." [13]

The year 1854 might be considered the real beginning of an educational program at Cherry Hill since it was during that year that Abram Boyer was appointed full-time teacher. He immediately supplanted the "three R's" with courses in "bookkeeping, phonography and mathematics." In addition he offered instruction in Spanish and German for those who cared and were able to absorb them.[14] In mid-1862, the inspectors, for some reason unknown, asked Boyer to describe his duties. The straightforwardness of his letter carries a pathetic ring.

I will give you a detailed statement of my duties in this institution. I spend two hours each morning in the center and blow the whistle

[13] *Thirteenth Annual Report*, 1842, p. 6.
[14] *Twenty-sixth Annual Report*, 1855, p. 27.

at stated periods, for the keepers to let out their men for exercise in the yards. The rest of the day I spend in teaching unless I am called off for other duties such as writing letters for prisoners, reading German letters and reporting their contents to the warden. A part of three days each week I spend in taking in, and giving out, the Library books through the house. At this time I have 71 scholars to which of each I give a lesson once in seven or eight days. My other duties preventing me seeing them oftener. My class is in the main making encouraging progress.[15]

A library is a necessary adjunct of any system of education, and the beginnings of one may be noted at Cherry Hill when the moral instructor reported "a valuable auxiliary in the department of instruction has been added in the new library presented by John Bacon, Esquire, a member of the Board." The year preceding a number of hymn books had been presented "through the kind interposition of Frederick A. Packard of the American Sunday School Union." Through the 1850s several publishers made relatively large contributions to the library of volumes which were primarily of a religious nature. However, there were many dealing with adventure, travel, and biography.[16] In 1900 a prominent Philadelphian, Edward T. Stotesbury made a donation of $1,000 for the purpose of replenishing the library.

There is little to report on the progress of Cherry Hill's school program until well after the turn of the century. Abram Boyer was followed by several other teachers, none of whom remained long. In 1882 John Storey was appointed as teacher and librarian. He remained until 1903 but thereafter a succession of librarians were employed to handle the duties of that important post. By this time the principle of separate confinement had completely broken down so that instruction in association was possible. In 1909 a building was set aside for school purposes.

In 1900 the newly appointed warden, Daniel W. Bussinger, who had for many years been the prison clerk under Warden Cassidy, organized a band which, he reported, gave concerts

[15] Boyer's letter may be found in the State Record Office at Harrisburg.
[16] For a sample of the type of books donated to the prison library at this time, see Teeters, *They Were In Prison*, pp. 510–12.

every evening from 7:00 to 8:30 in the center building. An orchestra was begun in 1904, and in 1909 a well-known musician from Philadelphia, Fred Weigandt, was appointed bandmaster. The warden purchased "one bass horn, two trombones, one clarinet and the necessary music;" other instruments were the personal property of the inmates.

The development of a prison school and library at the Philadelphia prison followed the pattern typical in practically all American prisons. Funds for such purposes have always been small. In the congregate prisons instructors have been recruited from those inmates who showed some capacity to teach. Books for the libraries have come largely from outside donations. As late as 1931 Austin MacCormick, eminent penologist, was obliged to appraise prison schools as mediocre and totally unrealistic after completing a study of educational facilities in the country's penal institutions.

PRISON VISITING

One of the basic features of the Pennsylvania System as practiced in the Philadelphia prison was the visiting program set up by the law of April 23, 1829, which permitted the members of the Visiting Committee of the Philadelphia Prison Society to be official visitors. The Society, from its inception in 1787, believed that kindly visits to inmates of jails and prisons was of extreme importance just as the exclusion of contaminating influences was necessary. The fact that the legislature, in creating the Philadelphia prison, gave the members of this reform group legal status is evidence that this visiting was one of the cardinal principles of the system. To this day, members of the Pennsylvania Prison Society are permitted by law to visit Cherry Hill.

The records of the Society show that thousands of personal visits were made each year. The organization divided itself into seven committees, each responsible for visits to one of the seven cell blocks. Taking the year 1862 as an example, we find from the records that 182 written reports were submitted. These embraced 776 visits to the penitentiary with an aggregate of

8,942 personal interviews with prisoners—6,149 being inside the cells and 2,793 at the cell doors. The interviews averaged about 15 minutes.

In addition to interviewing the prisoners in their respective blocks, comforting and advising them whenever it was thought expedient, the members of the Visiting Committee were charged by the Society to accumulate the following data:

1st.   The general health of the prisoners.
2nd.   The number received and discharged during the term and the number remaining—stating how many of each sex.
3rd.   How many discharged by expiration of sentence or removed by death and how many pardoned.
4th.   How many assisted pecuniarily by the institution or by the Society on their discharge and amount from each source.
5th.   How many sick and in the infirmary and how many on the list of the insane.
6th.   How many at each kind of employment.
7th.   How many associated together at labor and for what cause.
8th.   How many books loaned to the prisoners from the library during the term and whether any additions have been made.
9th.   How many prisoners are receiving instruction from the teachers.
10th.   He shall also report (leaving blanks to be filled in by the Sec.) showing the total number of visits made to the prison and how many times prisoners have been visited in their cells with such remarks in relation to the condition and government of the institution as may seem advisable.[17]

An example of the caution of the visitors is reflected in the following rules relative to visiting:

1st.   That we avoid taking children or grown persons into the cells of prisoners without authority from the warden or other proper officer.
2nd.   That we abstain from taking them even with permission unless with the consent of the prisoner.
3rd.   That we regard the feeling of such inmates, as have expressed a desire not to be visited; and avoid pressing our com-

[17] Drawn up at meeting, March 5, 1856.

pany upon them; similarly situated we should desire others to respect our feelings in that particular.

4th. That we carefully avoid reflecting upon prisoners for the offenses with which they may have been charged.

5th. That we exercise care, not to reflect upon, or speak disrespectfully of the form of Religion, in which the prisoner may have been educated or for which he manifests a preference.

6th. It is also suggested that no attempt be made to impress upon the inmates any form of belief not in accordance with the teachings of the Gospel; and also avoid anything of a sectarian character.[18]

The next year, 1861, the Society drew up the following guide for its visitors:

The members are expected to visit at least once a fortnight, or oftener if convenient; and to report monthly in writing to their respective Committees.

The more efficient mode of visiting is in the cells. Calls at the doors are to be separately reported.

The approach to the prisoners should be friendly; manifesting a feeling of interest and a desire to benefit them in any proper manner.

If visits be not acceptable to prisoners, they should not be pressed upon them.

Questions tending to criminate a prisoner should be carefully avoided; but simply inquiring what the charge is, and the sentence, is not offensive.

Expressing an opinion of either of the guilt, or of the innocence of the prisoner—or of the length of the sentence—or anything implying censure upon the administrators of the law—or of other persons—or encouraging such remarks by prisoners, are inexpedient.

Encourage obedience to the rules of the prison, and respectful conduct toward the officers.

Commend their diligence, or skill, in their work, as opportunity may offer; and encourage them to hopeful feelings as to their future.

Encourage them in the reverend daily reading of the Holy Scriptures, and committing portions of them to memory, as useful; and practice of these, with efforts to improve the mind by other useful reading, will be a remedy for morbid and unprofitable feelings.

[18] Report of Visiting Committee, October 11, 1860.

Reflecting upon the religious belief of others—or of teaching sectarian doctrines should be avoided.

Recommend cleanliness and good order in the cells.

Bathing the person daily with a towel; and active exercise, when practicable will be beneficial to their health.

Should any reasonable want be observed in relation to bodily or mental health—unemployment, exercise, instruction, or otherwise, mention it privately to the warden or other proper officer.

If a prisoner is unable to speak the English language, endeavor to have him visited by a person with whom he can converse; or report the case to the chairman of the committee for his care.

Should a prisoner solicit aid in obtaining a pardon, he should be distinctly informed that such is not our province.

No one is allowed to take a stranger to the cell of a prisoner, without the consent of an inspector or the warden; and also of the prisoner, proposed to be visited.

Neither letters nor messages are allowed to be carried without the consent of one of the officers. As the law prohibits, the giving to, or receiving anything from, a prisoner, care should be taken not to depart from this rule without the consent of the warden.

And finally, as our design in visiting is to endeavor to benefit the prisoner, morally and religiously, we should strive to do it in that spirit, which seeks their good; and in accordance with the precepts of the Gospel.

General Cautions

Before leaving the door of the cell, assure yourself that both doors are secure; and the wicket of the iron door turned down.

Be not too confiding; an appearance of penitence is often assumed to awaken sympathy.

The objects of the legislature in conferring upon the Acting Committee the privilege of visiting were:

1st. To secure a continuous supervision of our prison discipline— as to its effects upon the health and character of its subjects; and of the particulars in which its administration might be improved.

2nd. To give to prisoners the moral advantages of association with respectable citizens, desirous to aid their reformation, and to promote habits of reflection; good order and industry, and general amendment of life.

The committee members briefly noted their impressions, and when it is remembered that there was no such thing in those days as the "trained interviewer" it seems remarkable that these God-fearing citizens of Philadelphia seemed able to describe the personality of a prisoner in so few words. Here are some typical reactions of the visitors toward some of the prisoners:

No. 3949. George Norwood: a civil, quiet fellow.

No. 3630. John Mouse: says he was served right and hopes to be a better man.

No. 3791. Daniel McMullen: thinks the tendency of confinement here is to make him better.

No. 4059. Henry S. Hill: thinks he was not justly sent here.

No. 3855. Michael Clark: had the rheumatism before imprisonment, health improved by being here, a tender spirited man.

No. 3862. Isaac Smith: pleads guilty to the charge of larceny and likes the place.

No. 3873. Francis West: says through the help of God he will do right.

No. 3875. William Thompson: has sought repentance, feels the hardness of his heart.

No. 3874. James Robinson: has signed the temperance pledge on bended knee.

No. 3662. Tobias Eckert: thanks God he is here, has had more inward joy and peace in his cell than ever before, has been aroused from sinful slumber and trusts in Divine help in Christ and his atonement.

No. 3995. Lewis Wilson: was led astray by reading Paine's *Age of Reason* and was addicted to profane swearing; he has been favored to see the fallacy of his reasoning, and become convinced of the substantial truths of the Christian religion.

No. 3891. John Watson: a youth of 19 years informed his visitor that he had learned the ten commandments; and that the ejaculation of the Royal Psalmist, "Set a watch before my mouth, O Lord, keep the door of my lips" had risen before him with such power, as to prevent him from the sin of blasphemy.

No. 3512. John Toal: said he was thankful he was here; he should have been in a drunkard's grave, had broken himself of profanity since being here.

No. 4093. James Snodgrass: attributes his degradation to liquor, and says if the Almighty keeps him in his senses, he will never taste rum again.

No. 3814. John Lyons: admitted his confinement had been beneficial to him, that it had awakened in his mind a sense of his improper life, and had determined with God's help, to lead a different one, had given advice to those around him, to observe the rules of the prison, and to abandon their misconduct.

The following report is more lengthy. It shows a more sustained effort by the visitor to convert the prisoner.

No. 4287. Robert Shay: a pickpocket whose time of sentence expired on the 11th instant, said that when he got out of prison, he intended to follow his old business. I have labored with him to the best of my abilities to convince him of the awful consequences that must ensue to his present and eternal welfare, if he should continue in a course of crime, and I have the satisfaction of stating that in some of my last interviews with him, he said it was his intention to abandon his nefarious calling and also to strive and avoid lying, drunkenness, blasphemy, and dishonesty of every kind, which good resolutions I heartily encouraged him to adhere to. I gave him some religious tracts and an interesting little work entitled *No Lie Thrives*, and could have wished that I had a copy of the Holy Scriptures to have given him also. I think that every prisoner leaving the portals of the penitentiary should be presented with a copy of the Bible.

As we look back on those early days of Cherry Hill we are impressed by the large number of professional men, citizens of Philadelphia, who voluntarily visited the prisoners, month after month, year after year, in all sorts of weather. They met one or more times each month and made their reports to the Society, commenting on the reactions of their clients. Few types of volunteer work done in modern times can surpass, or perhaps even compare, with the work of this committee in honesty, singleness of purpose, and expenditure of time.

True, there were times when it was found necessary to remind the members of their solemn obligation. There were probably some who neglected their duties, and the records show that certain members apologized for being out of town, indisposed, pressed by business, all of which made it impossible for them to carry out their duties regularly.

Despite the sincerity of the Society members, there is at least one incident recorded which shows that their motives were considered suspect. It appears that the moral instructor of the prison, the Reverend Thomas Larcombe, in one of his sermons to the inmates questioned the work of the Visiting Committee. The minutes of the Society for March 16, 1858, record that Larcombe's sermon "endeavored to throw discredit on the visitations of the Society members—poisoning the minds of the prisoners with the idea that we are endeavoring to promote our own salvation, and establish a claim to the mercy of God by self-righteousness in visiting the prison." The secretary of the Society at the time, John J. Lytle, took the matter up with the moral instructor who "disclaimed any wrong motives."

The members of the Visiting Committee were especially diligent in their services to prisoners about to be released. "They visit[ed] each prisoner to be discharged several days previous to the expiration of his sentence, and aided him, so far as they deem[ed] possible, and the means within their control will allow, in returning to his friends or obtaining suitable employment after leaving the prisoner." The interest of the Committee for discharged prisoners is well borne out by the fact that many communicated for some time with the visitors who had befriended and encouraged them while in prison.

We have no way of knowing how the inmates reacted to the visits by these laymen. It is undoubtedly true that many were helped spiritually, and at the very least the visits broke the sheer monotony of their lot. Because we know the benefits of social intercourse it is safe to assume that many inmates in the earlier years were actually assisted not only upon their release but also while in prison. Prison visiting has always served as an integral part of the delicate process of reformation of the criminal.

Lay prison visiting has continued through the years at Cherry Hill, sponsored by the Pennsylvania Prison Society, now a casework agency, which works closely with many inmates through counseling and in parole planning. Through the services of the trained workers parole plans have been worked out and sponsorship and employment on release have been negotiated.

There is little information in the records of Cherry Hill regarding the visiting of prisoners by members of their families, or are there many allusions to the sending or receiving of mail by the inmates. We know, however, that family visits were made and that letters were sent out and received, especially in later years. The rule regarding family visits followed the pattern of the earlier practice in the Walnut Street Jail. A member of the prisoner's family could petition the visiting inspectors of the institution and, in due time, receive permission to come to the prison.

It is probable that the inmate was taken from his cell to the center building in the prison where he could converse briefly with his visitor. These quite inadequate visits were infrequent, probably not more than once every two or three months. It is likely also that only those visits considered absolutely necessary by the inspectors were permitted. Letters were allowed intermittently, but again there are few allusions to the practice in the records.

One lone reaction to the strict policy of the inspectors regarding family visiting is contained in a letter found in the prison records written by No. 1952, Jason Mahan, to a brother. Mahan, who had been convicted of counterfeiting, was apparently an intelligent person. He wrote in his letter, dated September 15, 1845,

The inspectors say it is their desire to treat every prisoner with humanity and kindness and I believe this is fulfilled on their part, with one exception, and that is the visitation of prisoners. It appears from the latter end of the 25th chapter of Matthew that visiting the prisoner was of an importance inasmuch as for the neglect thereof an everlasting curse is pronounced in verse 31st. I will not however censure the Inspectors here but I will merely observe that if the prisoner's family and friends were more frequently suffered to visit him there would be fewer cases of insanity than now are. I am very confident that this assertion can be substantiated by philosophical reasoning.

In later years it seems that the administration was more liberal regarding family visits. In a report of Warden Edward Townsend to the Board for 1872 we find, "One thousand persons have visited relatives and friends under proper restrictions" and 6,700 letters were received and 5,000 written by permission.

There are a few bundles of letters in the records of the prison that apparently were confiscated by the authorities as "contraband." Some register complaints, which may account for their being apprehended.

PUNISHMENTS

It was one of the proud boasts of the advocates of separate confinement that physical punishments were unnecessary to maintain discipline. They looked aghast on the brutality of the administrators of Auburn and Sing Sing prisons where floggings were meted out to the prisoners on the slightest pretext.

At Cherry Hill the only punishments, it was alleged, were the withdrawal of work or books from the prisoner and the restriction of diet to bread and water. For those prisoners who believed that work was a favor extended the inmate, a simple denial of this privilege for a short period of time would bring him around to accept his solitary lot. There were instances in which this was the only disciplinary measure; however, the investigations of 1834 and 1897 clearly demonstrate that drastic punishments were sometimes, if not often, inflicted.

A record of punishments was compiled by the wardens in their journals but they were written up in a very casual manner, failing to record the severity of the punishment and its effect on the inmate.

In 1843 a journal referred to as a "Record of Punishments" was begun in pursuance of Rules for the Government of the Prison passed by the Board of Inspectors June 3 of that year. It ended July 3, 1846, with no explanation for its discontinuance.

One of the inspectors, Thomas Bradford, refused to countenance the use of irons imposed on the prisoners by Warden George Thompson. In several cases Bradford voiced his protests in the inspectors' record. Examples are as follows: "I disapprove the use of hand cuffs in this and in all cases until such mode of punishment is sanctioned by the Board by rules adopted for punishment" and "I disapprove of irons in this case and as the punishment was inflicted without the previous order of the Inspectors as far as appears, I consider it to be illegal." The warden, for some unaccountable reason, ignored Bradford's protests.

Aside from a few instances of attempting to escape, the offenses for which the inmates were punished were attempting to communicate with other inmates or refusing to work. A few were punished for making noises, disturbing the quiet of the institution, or destroying their cell equipment.

In one case Warden Thompson had the following to record: "No. 1871, during his confinement in the dark cell, some part of the time of which he behaved in a most outrageous manner; I paid him a visit last evening which I am willing to hope we may both remember—and upon his acknowledgement of error and amendment—released him this morning."

Here are some samples taken from the punishment log that indicate the type of offenses and the punishments:

Record of Punishments

July 8: No. 1541 (James Hall) confined in dark cell on 10 oz. bread and one and a half pints of water—offence—disobedience to the Order of the President of the Board, visiting inspector, and assault upon the warden—period of confinement, one week—the above by order of vis. ins. Bradford and Bacon.

July 29: No. 1518 (Karl Goffin) for attempting to escape, same punishment.

July 29: No. 1615 (Daniel H. Hickok) confined by handcuffs for same period of time on prison allowance for aiding and abetting No. 1518, both the above submitted to and approved by Inspector Bacon.

August 8: No. 1547 (James McCue) at 6 p.m. was placed in the composing chair for threat of injury against Dr. Hartshorne, reported by Dr. Hartshorne and Overseer Clayton—approved by John Bacon, Esq., Visiting Inspector.

August 10: Released [the above] this morning on promise of good behavior by request of Dr. Hartshorne.

September 7: No. 1307 (John Maxfield) aged 11—Black Boy—
Put in the shower bath for three minutes for leaving his cell by with-
drawing the bolt and lock and secreting himself in the yarde—this
prisoner only laughed at the effects of the shower bath and seemed to
enjoy it.

Thompson records, "The warden made trial of the shower
bath himself and found it very agreeable for a short time, by
changing the position of the body the shower can be avoided and
little inconvenience sufficient during the time it is usual to keep
prisoners in."

Comment from the warden's Journal regarding John Maxfield:

From Montgomery County, in for arson; term 5 years; entered August 21, 1840, discharged August 30, 1845, illit. Dismissed and sent
to Alms House; in good health but considered unsafe to be at large
in consequence of a disposition to commit arson. Was born in the
Alms House, brought up and bound from there—consulted Judge
Parson on the subject of having him brought before the Court.

The Visiting Inspectors, upon whose shoulders fell the task
of visiting the inmates in their cells, also kept a journal. In this
they wrote routine reports of their visits, making such comments as seemed to them propitious. Samples of these notations
follow.

John Bacon, August 29, 1843: Attended and visited the prisoners
in South East Block. No. 1252 [Wm. Johnson, age 17, no trade, was
bound to a sweep, his master died. Parents dead, born in Long
Island, N.Y., cannot read or write; drinks beer] having refused to
work the warden was authorized in case he continued refractory to
punish him by confinement in the dark cell but let him have a taste
of the shower bath. All the other prisoners except 1492 (Samuel
Turner) and (Thomas Nicholson) appeared in good order. The
former continues as he always has been, a troublesome worthless
fellow—the latter labours under considerable aberration of mind and
made numerous complaints which were patiently listened to, and
suitable remarks made, unavailingly however.

Thomas Bradford, November 23, 1843: No. 1518 [Karl Goffin, born
in Smyrna, Turkey] complained that he had manacles or leg irons on
his legs for nine weeks. There does not appear to be any such punish-

ment ordered or approved inserted in the Book of Punishments an
as such kind of punishment is not authorized in any rules enacte
by the Inspectors, the Warden is forbidden to continue such punisl
ments any longer.

Richard Vaux, companion Visiting Inspector with Bradforc
took a different view of the case of No. 1518. He contende
that placing irons on this inmate did not constitute a punisl
ment but rather a restraint to keep him from escaping fror
his cell.

Each successive warden had different views of punishmen
While the dark cell was used intermittently throughout th
history of the institution, it is apparent that Warden Edwar
Townsend (1870–81) found it possible not to press it into us
He wrote in the annual report for 1880,

It might be said that there have been no punishments; we have r
dark cells, no appliances for administering correction, and no speci
apartments for refractory convicts. The violator of the prison rul
is kept in his own cell, fed on bread and water only, with no bool
but his Bible, and no intercourse whatever with any person excep
his official care-takers. The period of his rigid isolation depends upc
himself. He must be convinced of and acknowledge his error, b
fore any steps are taken to restore him his forfeited privileges. Th
discipline does not degrade the individual, nor cause rancorous fee
ings of resentment, such as are engendered by the infliction of thos
corporal punishments which are practiced in most of the prisons
this country.

Since imprisonment for convicted felons was introduced i
Pennsylvania as a substitute for physical punishments, the
was theoretically no need for physical pain to be inflicted c
the inmates of the Cherry Hill institution. The withdrawal
those pitiful privileges they enjoyed, such as work, exercis
a Bible or some other book, or food, seemed punishment enoug
for a violation of a rule. Yet physical punishments crept into tl
administration although the warden and the inspectors we
adept in rationalizing their use. A stern system of penalti
in a penal institution has almost always been deemed necessar
by administrators. The dark cell and reduced diet—often co

sisting of the traditional bread and water—are still widely used in our prisons.

SEX ANOMALIES

Modern prison administrators are constantly on the alert for signs of homosexuality among inmates. The separate system militated against homosexual relations between the inmates; hence we find no mention of this problem in the records of Cherry Hill while the separate system was in operation.

Females also were sent to the Philadelphia prison, but again there is no official record whatsoever of any attempts of the two sexes to arrange clandestine meetings. A few letters or notes written by inmates, some by females and a few by males, were apprehended by the officials, and may be found in the records of the institution, giving mute evidence that an occasional rendezvous was consummated. The females were segregated but many were out of their cells engaged in housekeeping duties.

Masturbation was the perplexing sex problem at Cherry Hill and many allusions to it are scattered throughout the records of the institution. The first mention made of masturbation among the prisoners is in the annual report of the physician, Dr. William Darrach, for the year 1838. His predecessor, Dr. Franklin Bache, made no mention of it in his reports from 1830 until his resignation in 1837. Dr. Darrach maintained that of 18 cases of insanity within the prison, 12 had been "caused" by masturbation. He further contended, as did other physicians who succeeded him, that many diseases were caused by the "secret vice." He stated, "The effects of this practice are first to produce dyspepsia, then acute dementia, and finally chronic pleurisy and pulmonary tuberculosis." He then recommended, "Remove the cause, and the diseases of this penitentiary will chiefly be those brought into the institution."

In Darrach's report for 1839 he contended that of 26 cases of mental illness, 15 were caused by masturbation. In his 1841 report he referred to one form of insanity as "erotic enervation" caused, as usual, by masturbation. His successors for the next 30 years held to the same position. Examples are:

1859—Dr. Thomas Newbold: "The few cases of mental aberration which have manifested themselves during the past year could generally be traced to the habit of self-abuse."

1871—Dr. H. M. Klapp: "Only one case of insanity occurred during the year caused entirely by self-abuse." He then added: "He has quite recovered and was discharged in as good mental health as when received."

1873—Dr. E. C. Bullard: [after recording one death from tuberculosis and another of inflammation of the brain, both due to masturbation] "I may here remark in connection with the death table, the serious effects caused by the habit of masturbation. Every effort has been made in the moral as well as in the physical treatment of the prisoners under our care, to combat this terrible vice, and evidence is daily given that our endeavors will meet much success. If we succeed as we hope, much of the sickness, physical and mental, will decrease."

It was not until 1876 that a physician began seriously to question the prevailing notion that self-abuse was the cause of the various physical and mental illnesses of the prisoners. Dr. J. W. White devoted his entire report for that year to this problem. He first referred to statements of his predecessors, samples of which appear above. Next he quoted from his own report: "In 1874, after a very short term of service, and under the influence of a decided bias from my reading, I wrote: 'I have found in my limited experience that the practice of masturbation is either the originating or predisposing cause of many of the cases of serious illness occurring among convicts.'" The following year he wrote in a more modified vein: "I have observed that those prisoners who became confirmed onanists are rarely or never originally healthy and vigorous, but are usually nervous, lymphatic, poorly nourished, and frequently of low intellectual grade, before the commencement of the habit," and "Instead of the vicious habit resulting in a pathological condition of the body or mind, the reverse is the case, and the mental or physical disease is at least the predisposing cause of the habit." This observation, strengthened by the physician's wide reading, marks a distinct turning from the dogma of that day regarding masturbation.

Dr. White further stated that the literature on masturbation "is of an extremely limited and highly unsatisfactory character, the consideration of the question having been so largely monopolized by quacks and charlatans . . . that reputable physicians seem to have dreaded the infection and to have religiously avoided it."

Other sources from which we gain an idea of the attitudes of prison officials toward masturbation and its alleged effect on prisoners are from the Journals of the Reverend Thomas Larcombe and the wardens. Warden Thomas Scattergood made the following notes in his Journal: "March 6, 1848, died last night, No. 1925. This man, always but little above the brute. I have no doubt, killed himself by masturbation." "January 25, 1849: Died this morning No. 2156, the consequences of self-abuse." In Dr. Given's report we find inscribed the causes of these two deaths: No. 1925, "softening of the brain"; No. 2156, "paraplegia." As late as 1889 Warden Cassidy could enter in his Journal about prisoner No. A 4622, who committed suicide by setting fire to his cell and inhaling the smoke, "primary cause leading to suicide, excessive masturbation."

Mr. Larcombe entered in his Journal, "No. 1096, by solitary vice became deranged, continued so a year and died April 28, 1841." Another, No. 690, "has greatly endangered his life by secret vice; in great distress on account of it and fears it will kill him; prays to God for help, subsequently hopes he will conquer."

We know something of the attitude of other sections of society regarding the extent of masturbation among prisoners by examination of the minutes of the Visiting Committee of the Philadelphia Prison Society. The first notation is dated March 11, 1851, when one visitor, A. T. Chur, reported "that an able essay had been submitted to him written by an intelligent German prisoner in his native tongue on the subject of masturbation which he thinks would be useful to circulate among the German prisoners." It was resolved that this essay be "revised by Dr. Demmé [local Lutheran minister and frequent visitor to the prison] . . . and to have published 250 copies."

In the minutes of July 12, 1860, the following item appears:

Some of the men are reported to be suffering from the habit of self-abuse and a member of the committee says that if a tract emphatically pointing out the inevitable mischief and debasement caused by this habit was placed in the hands of each prisoner on his first entrance of his cell, it is believed that it would act with much preventive power and efficiency.

The next item of concern regarding this practice among the inmates showed itself, apparently officially, in the following alarming statements printed on a card and hung in each cell. It is not known just when this warning was formulated, but we do know these cards were present in cells as late as 1883.

1. The effects of self-abuse are so numerous and so terrible, that all should be warned against it; the responsibilities of our relations to you make it our duty to give you this warning.

The result of this destructive vice appear; first in the derangement of the digestion, respiration, circulation and absorption of the secretions, which are most ruinous in their effects.

That insidious and fatal disease, pulmonary consumption, terminating in speedy death, is a common result.

It produces the most violent palpitation of the heart, tumors, scrofulous engorgements, derangements of the skin, blotches, dropsies, hemorrhages of the lungs, and a most troublesome marasmus, or, in other words, a consumption of the flesh.

It also weakens the genital functions and produces derangements of the nervous system, which are often incurable.

2. Among the disastrous effects produced is the entire destruction of the intellectual faculties, which become incapacitated for all useful occupations. Those who habituate themselves to this debasing vice, frequently lose all taste for society, and seek solitude under the idea that their crimes may be detected in their faces.

Self-pollution brings its victims to a level with the brutes; it deprives them of the best privileges of intelligence and reason; it exhausts all the pleasures of life, and confirmed insanity follows.

The statistics of the Insane Asylums of the country show that a large percentage of the inmates have been brought there by this humiliating and polluting vice.

3. The penalty incurred is sufficient to convince the sufferer that one of nature's holiest laws has been set at naught and violated.

4. It is a violation of the law of chastity, and leads to impurity of thought and licentiousness of life. It produces self-abhorrence, shame and remorse.

It debases the moral faculties, because it is a sin against nature and a sin against God, and whatever is wrong, is injurious to the whole man—Body, Mind and Soul.

It is wrong because it enfeebles both body and mind, and becomes almost an impassable barrier to the reformation of character.

He who continues this habit cannot have either a healthy body, a sound mind, or pure morals. He cannot perform his due share of labor in any of the departments of life. He cannot think and judge correctly. He cannot enjoy the truths of nature or of science, neither can he appreciate the doctrines and precepts of Revealed Religion. He destroys himself.

Let all who have been addicted to this loathesome vice thus described, *Stop, at once Stop.*[19]

In 1887, presumably to combat the high rate of "consumption," much of which was believed to have resulted from self-abuse, Dr. William D. Robinson opened a "gymnasium" for those who showed signs of the debilitating disease. The room, accommodating six properly masked inmates at a time, was equipped with "chest weights, Wortemburg apparatus, and other necessary paraphernalia." The calisthenics were in charge of an overseer appointed for the purpose, and each session lasted 30 minutes.

Masturbation has always been rife within our penal institutions, both in male and female prisons. In a prison like Cherry Hill where there were no contacts between inmates, the practice must have been widespread. We have no introspective evidence from the thousands of prisoners who were subjected to separate confinement that would give so much as a clue regarding resistance to or indulgence in this "secret vice."

THE USE OF TOBACCO

The law of 1829 specifically stated (Section 6) that "no tobacco in any form shall be used by the convicts and anyone

[19] From the *Journal of Prison Discipline and Philanthropy*, N.S. 24 (1883), p. 33.

who shall supply them with it, unless by order of the physicians shall be fined ten dollars."

The first recorded incident involving tobacco occurred January 25, 1830, three months after the prison was opened, when the warden entered in his Journal, "Philip Hahn informed me that No. 5 had been using tobacco and refused to tell where it came from—I directed that he should not be fed until he told." The next day No. 5 explained that "he found the piece of segar in the entry when he was employed in cleaning; stopped his breakfast but allowed him the other meals."

There is no way of knowing when or how frequently the prison physicians gave inmates tobacco or permission to use it, but by 1860 the use of tobacco was widespread among the inmates. From the records of the Philadelphia Prison Society we find that this group expressed much concern that prisoners were permitted to use tobacco. At a meeting held July 10, 1860, Dr. William Shippen offered the following resolution: "That the Acting Committee be requested to memorialize the Inspectors to do away with the use of tobacco in that institution."

In 1861 a committee was appointed by the Society to investigate the use of tobacco at Cherry Hill. It submitted a report denouncing the use of the weed among prison inmates. Mr. Alfred H. Love, long a member of the Society, presented a diatribe on tobacco as well as on its use among prisoners, protesting that almost every prisoner was granted tobacco. He reported his conversation with the physician of the institution.

Ninety-five per cent of the inmates ask for it upon coming to the prison, and are supplied with it until it is found to injure them. Of this percentage about ten per cent are deprived of it on account of its injurious effects. About five per cent are encouraged to discontinue its use by force of moral suasion and self-conviction of duty. The number deprived of it because of bad conduct is small, and such deprivation is but for short periods.

The allowance is one plug of chewing tobacco every two weeks. Some obtain half a plug more, as also for pipe-smoking and snuffing, the supply for smoking being sometimes quite liberal.

The yearly expense, previous to the late restriction of one plug every two weeks, instead of weekly, was $400.

Mr. Love stated that he had submitted the tobacco to "prominent tobacconists" who found it of inferior quality, being made of refuse tobacco and many foreign substances, besides containing "copperas." Aside from the opinion that the use of tobacco was injurious to the health of the prisoners, Mr. Love and his colleagues felt that the inspectors were not justified in spending the taxpayers' money in supplying something that was denied by law except on "recommendation of the physician." Nothing, however, was done by the Society.

The question of granting tobacco to inmates came up many years later in the meetings of the Society—in 1910, in a report by Joshua Baily, president.

I discovered at least one indulgence permitted the convicts to which I must take exception, that is, the use of tobacco.

Convict life is, and in my opinion, should be, a life of privation, and especially as to such a bad habit as the use of tobacco. Convicts are deprived of intoxicating liquors, and why should not the prohibition extend to tobacco? Do I hear it said that would be a great hardship? Is it not to many of them a greater hardship to be deprived of intoxicating liquors?

Still, no action was taken.

Whatever moral objections there were to the habit were soon overcome by the inexorable fact that most of the prisoners received at Cherry Hill were addicted to tobacco. We know that many inmates who smoked or chewed tobacco were furnished it free of charge; we do not know whether they could purchase it from their own funds. In prisons today tobacco of an inferior grade is furnished free of charge to those who use it, or they may purchase a better grade at commissaries with their own funds. The use of tobacco is no longer a moral question in or out of prison.

ESCAPES

The early annual reports of the warden and the Board of Inspectors are strangely silent on the escapes or attempted escapes from the relatively impregnable fortress of Cherry Hill, a fact which was attested to during the investigation of 1834.

Testimony brought out the details of several escapes during Warden Wood's administration, but it was pointed out that none of those who managed to make their getaway from the institution remained long at liberty.

During the long period when the policy of separate confinement was practiced it was extremely difficult for a prisoner to escape. First he had to get out of his cell or exercise yard, and second he must escape from the outer prison yard either by scaling the high wall or by climbing over the massive front building. Aside from the vigilance of the watchmen who patrolled the big yard throughout the night, there were always watchdogs near the front entrance that could be counted on to bark if unfamiliar persons appeared. There is an apocryphal story in the prison today—related by old-timers to members of the prison staff—that early inmates "made up" to the dogs and later counted on their friendliness to permit them to escape.

Because of the watchmen and the dogs, there was no need for firearms in the prison. Michael Cassidy as late as 1897 could state that there had never been a firearm of any kind in the institution. He later qualified that by adding that the night watchmen carried revolvers. Not until the separate system had completely been supplanted by the congregate system was it found necessary to place armed watchmen in the corner towers.

There is always a feeling of chagrin among prison administrators when an inmate manages to escape, even though his freedom is short-lived. This embarrassment probably explains why the reports coming from Cherry Hill seldom mention abscondings. Indicative of this silence, the reports of the Board of Inspectors show that only three inmates escaped from the opening date, 1829, until 1875. However, some of the wardens carefully recorded each escape or attempted escape in their Journals. Warden Cassidy testified in 1897 that there had been only five successful escapes throughout the history of the institution up to that time.

The best descriptions of the escapes or attempted escapes during Warden Wood's regime come from *McElwee's Report*. The first prisoner to escape was William Hamilton, No. 94, a Negro,

in 1832. He was employed in the institution as a baker and as a
waiter for the warden's table. One Sunday, in the warden's
absence from his apartment, Hamilton secured a bedcord to
which he affixed a block of wood. He got out on the octagonal
tower, dropped to the roof of the front building, placing his
stick of wood across one of the embrasures in the battlement,
let himself down to the ground, a distance of 50 feet, and walked
off. He took with him some clothes, razors, and silver spoons
which were the property of the warden. He was subsequently
arrested in Montgomery County for "stealing hogs" and was
returned to the prison and restored to his old quarters. On
January 1, 1837, Hamilton succeeded in getting out of prison
again. As Warden Wood wrote in his Journal for that date,

About ½ past 8 this evening the Gate Keeper heard footsteps in the
tower and gave the alarm, when George Dudley, he and I went up
and soon found a piece of cloth hanging from the chimney into the
street. I drew it up and then went out and tracked him in the snow
for some distance and finally sent Dudley and George Dargin in
pursuit. On examination found it was Hamilton, old No. 94, who
descended exactly as he had done before. From appearance I think
his iron door was left unbolted and he cut a hole in his wooden door
with his knife, large enough to get out at.

Two days later the warden reported that Hamilton had been
arrested in the possession of stolen goods and after giving fight
to the "watchman" had been lodged in Moyamensing County
Prison. The warden picked up the old man "himself badly
beaten" by the watchman.

The second escapee was No. 127, Washington Taylor, who
made his getaway in 1832. He had been permitted to leave his
cell to whitewash his yard. He reared his shoemaker's bench
against the yard wall and climbed over to the main yard. Car-
penters at work on the tower had gone off to dinner leaving
the door open. With his bedclothes, a towel, and a rope, he
ascended the tower and came out on to the roof of the wall. He
drove a large spike into the wall to which he attached a long
rope and started to descend to the ground. But the rope gave
way and he fell to the ground and was badly hurt. He was soon

discovered crawling along the outside of the wall and was returned to the institution. The warden makes no mention of this escape in his Journal, presumably because it was unsuccessful.

The third escape was in the summer of 1833 by No. 143, John Kennedy, a stonecutter. A temporary shop had been made for him. He simply left his shop, put on one of the workmen's hats and walked out the front gate with the other workers. He was arrested in the city and returned to the prison the same day. The warden records that the prisoner was back in his cell by noon, having been at liberty less than three hours.

Another escape, also in 1833, is that of William Johnson whose absconding recorded no peculiar details. He was soon apprehended in Trenton, New Jersey, and returned by his captors who received a reward offered by the prison authorities.

The most clever escape was that of Samuel Brewster, No. 145, the third to get out of the prison in 1833. He was a carpenter and was permitted on occasions to leave his cell to grind his tools. In this way he was able to size up his prison with a discerning eye.

On the day of his escape he took off the lock of the exterior or plank door, and placed a small block of wood under the tumbler, which allowed the bolt to be pushed back without the aid of a key. He inserted a thick piece of iron into a rod three feet long with which, after the keepers had retired for the night, he forced back the bolts and, cutting a hole in the door, threw off the bar. The iron lattice door was fastened with a spring padlock. He had taken care that the spring should not catch when it was closed, so that he had no difficulty with this door.

He was then in his exercise yard and without much trouble scaled the wall surrounding it. His next job was to scale the 30 feet, exterior, main wall. He had foreseen this difficult task by constructing a stout ladder in three parts. These sections, which had been concealed in his cell, were screwed together. At the top of the ladder was a board, attached to the sides on which were a number of sharp points for the purpose of affixing the ladder firmly to the top of the wall. This board also insured against the ladder's swerving as he climbed it.

Upon reaching the top of the wall, Brewster anchored a long spike in the masonry and to it attached the ladder which he had drawn up after him. But he had not reckoned with the layout of the land on the other side of the wall. At that particular point the wall was ten feet higher on the outside than on the inside, but he had no way of knowing just how far the end of his ladder was from the ground. Obliged to jump, he could not brace himself against the fall and accordingly sprained his ankle as he landed.

He was, however, able to effect his escape, but foolishly went to his home in Kensington where he was apprehended a few days later. The story goes that his wife betrayed him by notifying the authorities, and our contemporary informant, Thomas B. McElwee, stated, "He was betrayed by one, who, in accordance with the laws of Nature and its God, should 'shield him and save him, or perish.'" Warden Wood records this escape in his Journal.

The next escape was that of Charles Johnson, No. 264, which took place on September 15, 1834. As the warden reported it, "He had opened his cell and with a ladder made of boards fixed on trussels he had got to the top of his wall and descended by means of a rope made of his coverlets, shirt, etc. and had escaped. I immediately took measures to have him arrested but could gain no tidings of my man." Later, on September 22, the warden wrote, "Had an interview with some men who told me they thought they could get Charles Johnson, alias Thompson . . . and after a great deal of bargaining I agreed to give them $250 if they could procure him. They then told me they had him secure in the Lumberville, New Jersey, jail. I gave them the necessary papers and agreed to meet them at Trenton tomorrow when they promised to be with the prisoner." The next day the warden reclaimed his escapee, paid the $250, and "took him to the Steam Boat and thence to Philad. and safely lodged him in his cell." But there is no report of this escape in the annual report for that year.

The first escape recorded in the annual reports occurred in 1838. For the details of this event we must go to the warden's Journal where the following entry appears:

Bernard Teese No. 611 succeeded in opening his cell door and had made his escape over the wall. He had taken great pains to conceal the instruments of his escape, but they were discovered. I went at once to the city and saw the Inspectors and Blany and Young and set them to work. Thos. Bradford and J. Bacon came out with me and directed me to discharge the two outside guards.

There is no record that Teese was ever apprehended.

The warden may have been a little more than usually embarrassed when, on April 29, 1840, he discovered that one of his female prisoners had succeeded in getting out of his prison. He wrote in his Journal,

This evening about 7 o'clock as the carriage was returning from taking the inspectors home Letitia Hennard, no. 1209, who had been employed by the matron to do her house work took the opportunity to escape. She was pursued and caught by D. Scattergood at the corner of Coates and Schuylkill 5th St. and safely lodged in the 2nd. block.

Other attempted escapes recorded by Warden Wood were:

January 11, 1834: Received a note from No. 284 that No. 281 (Howe) and No. 270 (Gibbs) and another who I took to be No. 4 (John Lavrow), had agreed on a mode of escape and that No. 270 would begin to cut his door after dinner next the corridor. We watched and caught him in the act and found a rope made from his sheets. We also found a rope made of sheets in the cell of No. 181. Ordered both into a dark cell leaving No. 4 until tomorrow.

The next day he directed that No. 4 "should not be let out but removed to a room believing that he is guilty of the conspiracy yesterday." We noted earlier that this prisoner, John Lavrow, was given the run of the institution (see page 85).

August 1, 1834: No. 264 got out of his cell into the yard and attempted to get over the wall but failed and came and gave himself up.

October 15, 1835: No. 292 was found with a number of instruments designed to make his escape from his cell. They were shown me several days ago but being much engaged I had left the case until this morning. After a full investigation I found he had destroyed one of his tin vessels and made out of it keys and other instruments and had plated a rope, etc. I ordered him to the dark cell on short allowance.

But only two days later this same prisoner

had effected again his escape from his cell. He did this by cutting and breaking the end of the slide bolt which passes into the bolt of his iron door and cutting a hole in his wooden door large enough to get his body through. The prisoner in the next cell gave the keepers information and we believe on discovering this came and gave himself up.

The story of the escape of No. 1170, Joseph C. Myers (formerly No. 460 under the name of King), during the regime of Warden Thompson, is an interesting one. On December 15, 1841, Thompson wrote in his Journal,

Last night No. 1170 escaped by forming a ladder and mounting thereby the wall of the matron's yard—then affixing the ladder on the wall reached the roof of the main building from which he left himself down with a rope—his escape was discovered at nine o'clock and every exertion was made for his recapture which has not yet been successful.

The story of this man's capture can best be related by the warden himself as set down in his Journal. On December 18 he wrote,

At dusk a person called at the prison and stated for a reward of 100$ he would give me the opportunity of arresting Myers in the street— accepted his offer and followed him attended by overseer Wm. Blundin. After proceeding some distance and crossing the Commons passed two horses saddled and bridled and tied in a lot. He then proceeded a short distance and pointed out a light in the 2nd story window of a brick house and stated in that room the prisoner would be found—directed me to proceed to the yard in the rear of the house, enter by a side gate and into the house by the back door, ascend the stairs at the head of which the prisoner would be found; after which directions the guide ran off. Proceeding according to his directions, got into the house at the back room which was occu-

pied by two men, proceeded without stopping to the head of the
stairs and entered the room described, where found two men and
the convict. Arrested him with little resistance and succeeded in con-
veying him to the yard and street with little interruption from thence
proceeded to Market Street where I retained him in a store until
Blundin obtained a cab in which we returned to the prison and
lodged the convict in his cell. At 10 P.M. the guide applied for his
reward of 100$ which was paid him. Officer Blundin showed the
greatest coolness and determination and attention to the orders he
received. The manner of escape was as follows: A ladder had been
prepared in the workshop in sections—the watchman on duty at 8
o'clock did not stop as usual on his first round but was satisfied at
seeing the light. The prisoner then with his ladder proceeded from
the shop to the juncture of the matron's wall with the main building.
He then placed the ladder and ascended the matron's wall but had
to remain some time in consequence of some person being in the
yard.

Warden Thompson recorded three attempted escapes during his term of office.

July 2, 1840, No. 1021 (Henry Mitchell, colored) attempted to
work through the masonry of his cell with the wire taken from his
basin.

April 9, 1842, No. 1401 (Andrew Swope, a German) made a hole
under the wall of his cell by removing the boards near the privy. A
rope ladder was provided from chains from the loom, an iron hook
was attached, three long boards were taken from the cell floor, holes
morticed through them so that they might be secured to each other.
A chain from the loom was provided to descend with. He succeeded
in getting into the yard and returned to his cell being supposed ter-
rified by the watch and dogs. The prisoner was a German and did
not speak English and had been on the sick list for a long time. The
tin pan he used to dig with was covered with cloth to prevent noise.

October 25, 1842: Last night the same No. 1401 (Andrew Swope)
and No. 1490 (Louis Harborde, another German) attempted to escape by cutting off the rivets from their doors and making a ladder
from their bedding. They were detected by the watchman and both
placed in dark cells.

Warden Thomas Scattergood, whose incumbency extended
from 1845 to 1850, was more fortunate than were his predeces-

sors since no prisoner actually escaped during the five year period of his office. One prisoner did get out of the institution but was immediately apprehended. The details were:

April 3, 1848, No. 2330 (David Pledge) taking advantage of the short interval the wooden doors are left open during the time of serving breakfast for the purpose of ventilation, opened his iron door and came out and passed through the front gate (there the Gate Keeper was standing with the gate open) and thus into the street. The alarm being immediately given he was pursued and overtaken by S. B. Deal, nurse, and M. Larkin, coachman, and brought back and put in the dark cell.

Warden Scattergood recorded two attempted escapes as follows:

July 10, 1846: This morning about 4 o'clock watchman Hamilton discovered that some one had made an attempt to scale the east wall opposite the lumber yard. Upon reaching the spot, from the indications I was induced to believe that it was 2084 who has for some time been engaged at last making. Upon examining his cell our surmise proved to be correct. After a considerable hunt he was found on the west side of the gate way in the second story having made his way to the stable thence on top of Harriet Hall's matron yard wall intending for the top of the Front Building but the dogs foiled him. From the wall he got down into the yard and from thence through the cellar way to the place where he was found.

August 10, 1849: Watchman Smith upon going his round last night between 11 and 12 o'clock discovered a rope apparatus affixed for scaling the wall. He gave the alarm when No. 2235 who had been employed in the Blacksmith Shop was found in the Green House. He had bored the door of his cell and let himself out. The dogs prevented his attempt to scale the wall. He was ironed and placed in the dark cell.

The first Halloway regime (1850–54) witnessed two escapes, which are recorded in the warden's annual reports for 1853. The first one on October 9, 1852, is described in the warden's Journal.

About ten minutes past 4 o'clock was informed by Overseer Coxey (south side of 7th block) that No. 2928 (William E. Crissy) employed at tailoring had dressed himself in a suit of clothes that had been given to him to press, belonging to a prisoner whose term expires tomorrow, and had forced open his gate, he having a furnace in it to heat his irons, and had gone down to the front gate and been passed out by the Gate Keeper under the belief that he was one of the number of visitors then in the institution. The warden dispatched some keepers after the fugitive and he himself went into the city and notified the mayor, marshall and the police, offering a reward of $50 "with all reasonable expenses" for the return of Crissy.

On November 12, about a month later, Crissy was found at Skippackville in Montgomery County and was returned to the institution. A second escape during Halloway's first term occurred on January 27, 1853, and is recorded as follows:

On my arrival home from court about 2 o'clock was informed by the Gate Keeper that prisoner No. 2360, George W. Race, who was engaged in the blacksmith shop and who, with his overseer, was employed in repairing a wicket at the back gate of the prison. While his overseer was gone to dinner and those in other parts of the building were serving dinner to the prisoners, had come out of the shop unobserved and with the key they were repairing in the lock of the gate had passed down to the east gate and left himself out, the gate keeper at the time being in the privy in the side yard. The mayor and the police were informed.

While there is no record in the Journal that Race was apprehended, he must have been because in the same year, on November 25, he escaped again. The details of this event are thus recorded:

This evening about a quarter past seven o'clock was informed by the Gate Keeper that a person had been seen on the western wall. Started one of the watchmen round on the inside of the wall and went myself on the outside. Saw no one. Returned inside and upon going to the cell of No. 2360 found he was absent. In a few minutes Watchman Hamilton came into Center Building and stated he was at N.E. Tower from whence he was taken down a little after eight o'clock. This man was working at Shoemaking in the 5th Block under Overseer Hall and sleeping in a cell distinct from the one in which he worked. He had drilled the bolt with a shoemaker's awl so that it could easily be broken which gave him access to the lock on the outside door which he also prepared to suit his purpose and with a fixture made from wood from his bunk opened the door and went out soon after 5 o'clock or directly after all were locked up for the night and the keepers had left. The officers living in the neighborhood were summoned to attend as soon as information was received.

The warden does not record that this prisoner was captured in his second departure from the prison. One attempted escape is recorded by Warden Halloway:

January 10, 1852. Upon arrival home from the city about 1 o'clock where I had been on business of the institution, was informed by the Gate Keeper that prisoner No. 2447, an insane man, who worked in the ware room had secreted himself behind a cart and escaped into the street. He was immediately pursued and overtaken at the western corner of the prison and brought back. Deeming it an act of gross negligence on the part of the Gate Keeper I suspended him from duty for the present until an inquiry can be made.

Warden Strickland's short term of two years (1854–56) witnessed only one attempted escape. This occurred on Christmas Day, 1855. He recorded it as follows:

About a quarter before 8 in the evening Watchman Smith informed me that he had apprehended a prisoner in the large yard and that he was then in the Center Building. I immediately went up and made an investigation and found that No. 3067 had, according to his own statement, escaped from his cell in the Infirmary about 6 o'clock and passed thence to the 1st block smith shop and to the 2nd block where he had kept himself concealed until a few minutes before the watchman had detected him. He got from his cell, it appears, through a door not in common use, it having been left unlocked having been neglected by the nurse. The prisoner was put in a dark cell.

A recorded escape was by No. 4355, George Black, which took place March 3, 1861, during John Halloway's second wardenship. He was a third-timer under sentence of two and a half years of which he had served about six months. The warden, in his Annual Report for 1861, had this to say:

Owing to the negligence of an overseer he [the prisoner] opened his cell door into the yard and from thence escaped over the front building, eluding the vigilance of the watchman. A liberal reward was offered for him, but failed in securing his recapture. He passed into

New Jersey, where he was soon arrested for stealing and is now serving a five year sentence in the Penitentiary in that state.

The next escape under Warden Halloway occurred August 8, 1867. From his Journal we find the details.

I again have the mortification to record the passage of a prisoner through the front gate at about a quarter before 2 o'clock today. It proved to be No. 5222, Henry Vail, white. He had dyed his blankets with his shoe color and made himself an overcoat and pantaloons and cap, opened the backdoor into his yard, passed up through the center building and down the front gate where he was let out by Wm. Root who was on duty at that point while the regular gate keeper had gone to his dinner. Dispatched officers in pursuit immediately but without success.

Dr. Edward Townsend, who was warden from 1870 to 1881, recorded the following escapes in his Journal:

August 1, 1872: I have the extreme mortification to record that last evening three prisoners—6591, Thomas Dane, 6774, John Thomas, and 6775, Wm. Thomas (all mulattos) made their escape through the sewer coming out on Corinthian Ave. near Parrish St. Although rigorous measures have been resorted to, they have not yet been captured.

This, apparently, was the first time prisoners in Cherry Hill managed to escape through the labyrinthine sewer system of Cherry Hill, but in more recent times it has been used successfully by several inmates, one of whom was the notorious Willie (The Actor) Sutton in April, 1945.

Warden Townsend recorded two more escapes:

April 26, 1876: At dinner time today it was discovered that No. 7572 (James Reilly) was missing. Diligent search was made for him but nothing was heard from him.

Same day: This afternoon got word that our escaped prisoner had been arrested for pocket picking and was in county prison. Went to county prison and obtained our boy.

December 3, 1877: This afternoon about three o'clock No. 7873 (Timothy Boyle) made his escape in an empty molasses hogshead which was conveyed away in a truck. Wm. Fulton, yard watchman, was on duty at that part of the yard and I discharged him for negligence. Several of our officers have been unsuccessfully hunting for him.

Warden Michael Cassidy recorded an attempted escape in his Journal for November 24, 1884, as follows:

Last night was the stormiest high wind very heavy rain. On Sunday night 9829, Scotty, worked all night in the sixth block to get out of his cell by the back door. He succeeded in fitting a key to the lock on the bar of the outside door and by means of a contrivance made with a pully and twine attached to a strip of wood he took the outside bar off and then commenced to drill the staple off the inside iron door which would give him his liberty of the cell but the later operation took up more time than he counted on and daylight came which caused him to stop operations. Once out of his cell he intended to go over the wall off the roof of the sixth block which is practable. He had a line sufficiently strong to carry him as he is a light man. The line was made of stocking yarn and shoe thread. The attempt would have been successful if the work had been done in less time or he had not been delayed by the rain which wet his pully and caused the wood to swell and worked stiff. He says he counted on doing the work in about three hours commencing at 9 o'clock.

There may have been other escapes or attempted escapes from the prison but due to the fact that some wardens' Journals are apparently lost or mislaid it is impossible to get evidence regarding their occurrence. The Cherry Hill prison is formidable, as are all maximum-security institutions, but this has proved only a challenge to many prison inmates. The escapes recorded in this section testify to the amazing ingenuity of imprisoned men. Long, lonely, unoccupied hours in a prison cell are often occupied by planning escapes, and Cherry Hill's prisoners were no exception.

THE PARDONING POWER

When the fixed or time sentence was the practice of the day, the only avenues by which a prisoner could leave prison were to finish serving his entire sentence or be pardoned. It was only natural that any person sent to prison should use every facility at his command to win the coveted pardon from the governor, in whom the power was vested. Friends, the use of money, political influence, and even the intercession of prison officials were mobilized to exert influence on the state's chief executive. Truly, the pardoning of criminals was the Achille's heel of prison administration.

In several states, pardons were flagrantly sold by unscrupulous governors. Periodically, pardon scandals were brought to light and in some prisons almost as many prisoners were pardoned in a single year as were sentenced. For example, it was discovered that in 1813, 198 prisoners were received in Newgate prison in New York city and 134 were pardoned; in 1814, 213 were received and 176 pardoned; and between 1797 and 1822, 5,067 were admitted and 2,819 pardoned.

It was not uncommon for professional pardon agents to solicit a commission from a prisoner to extract a pardon from a governor. They would then go about their task in a businesslike manner, following a procedure such as this: first, poll the jurors who convicted the man and thus procure their signatures; second, secure as many signatures as possible from influential people in the prisoner's community; and third, present the signatures to the governor. Often signatures were bought. Warden Wood of the prison at Philadelphia wrote in a letter to Dr. Philip Tidyman of South Carolina in 1839 that he had known of cases where as much as $1,000 was used in securing a pardon.[20] Cases were even known in which jurors, after convicting a felon in court, immediately joined in signing a petition to have the culprit pardoned.

The menace of promiscuous pardoning was minimized considerably following the introduction of "good time" laws, a form of commutation by which a prisoner could, through good behavior, reduce his term of imprisonment somewhat. New York passed such a law in 1817 and other states soon followed its example, Pennsylvania delaying until 1861. However, it was declared unconstitutional so that real commutation did not materialize until 1869.

All through the years, from the opening of Cherry Hill until

[20] Philip Tidyman, *On the Abuse of the Pardoning Power* (Harrisburg, 1839).

1869, the practice of pardoning prisoners bedeviled the Board of Inspectors and wardens. While the figures indicate that only 16 prisoners were extended executive clemency during the first five years of Warden Wood's administration, he protested vigorously to the governor. The warden was less concerned regarding the wisdom of releasing men into society because of their criminal tendencies as he was disturbed at losing the labor of the potential recipients of such grace. This is noted in the letter he wrote to Governor Wolf in 1833.

Philadelphia 8 Mo 31st 1833

My Dear Friend:

About ten days ago George M. Dallas made enquiry of me relative to Thos. Wardle a prisoner in my custody, and stated his intention to apply to thee for his pardon—I have since received a letter from the Secretary of State respecting said prisoner which I answered yesterday. He was one of a gang of horse thieves, three of whom we got—Thee may get correct information respecting them from Schuylkill and Northumberland Counties in both of which they *traded*— I am inclined to believe that Wardle & Emmerson were the two best —The worst was not taken—

Thomas Biddle has also called on me for information respecting William Davis a young man who robbed his Country house of a pair of candlesticks—Now I can say as much in favour of Davis and Emmerson as I have done for Wardle "Their conduct has been unexceptionable since they have been inmates in the Eastern Penitentiary." But if this was good & sufficient cause to have *them* pardoned, a large majority of those under my care would be entitled to this favour— Now the fact is, that we have not three men at this time in the Penitentiary that we could so illy spare—They are all Smiths and better workmen than I have been able to procure for eight dollars per week—Indeed I do not know where I could replace them for ten dollars per week—We have now 354 iron doors to make; & iron fastenings for the same number of wooden doors: and on these three men I very much depend for the execution of this work—And I would therefore say if any men are to be pardoned for good Conduct, I would much rather let 6 or 8 others who do not earn 20 cts per day (but who behave equally as well as these men) rather than these three and some others of like kind—As the good conduct of one prisoner (& consequent pardon) cannot have any influence on another in our establishment; we have never taken nor I hope never will take this ground—I know my views look selfish; and I think it likely I feel so—If however there was any good & sufficient cause shewn, why these men should not serve out their time, I would be willing to say, the State might hire men—But if there is, I do not know it. Do not my dear friend think me too hard on this old subject of pardons—I know the importunities by which thou are beset, and feel for thee, and should be very willing if it were possible to take all the blame and censure of not granting them—I am satisfied the ground we have taken has had a salutary effect and I am very desirous that our list of pardons when presented at the close of the year will look small.

I remain with much regard & sincere friendship thy friend

Samuel R. Wood

George Wolf Esq.

Warden Wood was very frank regarding pardoning practices. He stated that "very seldom is the petition for a pardon got up on the grounds of innocence, improper evidence, severity of sentence, or new evidence." Rather, the reasons advanced were: "he the prisoner had a large family dependent on him," "he previously had a good character or this is his first conviction," "he is in poor health and may die if forced to continue in prison," or "his imprisonment has been effective and he is now a reformed and penitent man." During the early 1850s the prison records give the following reasons, among others, for conferring a pardon: "sufficiently punished," "sincerely repented," and "end of justice answered."

From the opening of the institution to December 31, 1875, out of the 8,187 prisoners received, 896 or 12.4 percent had won a pardon. Of this number, 927 were pardoned by the governor and 94 by the President of the United States.

On numerous occasions the wardens were opposed to pardons and registered protests in their Journals. For example, Warden Nimrod Strickland in 1854 wrote, "The warden protests the pardoning of Murphy No. 2458." Again, in connection with the pardon of Sarah Garber, a young girl who, as a baby sitter, allowed a baby to swallow pins, resulting in the baby's death, he wrote,

Discharged by pardon of Governor Pollack No 2851 (Sarah Garber) sentenced for four years on a 2nd degree murder charge. She is about 17 years old and is of rather a weak mind. Has been considerably benefited morally and intellectually since she came and has conducted herself with general propriety. The pardon states that, among others, Nimrod Strickland joined in the recommendation of it. If this means the warden it is an error, as he has not connected himself or his name with any application for pardon since he entered upon his duties.

While Warden Strickland might have objected strenuously to the granting of pardons, some earlier wardens or members of the Board of the prison must have been overly anxious to get rid of some inmates by this route. For instance, in 1850 Governor W. F. Johnston stated that his predecessors had been frequently approached with pleas for pardoning prisoners with "ill-health or insanity" on the grounds that "a change should be made in the laws so as to modify the severity of the system of separate confinement." [21]

CHERRY HILL AS A MECCA FOR SIGHTSEERS

Distinguished visitors from abroad, whether they were penologists, diarists, or novelists, regarded the Philadelphia prison as one of the *musts* to be seen in this country. Along with the celebrated Sing Sing prison, Cherry Hill rivaled the Falls of Niagara and the United States Capitol as a tourist attraction. Visitors from Philadelphia as well as from the rest of the nation were strongly drawn to see this remarkable American prison. Even during its construction many visitors trudged from the center of the city to Bush Hill, two miles away, to witness the elevation of the walls, the ornate front building, and towers. For instance, General Lafayette viewed the prison during its construction and spoke disconsolately of "the turrets which flank the corners of the wall" which are grim indeed.

The visitors' books opened with the first signature on October

[21] From the governor's message, *Journal of the Senate of Pennsylvania,* II (1850), 608. For the record of pardons granted from the Eastern Penitentiary from 1829 through 1871, see Richard Vaux, *Brief Sketch of the Origin and History,* p. 138.

25, 1829—the day on which the first prisoner was received. Entries through the many long years compare favorably with similar present-day visitors' logs of such shrines as Independence Hall in Philadelphia and Washington's home at Mount Vernon.

The first visitor to sign his name in the log at Cherry Hill was George Washington Smith, prominent Philadelphian and author of an informative pamphlet on the prison system, *A Defense of the System of Solitary Confinement.* The second person to sign the register on November 2 was one Charles Wells, also of Philadelphia. On November 12 Mr. C. C. Biddle signed his name. The fourth and fifth visitors were members of the Philadelphia Prison Society, James J. Barclay and David Wetherly, who were the first of the many lay visitors appointed by law to visit the inmates of the prison.

On November 20 Mr. Gershom Powers of New York, for many years identified with the rival Auburn prison, came to inspect the Philadelphia institution. On January 24, 1830, the Reverend Louis Dwight, often referred to in this book, visited the establishment, the first of several visits he made to the prison he so frequently condemned.

The first visitors' register extends in time from the opening of the prison to its first inmate through about half the year 1841. There were relatively few visitors from 1829 to 1834, the yearly average being about 100. But in 1835, 1,108 visitors' names were recorded; in 1836 there were 2,062; in 1837, 2,538; in 1838, 3,133; in 1839, exactly 4,000; and in 1840, 3,385. On some days as many as 100 persons visited the institution.

Aside from single visitors, many delegations were received; legislators from Pennsylvania and neighboring states, students from Philadelphia schools, and commissioners were sent to the prison to study the Commonwealth's system of penal discipline, which was rapidly making a reputation throughout the world. The bulk of the visitors was, of course, from Philadelphia. One interesting entry appears on the register: "Thomas Jefferson Trist, Virginia, grandson of the late T. J., President of the U.S. (one of the students of the Penna. Inst. for the deaf and dumb) visited the E. P. June 9, 1838." On September 13 of the same year, "76 members of the United Fire Co. of Baltimore."

There were many family groups both from Philadelphia and from out of town. Typical of the latter were: "the 6 Brodheads, Milford, Pike County, July 1, 1836;" "H. C. Rowden, Lady and Sister, New York July 6 1836;" "Cyrus Curtis, Lady and two sons, Hudson, N.Y., October 27, 1840."

Among the distinguished visitors interested in some aspect of penology whose names are recorded in the first visitors' book are: Edward Livingston; Dr. Francis Lieber; Alexis de Tocqueville; Gustave de Beaumont; Thomas U. Walter, architect of Philadelphia's Moyamensing Prison and the first building of Girard College; Dr. Nicolaus Julius from Berlin; Dr. James Mease, Philadelphia, a strong supporter of the separate system; Abel Blouet the French architect and collaborator on a book concerning the architecture of American prisons; Judge Frederic Demetz; and John Joseph Gurney, brother of Elizabeth Gurney Fry, famous prison visitor to London's Newgate Prison.

There are signatures of at least three out-of-state governors: Cass of Michigan, Carroll of Tennessee, and Camay of Arkansas.

There are many entries recording the visits of statesmen, literary figures, and other well-known men and women who apparently found it interesting to inspect the famous Philadelphia prison. In chronological order, among those who appeared during the first decade or so, we find: Matthew Carey, Philadelphia printer and publisher; Josiah Quincy of Boston; Nicholas Biddle, the Philadelphia financier who accompanied John Quincy Adams to the institution on April 13, 1833, just one month after Adams had been succeeded to the presidency by Andrew Jackson. "His Excellency, Andrew Jackson, President, United States" also came to Cherry Hill on June 11, 1833, but did not personally sign the register. Several years later, on Christmas Day of 1838, Nicholas Biddle again visited the prison, accompanied by a foreigner, Maria Amerigos des Vespucci, who claimed to be a descendant of the explorer but appears to have been merely an adventuress.

Mahlon Dickinson, Secretary of the Navy, entered his name

on the record of the prison on June 16, 1835; Harriet Martineau, the British author, signed her name on November 27, 1834; and Captain Frederick Marryat, British naval officer and novelist, came on September 28, 1837.

Groups of American Indians occasionally came to Cherry Hill. Warden Wood records in his Journal on June 13, 1833, "Had a visit today from Indian Chief Black Hawk and his company." Earlier, on December 29, 1830, Colonel Stambaugh signed the record as "Indian Agent, Green Bay [Wisconsin] with 14 Menomonie Indians." Six years later, on March 30, 1836, Mr. L. Slater and three Ottawa chiefs from Michigan came to the institution. The names of the chiefs, the handwriting of which is difficult to read, appear to be: "Chief Wynemewh-ge, Chief Maketaeso, and Chief Wa-job-equam."

Another interesting entry of about the same time is, "N. Roosevelt of Hyde Park, New York, December 14, 1837." Others of some interest are: "Rev. E. M. P. Wells, superintendent of the House of Refuge, Boston, September 6, 1838; Ezekiel Hale Barstow, Dartmouth College, Hanover, New Hampshire, November 23, 1838; Elihu Pickering, Penn Township, Pa., October 31, 1840; Nathan Lampsman, Coxsackie, Green County, New York, July 18, 1845, '7 feet 3 inches tall.'" Other visitors included the Reverend Sam Hollingworth, April 2, 1840, from far-off Botany Bay, Australia, notorious penal colony of Great Britain; Horace Mann, down from Boston on March 26 of the same year; and John Haviland, the prison architect.

On June 14, 1837, the Reverend I. R. Goodman, chaplain of the United States Senate, visited the prison, and on June 22 of the same year, one "Mrs. Jane Spangler, Gentle Woman, Philadelphia" ventured into the forbidding fortress. Men, accompanied by their wives, almost invariably registered their names as "Mr. Jones and Lady." But when Thomas A. Nelson of Booneville, Missouri, visited Cherry Hill with his "Lady" on April 25, 1840, that independent female crossed out the "Lady" and signed herself "Mrs. Mary Gay Nelson." This may be one of the first indications of feminism in this country.

We have already mentioned some foreign visitors but there

were many others. Delegations came from Antigua, Leeward Island, Jamaica, Puerto Rico, and many individual visitors came from such glamorous places as "New Granada," Bogota, Rio de Janeiro, Santiago, Chile, and Madeira. A Mr. Aspinwall, Stockholm, Sweden, recorded his name on November 3, 1832; T. F. C. Brün and T. Bille, both from Copenhagen, Denmark, came to the institution on September 6, 1837; Eduard Hasle, from "Berlin in Prussia" was at Cherry Hill on October 18, 1837; while Edler von der Planitz from "Dresden in Saxony" came two days later. Two other Germans, F. Steinheit and John Philip Stürmer, both from Frankfurt came in January, 1838.

One visit was for a grim purpose when on May 19, 1837, Captain James McCauley of the United States Marines registered and entered the prison with a contingent of 50 enlisted men to conduct James Moran, No. 750, to his execution. Moran, a 19-year-old seaman, had been convicted of murder on the high sea. Samuel Wood, warden at the time, wrote in his Journal regarding the event, "We left the prison about a quarter before eleven o'clock and at 27 minutes after 11 the drop fell and a few minutes more the unfortunate man was no more. Hanged May 19, 1837." [22]

A number of traveling noblemen took time to visit the penitentiary during its early years. On October 10, 1860, the Prince of Wales and his entourage came to the prison. He did not sign the register but from Warden John Halloway's Journal we find the following story:

The institution was visited this morning by the Prince of Wales traveling as Baron Renfrew, accompanied by the Gentlemen of his Suite, viz., Duke of Newcastle, Lord Lyons, Earl St. Germaine, Col. Bruce and others. All the members of the Board of Inspectors were present to receive them. They spent rather more than half an hour in the institution and expressed themselves much gratified with their visit.

Thirty years earlier such noblemen as Baron de Behr, Belgian Minister, Le Comte de Estoumel, member of the French Cham-

[22] J. Thomas Scharf and Thompson Westcott, A History of Philadelphia, 1609–1884 (Philadelphia, 1884), I, 649.

ber of Deputies, the Earl of Selkirk, and Lord Gosford visited the institution.

We mentioned above that John Haviland visited the establishment he had designed. He made several visits throughout the years. One entry is of special interest: "On April 15, 1837 Wm. C. Crane, New Jersey, with the master Haviland" visited. At that time Haviland was at work supervising the erection of a new prison at Trenton. Crane may have been a helper or one of the building commissioners.

The number of visitors increased as the years advanced. In 1859, Warden John Halloway reported that during the preceding five year period over 40,000 people had visited the prison. In 1858 alone almost 10,000 people went through the institution. These figures do not include the friends and relatives of the prisoners or those coming to the prison on official business.

How these sightseers were handled by the staff is not recorded. But it must have taken endless hours of conducted tours to satisfy the understandable interest the public had in this famous model of the separate system of prison discipline of which the state of Pennsylvania was so proud.

≡7
The Rise and Fall of the Pennsylvania System

PREVENTING the contamination of prisoners, one by the other, was the basis for the philosophies of both the Auburn and the Pennsylvania Systems. The literature of the day is specific on this point. But the founders of the two systems and the state legislators who were charged with the responsibility of developing prison systems differed on details as to how this contamination should be prevented.

Many states made provision for solitary confinement, but there was considerable variation as to the portion of the sentence to be spent in solitude. There were also differences of opinion as to the types of criminals to be completely separated. The following data indicate the extent of the adoption and the dates of the abandonment of the Pennsylvania System in other states: Maryland introduced solitary confinement in 1809 and abolished it in 1838; Massachusetts authorized it in 1811 and abandoned it in 1829; Maine carried it out from 1824 to 1827; New Jersey introduced it in 1820, abandoned it in 1828, reintroduced it in 1833, and finally gave it up completely in 1858; Virginia experimented with it from 1824 to 1833; and Rhode Island practiced it from 1838 to 1844.

But these states adopted only the "solitary" feature of the Pennsylvania System without recognizing such essential ingredients as prison visiting, recognition of the prisoner as a human being rather than a wage slave, and a firm kindliness as exemplified by the Quaker philosophy of life. Architecturally the prisons in these other states were not suited for the system —the cells were usually smaller and no exercise yards were provided—and it is no wonder the system failed in these states, in some cases after only a preliminary trial.

During this experimental period even the inspectors of the Auburn prison thought that complete separation of prisoners with restriction of labor might be the answer. In 1821 they ordered that a selection of the "oldest and most heinous offenders" be placed in complete solitary confinement for the purpose of observing the disciplinary effects. In addition, a second group was put in separate cells for three days of each week, while the younger offenders were allowed to work in the shops with separation only at night.

This experiment continued throughout 1822 and 1823 and it proved to be a ghastly failure. What happened to these Auburn inmates is best described by the French commissioners, De Beaumont and De Tocqueville:

The unfortunates, on whom this experiment was made, fell into a state of depression, so manifest, that their keepers were struck with it; their lives seemed in danger, if they remained longer in this situation; five of them had already succumbed during a single year; their moral state was not less alarming; one of them had become insane; another, in a fit of despair, had embraced the opportunity when the keeper brought him something, to precipitate himself from his cell, running the almost certain chance of a mortal fall.[1]

Twenty-six of those who survived this rugged treatment were later pardoned.

All this experiment proved was that the mere separation of prisoners, without any of the basic features of the Pennsylvania System, induced tragic results at Auburn. Yet, because of this experiment, many who were undecided between the two systems repudiated the Pennsylvania System and recommended the Auburn, convinced that contamination could be prevented by means of the strict rule of silence. But the only hope of maintaining this rule was by free use of the lash.

Elam Lynds, warden of Auburn, regarded flogging as the

---

[1] De Beaumont and De Tocqueville, *On the Penitentiary System in the United States and Its Application in France*, trans. Francis Lieber (Philadelphia, 1833), p. 8.

most effective and humane of all punishments. He contended that reformation of a criminal could not be effected until his spirit was broken and it was the purpose of penal discipline to accomplish this. Only then could the prisoner develop good habits, embrace a more religious attitude, and accept all elements of reformation. Lynds looked upon prisoners as cowards and charged his officers to regard them with contempt. He was insensitive to the sufferings of his prisoners. Contemporary accounts state that a rawhide whip was used but sometimes floggings were applied with a cat made of six strands of twine. Five hundred blows on a stripped convict were not unusual as punishment. The insane were flogged as well as those who were subject to fits. Punishments were supposed to be witnessed by the inspectors, but frequently those officials asked to be excused from this duty because it gave them "such painful feelings."

Another disciplinary technique was developed by Lynds's deputy, John Cray, which aided in repressing all forms of communication. Known as the lock-step, it consisted of a close order formation of the men as they shuffled to and from their work, each with one hand on the shoulder of the one before him, with downcast eyes (or all facing the officer) and, of course, no talking or moving of the lips.

This was the Auburn System which generated the enthusiasm of legislators and of some prison reformers. The name of the Reverend Louis Dwight, secretary of the Boston Prison Discipline Society, has been mentioned on numerous occasions. His fervent support of the Auburn System and his repudiation of the admittedly more humane Pennsylvania System is difficult to understand at this late date. In the first report of his society he penned the following eulogy which has become a classic:

At Auburn, we have a more beautiful example still, of what may be done by proper discipline. . . . The whole establishment from the gate to the sewer is a specimen of neatness. The unremitting industry, the entire subordination and subdued feeling of the convicts, has no parallel. . . . In their solitary cell, with no other book than the Bible, they spend the night and, at sunrise, they rise and proceed, under military order, under the eyes of the turnkeys, in solid columns, with the lock march, to their work-shops; thence, in the same order, at the hour of breakfast, to the common hall, where they partake of their frugal meal in silence. Not even a whisper is heard through the whole apartment. The convicts are seated in single file, at narrow tables, with their backs toward the center, so that there can be no interchange of signs. If one has more food than he wants, he raises his left hand; and if another has less, he raises his right hand; and the waiter changes it. When they have done eating, at the ringing of a little bell, of the softest sound, they rise from the table, form the solid columns, and return under the eye of their turnkeys to the workshops.

At the close of day, a little before sunset, the work is all laid aside at once, and the convicts return in military order to the solitary cells; where they partake of their frugal meal, which they are permitted to take from the kitchen. . . . After supper, they can, if they choose, read the Scriptures undisturbed, and then reflect in silence on the error of their lives. They must not disturb their fellows by even a whisper.

While Dwight thus described the system he admired, the inspectors of the prison published this report in January, 1823, which presents another side of the convict's life at Auburn:

Very different would be the conclusion if they [visitors] could know and judge from the facts; if they could realize the unceasing daily toils, and nocturnal solitude, even of the industrious and orderly; brooding over their crimes and sufferings, till their terms of sentence expire, or death shall relieve them, and deliver their bodies, not to the peaceful grave, but to the surgeon for dissection, or if they could witness the stripes and galling chains of the stubborn or disobedient; or could they discover the feel and condition of those (the most depraved and incorrigible) who are doomed to uninterrupted solitude, —who, on hearing distant footsteps, strain their eye-balls to catch but a glimpse of the human face, and whose haggard looks fearfully express their mental agony and distress; the recollection of better days, the endearments of home, of family and friends; all combining with an agonizing sense of guilt, to fill up the greatest measure of suffering that human nature can conceive or endure.

About the time that the Auburn System was attracting favorable attention, the New York legislature, by an act passed March 7, 1825, authorized another prison near New York city.

So confident was Elam Lynds of his disciplinary system at
Auburn, that he volunteered to build the proposed prison,
transporting convict labor to the new site from Auburn. The
story of the erection of the prison, first christened Mount Pleasant but later known by its present name Sing Sing, is dra-
matically told by the late Lewis E. Lawes, long a warden of
Sing Sing, in his book *Cell 202*.[2]

The site of this new prison is a tract of 130 acres known as
the Silver Mine Farm, since prior to and during the American
Revolution it had been worked somewhat extensively for silver.
It is situated on the east bank of the Hudson River, 33 miles
from New York city and not far from the little village of Sing
Sing, now Ossining. The term Sing Sing is from the Indian,
ossine ossine meaning stone upon stone. This particular land
was chosen because of the presence of good building stone not
difficult to quarry. The prison was erected by the convicts who
were thus given "useful, healthful, and it is believed, profitable
employment."

During the 1830s, a number of distinguished Europeans,
many of whom were commissioned by their respective govern-
ments, visited the two rival prisons, the one at Sing Sing and
the one at Philadelphia. From France came the publicist, De
Beaumont, and the jurist, De Tocqueville, whose report was
calm, judicious, and reasonably objective. These gentlemen
were somewhat inclined to favor the Auburn System as epitomized in the Sing Sing prison; Mr. William Crawford of the
London Society for the Improvement of Prison Discipline submitted a glowing report in 1834 in favor of the Pennsylvania
System; Dr. Nicolaus Heinrich Julius of Prussia who came to
America in 1834 became a thorough convert to the Pennsylvania
System. In 1836 France, dissatisfied with the report of De
Beaumont and De Tocqueville, commissioned the noted jurist
Frederic A. Demetz and the architect Guillaume Blouet to make
a survey of the two systems. These gentlemen were more critical
than some of the other investigators, but in the end they were
disposed in favor of the Pennsylvania System.

The recommendation of the Philadelphia prison by such dis-

[2] Lawes, *Cell 202* (New York, 1935).

tinguished visitors led to a wide adoption of the Pennsylvania System throughout Europe. England adopted it in 1835 and erected its model separate prison at Pentonville in London in 1840. Other countries adopting the system were: Belgium in 1838, Sweden in 1840, Hungary in 1841, France in 1844, Prussia at about the same time, Denmark in 1846, Norway and Holland in 1851.

It is true, of course, that in few countries was the adoption as complete as in Pennsylvania, but in every case it was sufficient to leave the imprint of the "separate" system upon the administration of the penal institutions. Down to the present day the Pennsylvania System with various modifications may be found in several European countries.

While most protagonists of the Pennsylvania System were Pennsylvanians, there were several from outside the state. The same is true of its critics. But the most vocal and consistent critic of the system, as we have pointed out, was the Reverend Louis Dwight. His criticism was especially effective because he had the advantage of a journal with a wide circulation. Not until 1845 could the Philadelphia Prison Society boast a publication that could champion the cause of separate confinement. This was the *Journal of Prison Discipline and Philanthropy*. Hence Dwight had a clear field for his carping criticism for almost 20 years.

Though justifiably shocked at abuses he found in county jails of the country as well as in the Walnut Street Jail in Philadelphia and other congregate prisons, Dwight early embraced the Auburn silent system with all of its repressions and inhumane floggings. He accepted the necessity of punishments but, like Warden Lynds of Auburn, recommended the lash as the most humane.

Dwight convinced state legislatures that New York's system, as developed at Auburn and Sing Sing, was far superior to that of Pennsylvania. Starting as early as 1827 he condemned the prison at Philadelphia (then under construction) in his publication, almost annually. His critical comments, while violently partisan, are worthy of note since they constitute a basis of comparison with the equally partisan contentions of the exponents of the separate system.

In his 1827 report he presented a vigorous protest against the establishment of a system of solitary confinement in the Cherry Hill prison.[3] In 1828 he stated that he and a companion had visited a completed cell block in that prison and had experienced no difficulty in conversing from cell to cell and from exercise yard to exercise yard.[4]

In 1835 he condemned cruel methods of punishment such as the water douche and the gag and declared that there was an unjustifiable mortality and an abnormal degree of insanity in the institution.[5] The following year he made the sweeping assertion that the Pennsylvania System was a proved failure with respect to the elements of health, reformation, earnings from industry, and moral and religious instruction.[6] In 1839 he accused the authorities of the Eastern Penitentiary of attempting to suppress information regarding the abuses in discipline in that institution which had been revealed by Thomas McElwee in the investigation of 1834.[7] He explained that it had taken him four years to obtain a copy of McElwee's volume describing the cruelties practiced.

In 1842 Dwight stated that the authorities of the prison had persuaded the legislature to pass a law in 1833 taking away the right of the grand juries to visit the prison.[8] But the most trenchant and comprehensive indictment presented by this perennial critic is found in the report of his society for the year 1843.[9] Following a voluminous condemnation of the Pennsylvania System, accompanied by a large number of citations from reports and other documents and a recital of the instances of its failure before and after 1829, he made the following categorical arraignment of the separate system:

1. The Pennsylvania System fails to answer the expectations and designs of its friends in dispensing with labor.

2. The Pennsylvania System fails to answer the expectations

---

[3] *Report of the Boston Prison Discipline Society* (Boston, 1827), pp. 121–28.
[4] *Ibid.* (1828), pp. 39–47.   [5] *Ibid.* (1835), pp. 20–22.
[6] *Ibid.* (1836), pp. 38–40.   [7] *Ibid.* (1839), pp. 48–53.
[8] *Ibid.* (1842), p. 62.   [9] *Ibid.* (1842), pp. 49 f.

and promises of its early friends in preventing evil communication.

3. The Pennsylvania System fails to answer the promises and expectations of its early friends in deterring from crime and preventing recommitments.

4. The Pennsylvania System fails to answer the promises and expectations of its early friends in regard to its effects on health and life.

5. The Pennsylvania System fails to answer the promises and expectations of its early friends in regard to its effects on the mind.

6. The Pennsylvania System fails to answer the promises and expectations of its early friends in regard to self-support.

7. The Pennsylvania System fails to answer the promises and expectations of its early friends by dispensing with severe punishments for misdemeanors in prison.

8. The Pennsylvania System fails to answer the promises and expectations of its early friends in regard to its extension in America.

In his reports for 1849 and 1850, Dwight made a special attack on the Pennsylvania System for what he alleged to be its production of an abnormal amount of insanity among the inmates. He maintained that ten inmates became insane in 1848, and that the Canadian penal commission which had visited the Cherry Hill prison asserted that out of the total of 300 inmates, no less than 50 were insane.[10]

There is little evidence for believing that his criticisms did more than stir the exponents of the Pennsylvania System to a more determined defense of their philosophy and methods. Yet, penal gadfly that he was, there must have been a sigh of relief from the Board of Inspectors and especially from Richard Vaux, who, as we shall see, dominated the management of the prison when the Reverend Louis Dwight died in 1854. Dr. Orlando F. Lewis, for many years a close observer of penal practices in this country, wrote in 1922 concerning Dwight:

His enemies claimed—and in the light of these later years, correctly —that at times he distorted the truth, and misrepresented facts. It was this failing in Louis Dwight that stood in the way of his becoming a great man in his profession. Toward all that pertained to the Eastern Penitentiary he was highly biased, seemingly incapable of

[10] *Ibid.*, 1849, p. 70; 1850, p. 37.

calm judgment, and he was persistently unfair, although his motives were in no way low or sordid, or for his own gain. . . . He was severely arraigned in public by Charles Sumner, of his own Society, for the distortion and suppression of facts regarding the Pennsylvania System.[11]

Three of the charges lodged against the Pennsylvania System by Dwight and others are worthy of some comment. First, its expense in construction and in its operation; second, the mode of labor developed for the prisoners—handcraft as opposed to power machinery which required workshops for the inmates working together; and third, its tendency to induce insanity or mental deterioration because of the "complete solitude" imposed on the inmates.

These were, of course, serious charges, but they were elusive of proof. So far as expense was concerned, taxpayers, then as now, were disturbed at the high cost of maintaining prisons. Any feasible work plan for prison inmates that would help defray the cost of maintenance was likely to be acceptable, even though the more laudable objective of imprisonment, that of reformation, might be partially nullified. The prison movement was ushered in during the early days of the Industrial Revolution when power machinery was slowly supplanting hand labor.

It seemed absurd to prudent administrators as well as to legislators to maintain a handcraft prison labor policy when the trend was definitely in the direction of power machinery. Yet the zealots who believed implicitly in reformation as the aim of imprisonment were never much impressed with such an argument.

Charges that solitary imprisonment tended to induce insanity were heatedly debated by advocates of both systems. It must be remembered that in those early days there were mental hospitals only for those who could afford private treatment, that not too much was known regarding mental diseases, and that mental disease and mental defectiveness (feeblemindedness) were confused in diagnoses by some of the best physi-

[11] Lewis, *The Development of American Prisons and Prison Customs, 1776–1845* (Albany, 1922), p. 291.

cians. Perhaps the first discussion of insanity in prisons, at least in America, was that by Dr. Franklin Bache, the first attending physician in the Philadelphia prison. In 1837 he wrote,

A certain number of cases of insanity have presented themselves, some of them existing prior to entrance, and continuing, others had given signs of insanity prior to entrance. The subject of insanity in relation to prisons is a difficult one. One must, in many instances, distinguish between criminal actions and those caused by insanity. Judges and juries are very reluctant to admit insanity in defense. In every prison there will be a larger or smaller number of cases of insanity. I have seen more cases of insanity in Cherry Hill than in Walnut Street Jail.

We gather from his reports that Dr. Bache denied that the separate system induced mental deterioration. For example, his records show that in 1829, the opening year of Cherry Hill, and in 1830, no cases appeared. In 1831, there were four, but he said they did not originate in prison. In fact, his reports from then on give no cases as originating in the prison. His successors, Doctors Hartshorne and Given, also disclaimed any responsibility of the prison discipline for causing insanity. Whenever the management of Cherry Hill was attacked in this area, it retaliated by pointing out the number of insane in other prisons of the congregate variety. Thus, aside from the biased studies made by friends and foes of the separate system, there is nothing in the early literature of the American prison that would give more than a hint as to the effects of imprisonment on the mental stability of the prisoner.

In one annual report the inspectors of Cherry Hill would claim that separate confinement had no deleterious effect on inmates of high mentality although those of an inferior intelligence might be somewhat affected; whereas in another report, they would reverse this by stating that dull-witted persons might stand the rigors of separate confinement much better than the more intelligent groups (only a few of which ever got to prison).

Looking backward from this date we can only state that both groups were distinctly partisan and almost unscrupulous in editing their data to bolster their position and that so little was known at the time concerning mental aberrations, their causes, and progression that the charge was not susceptible of proof.

From time to time, Dwight could cite instances of certain prisoners placed in solitary confinement—usually in congregate prisons—and get testimonials from either the victims or guards. In some instances, he stated that they deteriorated while undergoing this punishment; in others he found that certain prisoners thrived on it and preferred complete solitude for indefinite periods of time to work in the shops or a good flogging.

Such comments by Dwight or any other critic of Pennsylvania's system of prison discipline were actually irrelevant. The system in operation at Cherry Hill, severe and unrealistic though it was, could not be compared to complete solitary confinement, a point which seems to have been missed by Dwight and others.

At all times there were several insane criminals sent by the courts to Cherry Hill. Many of the infractions of the prison rules were committed by those who were mentally unbalanced. The overseers and watchmen had to be constantly on guard against attacks by those who were insane. In the investigation of the institution in 1897 it was disclosed that some inmates were seriously clubbed by the overseers. In all of these cases the victims were either insane or were, according to the testimony, malingerers—that is, feigning insanity. At that time there was some agitation throughout the state for the establishment of a hospital or institution for the criminally insane. The prison inspectors and Warden Michael Cassidy were convinced that the criminally insane could be better treated within a prison if a separate wing or cell block could be provided than in a special hospital. However, in 1905 the legislature passed an act calling for an institution for this class of criminal, and it was opened in 1912 at Farview in Wayne County.

As to the charge that inmates could converse with one another, it is obvious that they could and did. As one reads the journal of punishments kept for a time by the wardens, the number of cases in which the offense was "talking with another prisoner" exceeds all others. Inmates obviously went to great lengths to contact those near at hand by means of water pipes, by tapping on cell walls, by communicating with others while in exercise yards, and by actually shouting in their cells. But at best such breaches of the rule could give little comfort to the vast majority of the inmates, as sustained conversation was almost impossible unless the rule was violated through the carelessness or apathy of officers.

CHERRY HILL UNDER RICHARD VAUX

The first period in the history of the Eastern State Penitentiary at Philadelphia began with its inception (1818) or with its opening (1829)—either may be argued—and ends with the appointment of Richard Vaux as a member of the Board of Inspectors. The date 1842 may not have been noted at the time, but as we view this famous establishment today we see that Richard Vaux was symbolic of its administration as well as its philosophy.

When Richard Vaux accepted the important post of inspector of the prison, he was only 26 years old. Born in Philadelphia on December 9, 1816, he was the son of the distinguished philanthropist and public servant, Roberts Vaux. Richard Vaux was later to become one of the city's leading citizens. He was elected mayor of the city on the Democratic ticket in 1855 and was one of the very few of that political party ever to hold the office. His career in connection with the Cherry Hill institution is remarkable. He was inspector for 53 years, secretary of the Board for nine years, and its president for 43 years. He was a man of great attainments and possessed a dominating personality. Michael Cassidy, warden from 1881–1900 and an employee of the institution in various capacities as early as 1862, wrote of Mr. Vaux,

His life work is without parallel in penology for it can truly be said that the oversight and care of the Eastern Penitentiary and of its inmates was his distinctive life work. He was an authority on penology, not only in Pennsylvania, but in Europe. . . . For many years it [the prison], was denounced as cruel and barbarous, tending to melancholia and insanity. Time has refuted all such assertions, and now the solitary system as practiced in this institution is commended everywhere, and is being copied and put into practice in Massachusetts and elsewhere in the United States, and in many cities in Europe.

The separation of prisoners into individual cells in which they work, as distinguished from the congregate in workshops, is the peculiar feature of this system. Mr. Vaux was the exponent of the system, and the Eastern State Penitentiary will never be mentioned or remembered without associating his name with it. He has stamped it with his own individuality and characteristics. To serve continuously for fifty-three years for the good and uplifting of unfortunate human beings, and that without pay, reward, or advantage, is such a noble self-sacrifice that it should enshrine the name and memory of Mr. Vaux as a great benefactor of his race.[12]

The wardens of the Eastern Penitentiary who served while Richard Vaux was a member of the Board of Inspectors include George Thompson (1840–45), Thomas Scattergood (1845–50), John Halloway (first appointment, 1850–54), Nimrod Strickland (1854–56), Halloway (second appointment, 1856–70), Edward Townsend (1870–81), and Michael Cassidy (1881–1900). Accepting as true what has been said about the dominance of Richard Vaux, it is understandable that all these wardens were subservient to him. He *was* the prison during most of his 53 years' connection with it. Vaux died March 22, 1895, with "the utmost serenity and peace," as stated by the Philadelphia *Times.*

While Richard Vaux may have dominated the wardens who worked under him, he was obliged to collaborate with his colleagues on the Board. When he was elected as inspector, there were two men, John Bacon and Thomas Bradford, who had been on the Board since the opening of the prison. Bacon, a merchant, had long been active in the Philadelphia Prison Society (he joined in 1801 and was its president from 1838 to 1840) and was one of the original members of the Board of Commissioners appointed to transact the business incidental to

12 Cassidy, *Prisons and Convicts* (Philadelphia, 1897), p. 5.

erecting the Eastern State Penitentiary. He was also active
for many years as a member of the Board of the Walnut Street
Prison. Bradford, also a member of the Prison Society (he
joined in 1805) and a Board member of the Walnut Street
Prison, was a member of the original Board that drew up the
act of 1829 by which the Eastern Penitentiary was first governed. Both of these men served actively and faithfully in the
arduous duties of prison inspectors for more than 30 years.
Bradford died in 1851 and Bacon in 1859.

There is some evidence from the records that Bradford and
Vaux clashed during the 1840s. Bradford was opposed to the
use of irons as punishment and led a lonely attack on their
use. He also resented the absence of the second "visiting inspector" when duty required a team of two inspectors to issue
any orders to the warden or the staff of the prison. As one reads
the reports submitted by this faithful, elderly man, one can
sense the loneliness and perhaps bitterness he must have experienced as he "went the rounds" during his periodic stints
of visiting and inspecting the prisoners and institution. His
testiness and Vaux's impetuousness may be ascribed to the
differences in their ages; the former was a tired and sick man
approaching 70, while the latter was virile and in his early
30s. Bradford was a deeply religious man, a staunch Presbyterian who frequently preached to the prisoners on Sundays.
Uncompromisingly opposed to the use of physical punishments,
he argued with the warden over the use of irons although he
seems not to have objected to the dark cell or the shower bath.

Little is known of the personal lives of the various wardens
who administered Cherry Hill during the regime of Richard
Vaux. They signed the annual reports together with the inspectors and they kept up the wardens' Journals. But so far as
the writer has been able to ascertain, they were almost totally
anonymous in the life of the city. Warden Thompson had his
little tiffs with the inspector, Bradford, and also with the physician, Dr. William Darrach. It seems that in March, 1843, the
doctor refused to visit some sick prisoners. From Thompson's
Journal we read,

March 23, 1843: Dr. Darrach here. Called upon him and requested him to visit 9 sick persons. This he refused to do and left without seeing them.

Observed in the doctor's *Journal* under date of March 22—7½ par., a notice of his visit of that time containing a gross falsehood evidently designedly put upon record to convey false impression, the remainder of the notice has the appearance of being the production of a disordered man. Shall call upon witnesses and require a hearing of them and examination into the case by the Inspectors.

March 27: Darrach agreed to erase entry. Matter closed.

Richard Vaux as spokesman for the prison was a sort of public relations man. He was very well-known throughout the state and even better known and respected in his native city of Philadelphia. Later in life he wrote many articles and a book on penology. He traveled in Europe where he spoke of the virtues of the separate system of prison discipline. While there were other distinguished members on the Board of the prison, it was Vaux who spoke for the Board and who wrote the annual reports. His complete domination of the prison may be dated from 1859 when John Bacon died.

Warden George Thompson carried on the policies laid down by the law of 1829 by which the prison was operated and developed by his predecessor, Samuel R. Wood. He was succeeded in 1845 by Thomas Scattergood. Of this Quaker, Louis Dwight wrote, "Friend, thou art rightly named; for I perceive thy mission in the Penitentiary is to Scatter Good."

ENDORSEMENTS FOR THE PRISON FROM OUTSIDERS

The noted Fredrika Bremer, Swedish gentlewoman and novelist (1801–65), eulogized the separate system under Scattergood's administration. She stated that at times on leaving the prison she was "more edified" than on leaving church.[13] Other female visitors of note wrote glowingly of Cherry Hill. Harriet Martineau (1802–76), English authoress, wrote in her *Society in America* (1837) that every one of the prisoners told her that they were under obligation to the management for

[13] *America in the Fifties: Letters of Fredrika Bremer,* ed. Adolph Benson (New York, 1924), pp. 154 f.

treating them with respect. Dorothea Lynde Dix, noted reformer of mental hospitals, wrote, "Pennsylvania has the high praise of having established a model prison . . . which in its whole plan and government is worthy of being copied wherever civilization makes the establishment of prisons necessary, for the security of society." [14]

Captain Frederick Marryat (1792–1848) of the British navy and a famous novelist visited both the Eastern Penitentiary and the Sing Sing prison. He interviewed a man who had served time in both prisons who stated that the treatment of the inmates at Cherry Hill was much more humane than in the New York prison. At Sing Sing it was the lash; at Cherry Hill the inmate was treated like a man.[15]

In 1843 two members of the Board of Managers of Sing Sing visited Cherry Hill and reported on the good order and quiet atmosphere of their rival prison. They were impressed by the opportunity afforded the inmates "for thought and reflection;" "the humbled and the penitent incurred no hazard of being compelled to transgress;" "the last moments of the dying man were not disturbed by ribald songs or abominable blasphemy." They were surprised to find that the prisoners who had served time never assaulted the officers and were unable to fight among themselves as they did at Sing Sing where "confusion and discord reign." [16]

It seems there was something about the Pennsylvania System as practiced at Philadelphia in the 1840s and 1850s that appealed to humanitarians and deeply religious people of the era. One will look in vain for such testimony of the Auburn System under such administrators as John Cray or Elam Lynds.

AN APPRAISAL OF THE SYSTEM

The Pennsylvania philosophy of penal discipline was almost sterile so far as reformation is concerned. The inspectors failed

[14] Quoted in *Journal of Prison Discipline and Philanthropy*, Vol. I, No. 2 (1845), p. 246.

[15] Marryat, *A Diary in America with Remarks on its Institutions* (London, 1839), II, 265–69.

[16] Quoted in Lewis, *The Development of American Prisons*, p. 225.

to comprehend that the reformation of a criminal involves training for a normal adjustment to the outside social environment and, as Harry Elmer Barnes has stated, cannot be successfully based upon the practice of developing broken and unoffending hermits. He further asserts that a successful prison system can scarcely be tested by its ability to turn out Robinson Crusoes, and such was, at best, all that the Pennsylvania System could make any serious pretension of doing. Years ago Thomas Mott Osborne, a discerning observer of prisons, wrote of the system, "It showed a touching faith in human nature, although a precious little knowledge of it." One is reminded of the astute remark made by the late Alexander Paterson, for many years a member of the prison commission of England. Defining a prison he likened it to "a monastery inhabited by men who do not choose to be monks." If that is true today, how much more applicable it was to Cherry Hill in the old days.

It would be impossible for anyone to write on the history of Cherry Hill or the more inclusive Pennsylvania System of prison discipline without paying tribute to Harry Elmer Barnes. In his *Evolution of Penology in Pennsylvania,* he has told the story of the famous Philadelphia prison as well as its sister institution in Pittsburgh. Most of his sources are the annual reports of the inspectors of the two establishments and the writings of many of the opponents of the system of solitary or separate confinement. The material in the next few paragraphs is taken from Barnes's account of the Philadelphia institution.

The fundamental character of the Pennsylvania System, as interpreted by its exponents, passed through several stages. During the period between 1790 and 1841 (or more specifically between 1829 and 1842) the system was erroneously known as the "solitary" system. In the thirties, however, the alleged barbarities of the system of imprisonment in enforced solitude and silence became the center for attacks by the opponents of the system, and the word "solitary" came to be a stigma rather than a mark of special virtue in penal discipline.

In order to answer this criticism, the officials began, during the early forties to refer to the system as "separate." They pointed out that "separate" confinement did not mean solitude or silence. Great emphasis was laid upon the alleged facility of the inmate to associate and converse with the officials of the institution as well as with the legal visitors, members of the Philadelphia Prison Society. The technical name of the system from 1842 to the middle of the 1860s was the "separate method of confinement with labor and moral instruction."

After 1866, however, it could no longer accurately be described as a system of separation, because in that year overcrowding forced the inspectors to place two men in a cell. The *Thirty-eighth Annual Report* (1867) states,

The number of prisoners in excess of cells is 29. This induces the temporary necessity of putting more than one in some cells and after great deliberation this has been done with due regard to safety and convenience. There are many convicts of such a low grade of mental capacity as to render them unfit for any punishment but restraint, and these have been so placed as to render association harmless, but the effect has been prejudicial to the system of discipline.

If, despite communication between cells and violations of the solitary discipline, there had persisted some semblance of the purity of separation, certainly the year 1866 marks the beginning of the end of the Pennsylvania System in the prison of its birth.

To save themselves from inconsistency the inspectors were obliged to cast about for another title descriptive of their cherished system. They now invented the phrase "individual treatment system." This appeared first in the report of 1872 and remained the official designation until the system was legislated out of existence in 1913.

In the midst of the conflict between the advocates of the two major penitentiary systems, a new philosophy began to be discussed and urged by many progressive penal administrators. This was a system developed in one of the Australasian prison camps, on Norfolk Island, by Captain Alexander Maconochie and called by him, the Mark System. Based on a series of progressive stages through which a prisoner could pass by means of his own efforts, an eventual parole or conditional release under supervision was possible. The system was adapted to conditions in Ireland by Sir Walter Crofton and thus it became known in America as the Irish System. Many of the more alert penologists in this country recognized the system as a means of ending the senseless struggle between the Pennsylvania and Auburn Systems and of creating a new type of prison to be known as the reformatory.

But the report of the inspectors of Cherry Hill for 1860 shows evidence of tilting with the Irish System. One sentence of this report is revealing: "It can now be fairly claimed that no improvement has been adopted in any country that was not initiated by this Commonwealth, and [by] the wisdom of her law-makers." Yet at the time the separate system was nowhere in existence in this country, and in some European countries the progressive-stages system was being advocated.

In 1868, in anticipation of the swing toward the Irish System in this country, the inspectors of Cherry Hill expressed skepticism of its possibilities. "Like all novelties," they wrote, "it is highly estimated. Experience will divest it of all its attractions. Just now, it is the newest phase of convict treatment, and most applauded where least understood." They concluded, "At last the philosophy of our penitentiary discipline and the laws essential to its integrity, as a system, must conquer opposition."

The inspectors watched with interest and even alarm the swing toward the reformatory as it developed in this country. It was put into operation in Elmira, New York, in 1876, and the Commonwealth of Pennsylvania opened a counterpart at Huntingdon in 1889. But despite all that was transpiring in penological circles and also despite the doubling up of prisoners at the Cherry Hill prison, the annual reports of the inspectors still glowed with eulogies of the separate system. By 1889 they apparently despaired of its inherent effectiveness on the basis of its own strength and held that divine aid might be necessary to supplement its reformative workings.

In 1891 the inspectors maintained that the new disciplinary methods which constituted the reformatory system had not "yielded any marked benefits" but contended that "great success had attended" the Pennsylvania System. In 1893 they violently condemned the legislation introduced throughout the country that called for the development of the reformatory system with its training for trades and parole.

But after the death of Richard Vaux in 1895, zealous defense of the separate system began to wane. Warden Cassidy still talked about the system before prison groups, but even as he spoke Cherry Hill was gradually merging into just another congregate prison.

THE LAST DAYS OF THE SEPARATE SYSTEM

Pennsylvania's system of separate confinement never worked completely. The last four cell blocks designed by Haviland, erected between 1829 and 1835 (Blocks 4, 5, 6, and 7), were two stories high. This architectural expediency deviated from Haviland's original plan and obviously made supervision more difficult since communication between prisoners in the lower and upper tiers was much easier. This was an initial wedge in the breaking of the system.

Earlier we pointed out that in the first investigation of the prison in 1834 it was proved that many inmates were out of their cells, some of whom were engaged in housekeeping or maintenance duties. There was likewise testimony presented by ex-prisoners that considerable communication was had between "favored" inmates. The record of punishments through the years also indicates that most of the infractions of the rules dealt with communication between prisoners.

Even if these exceptions are charitably overlooked, certainly it can be claimed that doubling up of inmates in the cells represented a serious breach of the system. This was admitted to have been resorted to as early as 1866, and as the years advanced more and more cells were used to house two inmates. The excuse was that cell construction could not keep pace with admissions. It was the acceptance of this situation that prompted the administration to substitute the philosophy of "individual treatment" for that of the separate system.

Warden Cassidy was succeeded in 1900 by his prison clerk, Daniel W. Bussinger, who, in 1904 was followed by the eminent prison administrator, Joseph Byers. Byers recognized that the separate system had completely broken down and was quite outspoken regarding the insurmountable difficulties of longer maintaining the fiction of the Pennsylvania System of prison discipline. Byers had grown up professionally in congregate prisons and, even though he remained at Cherry Hill for only a year, brought heretofore shunned concepts into the institution. By that time the inspectors were able to accept them. Cherry Hill had become just another congregate prison.

The history of this famous Philadelphia prison from the turn of the century until the present time would make another interesting story but it has no part in this book. The transition from the separate system to the congregate system was piecemeal. The introduction of power machinery to replace the historic handcraft work called for ingenuity. The change was accomplished primarily by tearing out the exercise yards and converting the space into shops. The resourcefulness of the administration was taxed to the limit to provide room for medical and hospital facilities, the preparation and serving of food, setting up school and religious programs, and identification and later classification of new admissions. Rooms were made by tearing out walls of cells, or buildings were constructed by legislative grants in the already cramped space between the cell blocks. A new hospital building and a boiler room were erected in 1901, a storehouse in 1905, a new industrial building in 1906, a shop building in 1907, and an emergency hospital in 1908. Today the ten-acre enclosure of the prison is an architectural nightmare, giving one the impression of a hodgepodge.

Security measures had to be completely overhauled as Cherry Hill emerged into a congregate prison. With men out of their cells, unmasked, moving from one assignment to another, engaging in exercise in communal yards rather than in the outmoded and pathetically little individual yards, there was need for custodial alertness undreamed of by earlier

prison guards. Accordingly, sharp-shooting custodial officers
were placed on the towers of the wall, and the officer in the
central observatory was obliged to develop a new type of surveillance. The silence rule, universally a significant part of
early prisons, began to be observed at Cherry Hill. It was enforced in the shops and at mess but relaxed during recreation
or "yard out" and, of course, in the cells at night between cell
mates. The process of changing the prison from a separate
system to the congregate type went inexorably on its way.

Some insight into the degree to which the system had disappeared in practice before its legal termination may be obtained from the fact that the act of 1913 repealing the system
did not receive the slightest reference or comment in the report
of the inspectors or of any of the officers of the institution at
Cherry Hill. Yet this act meant the end in America of one of
the most important and influential systems of prison discipline
ever devised. It was actively defended for 30 years after it
had ceased to exist in its true form, and it lingered on as a legal
ghost for nearly 20 years after it had ceased to have any conspicuous apologists except Richard Vaux and his doughty
warden, Michael Cassidy.

Were De Beaumont or De Tocqueville, William Crawford,
Frederic Demetz, Dr. Nicolas Julius—early Europeans who
extolled the system—or even Richard Vaux to visit Cherry
Hill today, they would doubtlessly regard themselves as victims
of an optical illusion to behold groups of men milling about
in the yard for purposes of recreation or daily tasks and engaged in practically unrestricted conversation.

Periodically, through the years, there had been expressed a
fond hope that the Cherry Hill prison could be completely
abandoned along with the Western Penitentiary at Pittsburgh;
this was to be accomplished by erecting a state penitentiary
in the central part of the Commonwealth. As a culmination of
this abortive hope, the legislature passed the act of June 14,
1915, calling for the erection of just such a plant at Rockview
in Center County. However, great opposition developed to
this proposal—but not before a grand façade and maximum-

security cell block were erected—primarily because of the great distance to be traveled to visit prisoners. The plans were hurriedly altered and a minimum-security prison was erected. It was administered as an annex of the Pittsburgh prison, and in January, 1954, it became a part of the state system of prisons under a Commissioner of Correction.

In 1925 the legislature passed an act providing for an annex to Cherry Hill, which was built at Graterford, Montgomery County, and was opened to prisoners in 1929. It was administered by the inspectors of the Philadelphia institution until 1954 when it, too, became an integral unit of the state system of prisons.

The inspectors of Cherry Hill had long complained because women were housed in the Philadelphia prison. Several petitions were sent to the legislature calling for a special institution for female convicts. Eventually the plea was recognized, and the act of July 25, 1913, provided for the creation of the State Industrial Home for Women, located at Muncy in Lycoming County. This institution was ready for the reception of convicted females who had been housed at Cherry Hill and in the various county jails of the state. The women were removed from Block 2 of the Philadelphia prison during the autumn of 1923, much to the relief of the staff and doubtlessly also to the women themselves. The last woman to be removed was taken to Moyamensing County Prison in Philadelphia on December 12, 1923.

☰ 8
Influence of the Pennsylvania System

THE Pennsylvania System of prison discipline was but one phase in the history of penology. While its philosophy is obscurely rooted in the Middle Ages, in the monastic practices of the Church, it is to John Howard that we turn for its implementation. He favored imprisonment for all criminals as a substitute for public, physical punishment. He advocated "penitentiary houses" in which each prisoner should have his own individual cell.

This philosophy of Howard was enthusiastically accepted by the reformers of Philadelphia. To them goes the credit— or discredit—for the system. As early as 1787 the eminent physician Dr. Benjamin Rush, who was familiar with the works of Howard, published his ideas on penal treatment.[1] Prefacing his program with the remark that "ignominy is universally acknowledged to be a worse punishment than death," he contemplated "secret" punishment "in a large house of a construction agreeable to its design in a remote part of the state" of Pennsylvania. He refrained from calling this place a prison because these establishments were at the time associated with promiscuity and debauchery. He chose to call it a "house of repentance." Benjamin Rush lived in a period when expiation and repentance were considered necessary for salvation and reformation. Here is how he described his dream institution for criminals:

Let the avenue to this house be rendered difficult and gloomy by mountains and morasses. Let the doors be of iron; and let the grating occasioned by opening and shutting them be increased by an echo from a neighboring mountain that shall extend and continue a sound that shall deeply pierce the soul. . . . Let all officers of the house be strictly forbidden ever to discover any signs of mirth, or even levity, in the presence of the criminal.

[1] See p. 7.

Here was, in effect, the nebulous forerunner of the separate system as conceived by the Philadelphia reformers. Terrifying though his conception of a prison is, Benjamin Rush anticipated many phases of modern penology, which place his name among the most enlightened leaders in the field. The program, the ideas of sentencing, and other phases of penal discipline suggested in his writings are testimony to his foresight in predicting what we now understand as treatment.

His plan called for the inmates of his "house of repentance" to be self-supporting. "The labor should be so regulated and directed as to be profitable to the state. Besides employing criminals in laborious and useful manufactures, they may be compelled to derive all their subsistence from a farm and garden, cultivated by their own hands adjoining the place of their confinement." This clearly anticipated the state farm so wisely advocated today. Rush added that such an establishment would not cost as much as one-fourth that of maintaining the several jails scattered throughout the state.

He advocated the classification of prisoners by which would be decided a form of treatment suitable to each one's disposition and temperament and to the atrocity of his crime. The scale of punishments proposed included the infliction of bodily pain (not specified), labor, watchfulness, solitude, and silence. Such punishment or treatment might be used "separately or more or less combined." The purposes of such punishment were reformation, the prevention of crime, and the removal of persons from society who have demonstrated by their tempers and crimes that they are unfit to live in society.

Sentencing of criminals, according to Dr. Rush, should be imposed "by a court properly constituted for that purpose whose business it should be to visit the receptacle for criminals *once or twice a year*." Anticipating what is now known as the indeterminate sentence, he recommended, "Let the various kinds of punishments that are to be inflicted on crimes be defined and fixed by law. But let no notice be taken, in the law, of the punishment that awaits any particular crime. . . . Punishments should always be varied in degree according to the temper of the criminal or the progress of his reformation." He further added: "Let the duration of punishments for all crimes be limited, but let this limitation be unknown [to the criminal]. I conceive this secret to be of the utmost importance in reforming criminals and preventing crimes. The imagination, when agitated with uncertainty, will seldom fail of connecting the longest duration of punishment with the smallest crime."

This injunction unquestionably parallels the indeterminate sentence which has not yet been completely realized. Most penologists agree that the flat-time sentence is inadequate. According to this great colonial physician, release from prison should not come until there is assurance that the inmate has been rehabilitated. He stated, "To obtain this great and salutary end, there should exist certain portions of punishment, both in duration and degree, which should be placed by law beyond the power of the discretionary court, to shorten or mitigate." Productive labor, instruction, and religion were handmaidens of proper treatment in effecting rehabilitation in this imaginative house of repentance.

Much of what Dr. Rush urged in his pamphlet of 1787 was overlooked when the penitentiary was finally adopted in the Walnut Street Jail by the legislative act of 1790. The Philadelphia Prison Society, of which Rush was a charter member, was obliged to compromise with the architectural shortcomings of the institution, although a "house of repentance" for hardened criminals was erected in the jail yard. This building, similar to that suggested by John Howard in 1777, was the first penitentiary house. The inmates sentenced to solitary confinement without labor were placed in this three-storied building. The rest of the prisoners were productively employed, classified, and humanely treated. Cleanliness and "contentment" prevailed. Rush himself was pleased with the program because he wrote in his commonplace book in 1794 that all prisoners were busy at various productive tasks. He sent them watermelons in August, 1796, and turkeys for Christmas of the same year.

Benjamin Rush died in 1813, 15 years too soon to see more of his ideas set in motion at Cherry Hill prison. Here he would have witnessed prisoners in "solitude," working at tasks in their cells, some growing vegetables in their little yards, and receiving individual instruction in religion.

The Pennsylvania System was conceived by honest, courageous, and understanding men. These pioneers were sincere in their belief that such a system was the answer to the problem of penal treatment. They were violently opposed to the "schools of debauchery" that were prevalent in the local jails of the day and looked with abhorrence on the contaminating influences of such establishments. In advocating a system whereby each convicted criminal should be separated from all others, they may have been correct. They were incorrect in at least one vital area: there was simply not enough human contact provided the prisoner. Conceived before the development of social psychology, the founders of the system could not know that the human spirit, however depraved, must communicate if it is to thrive in a healthy fashion.

While the system was repudiated in the country of its development, its advocates had every right to be elated at its reception abroad. Aside from its adoption in most European countries as well as in South American countries, it was endorsed at the First International Penitentiary Congress which held its meeting at Frankfurt-am-Main in 1846. One of the resolutions adopted at that famous meeting of prison administrators and students of the crime problem reads as follows:

Separate confinement shall be applied generally to convicts, with aggravations or alleviations commended by the nature of the offenses and of the sentences, by the individuality and the conduct of the prisoners; in such a way that every prisoner shall be employed in some useful labor; that he may enjoy daily exercise in open air; that he take part in the benefit of religious, moral, and school instruction, in the worship of his confession, and that he receive regularly the visits of the clergyman of his creed, of the warden of the prison, of the physician of the prison, and of the members of the committees of inspection and of patronage [prison visitors], besides other visits, which may be authorized by the by-laws of the house.[2]

While the above endorsement referred primarily to prisoners with short sentences, the next resolution adopted by the Congress stated, "[it] shall likewise be applied to imprisonment for longer terms, being combined with all the progressive alleviations which may be brought in harmony with maintaining the principle of separation." Louis Dwight, the nemesis of the Pennsylvania System, was the lone delegate to this Congress from the United States. In his remarks before the assembly he said nothing against the separate system despite the fact that the delegates expected him to present his standard arguments.

The system as adopted in European countries had variations. The prisoners were usually exercised in the prison compound instead of small exercise yards attached to the cells as at Philadelphia. In the British prisons the inmates undergoing exercise were masked. They merely walked around a circle, each grasping a rope so they would keep together. In the Danish prisons, inmates were placed in a huge cartwheel structure about 60 feet in circumference with "rim and spokes" eight feet high. They were exercised separately with the eyes of the guard constantly upon them. This type of exercise is still used in some of the prisons of that country. Religious services were conducted in chapels fitted up with small, individual cubicles or stalls. The inmates walked to the chapel wearing masks and only after entering their little stalls could they remove them. Some of these odd chapels may still be seen in certain countries of Europe.

In this country the Auburn System finally fell into disrepute because of its inherent cruelties. The exploitation of prisoners by labor contractors was beginning to be exposed by humanitarians and, for different reasons, denounced by labor unions. Inmates worked together but under an unmitigated rule of silence, the breaking of which resulted in prompt and often cruel punishment. Rebellion smoldered in many prisons. Even

[2] See Negley K. Teeters, "First International Penitentiary Congresses," *Prison Journal*, Vol. XXVI, No. 3 (1946).

as early as 1815 Massachusetts prison guards "were exhorted to think of the prison as a volcano filled with burning lava, which, if not restrained, would destroy both friends and foes." This has ever been the injunction of prison administrators.

By 1870 prison authorities throughout the country were convinced that something drastic should be done to improve penal discipline. The Irish System seemed to offer a solution to American penologists, and eventually there grew out of this new concept the reformatory system.[3]

At a meeting of prison administrators and penologists held in Cincinnati, Ohio, in 1870 there was drawn up a Declaration of Principles, reflecting ideas regarding sound, humane prison policies and practices. Under the inspiration of the leaders of the reformatory movement, there was some hope that decent standards could be implemented in penal establishments.

We now know that the dreams of the stalwarts who attended the Cincinnati meeting were not realized. They succeeded in launching the reformatory system but even that movement failed to fulfill expectations. After a few years of initial success at Elmira, New York, and in some other states, reformatories became merely junior congregate prisons wherein all the same repressions, cruelties, doubling up in cells, and mismanagement inevitably resulted. The history of these penal institutions once again demonstrates the questionable possibility of imprisonment as a rehabilitative device.

The best the reformatory system could do was to instill in inmates "good habits of industry." Its grading system broke down and, as the *Attorney-General's Survey of Release Procedures* stated, "The tendency was to put everyone who behaved himself into the first grade, leaving only a few in the second and those actually under punishment in the third grade. The old prison discipline that placed the emphasis on being a good prisoner regardless of anything more fundamental, such as achievement in school or shop or in a change of character, was dominant still." [4]

[3] See pp. 218–19 for discussion of this system.
[4] "Prisons," *Attorney-General's Survey of Release Procedures,* V (Washington, D.C., 1940), 25.

Perhaps the Philadelphia skeptics, walled in by the parapets and embrasures of Cherry Hill, felt vindicated by the failure of the reformatory. But their system was also failing. In truth, both the advocates of the reformatory and the separate system were victims of the relentless dry rot of imprisonment. Its failure has been admitted by numerous people throughout the country.

The members of the Philadelphia Prison Society, watching the administration of the Walnut Street Jail, stated despairingly in 1820 that no reformation had been effected in that institution due to: (1) The unfitness of the plant, (2) The want of classification, (3) The crowded state of the prison, and (4) The want of employment. Years later, Franklin B. Sanborn, an astute student of penology from Massachusetts, asked the rhetorical question, "But do our prisons work reformation of the criminal?" and answered it with, "Go to our prisons as I have done . . . inquire of the officers, hear the story of the convicts, watch the workings of the system and you will see that instead of reforming they harden the criminal." [5] The same year (1866) the Commissioner of Public Charities and Correction for the state of New York made this bleak statement: "The system of prison discipline is defective. Instead of reforming persons convicted of crime, by its harsh and undiscriminating character, confirms the prisoner in his criminal pursuits, and that on his discharge from prison he is prepared for the commission of graver crimes than when he entered it." One year later, two of the best known penologists of their day, Theodore Dwight and Enoch C. Wines, after surveying the prison scene, sadly remarked, "There is not a state prison in America in which the reformation of the convicts is the supreme object of the discipline."

During the decade of 1920–30 a more modern approach to the problem of imprisonment was adopted. In the parlance of the penologist this is referred to as "classification." The theory underlying classification is that those sent to prison

[5] Quoted in the *Thirty-seventh Annual Report* of the Board of Inspectors of the Eastern State Penitentiary, 1866, p. 23.

should be studied as to personality, previous work, and school record, and then placed in units composed of those of similar assets. Classification was initially developed by the states of New Jersey and New York and by the Federal Bureau of Prisons. Centralized classification procedures were developed according to states, and all prison facilities were placed under a Commissioner of Correction. In addition, parole planning and parole authority were strengthened. Much attention was placed on prison administration during that decade. An era of hope was ushered in by the happy phrase, "The New Penology." The Federal Bureau of Prisons under the able leadership of Sanford Bates and his equally capable successor, James V. Bennett, certainly led the nation in implementing the New Penology. The Federal Bureau has served as a model in establishing progressive techniques and skills in prison management and has insisted on developing personnel to staff its prisons. A few other states have accomplished much in developing a good penal program. California, for example, has become a leader in progressive penology. Pennsylvania, at present, stands on the threshold of developing a system of correction, that will compare favorably with some of the more progressive states in the country. The legislation of July, 1953, that created the Bureau of Correction makes this possible.

Regardless of the fact of classification and the New Penology, the old evils of the prison still remain. It has been somewhat cynically stated that the only efficient classification would be to approach the ideal of one man to a unit. In this way the Pennsylvania reformers' old fear of contamination could be avoided. Complete separation of inmates is exactly what the Pennsylvania System of penal discipline attempted to do for almost 75 years.

We cannot review here the many difficulties and problems of the modern prison. However, it is of some moment to state that the so-called New Penology with its inadequate and superficial classification procedure is merely a "patch-quilt" process. The evils of imprisonment still remain.

We do not intend to defend the system of separate confinement. But we submit that the pioneers of the penitentiary, especially those who were citizens of Pennsylvania and more specifically of Philadelphia, could not have been completely wrong in their analysis of penal treatment. Aside from their ignorance of social psychology, in what way were the following intellectual leaders of Philadelphia in error: Roberts Vaux, Bishop William White, Thomas Bradford, Samuel R. Wood, John Sergeant, Judge Charles Coxe, the earlier Dr. Benjamin Rush, and the later militant Richard Vaux. Added to these luminaries of nineteenth century thinking we may mention Edward Livingston, Francis Lieber, and George Sumner of Massachusetts, who were defenders of the Pennsylvania System. Can we indict the dozens of brilliant European penologists who adopted the system in their native countries? We do not know how successful the modified system of separate confinement is in European countries where it is still maintained. We know it would be impossible to turn the clock back and revive it in this country.

But if it can be assumed that modern imprisonment in this country is failing to rehabilitate the criminal, perhaps this may be due to the process of contamination that unhappily is its chief characteristic. Those alert observers of social conditions, including prisons, De Beaumont and De Tocqueville, made the following significant statement which is as true today as when they made it:

Whoever has studied the interior of prisons and the moral state of their inmates, has become convinced that communication between these persons renders their moral reformation impossible, and becomes even for them the inevitable cause of an alarming corruption. . . . No salutary system can possibly exist without the separation of the criminals.[6]

The provision of smaller and smaller diversified units, all staffed by men and women who understand people who have erred, might be the next step in penal philosophy and practice.

[6] De Beaumont and De Tocqueville, *On the Penitentiary System in the United States and Its Application in France,* trans. Francis Lieber (Philadelphia, 1833), p. 21.

This presupposes a centralized diagnostic clinic in each state, to which all persons convicted of crime would first be sent. In making a concession to the philosophy of separate confinement, there should be permitted as few contacts between prisoners as possible in this diagnostic unit. Here they would be carefully examined and interviewed so that the trained personnel of the unit would be able to classify them in terms of security and treatment program. The term "individualized treatment" would have to take on meaning in such a program. None of the units to which the prisoners would be sent should house more than 100. Many of the prisoners would need little custody; thus the units would be more like farms, horticulture centers, forestry camps, salvaging units, and the like. Those whose records indicate poor prognoses would need certain degrees of custody and would be sent to walled institutions. Others with emotional problems would also be sent to custodial units equipped to deal with the problems represented.

It is not our concern here to spell out a rational penal program. But if imprisonment is to continue it is obvious that the curse of contamination, one prisoner by another, must be minimized if not completely eliminated. This can be done only by separating individuals convicted of crimes into small groups differentiated by attitudes, cultural assets and liabilities, and potential danger to society.

One other alternative would be to develop and expand substitutes for imprisonment.[7] The strengthening of probation, imposition of fines based on one's ability to pay, revocation of rights, privileges, opportunities—these and others might be explored by an imaginative society and, if invoked, would reduce the large number now being sent to prison. It is imperative also that penal codes should be radically revised and court sentences greatly reduced. It is agreed by most penologists that excessively long sentences are pronounced. There are men in prison today serving out sentences of 100 years. One inmate

[7] Negley K. Teeters, "Substitutes for Cellular Confinement," *Prison Journal,* Vol. XXX, No. 3 (1950).

left the Illinois prison in 1954 after serving 46 years. The philosophy of long sentences is absurd if we contend that the function of the prison is to rehabilitate.

The champions of separate confinement would have insisted that its failure was due to the inability or unwillingness of the legislature to construct enough cells to house privately the growing number of inmates. This is part of the truth but it is not the whole reason for failure. The advocates of the system were impervious to the slow march of penal progress in this country that represented a philosophy diametrically opposed to that to which they desperately clung. Their intentions were kindly and humane but they were impractical. The future will probably indict the modern prison in a similar fashion since it can be amply demonstrated that it, too, is practically ineffectual.

Appendix I

Building Commission

Minutes: Vol. I, April 6, 1821–March 29, 1825
  Vol. II, April 1, 1825–September 20, 1832
  (also Rough Drafts of Minutes for period 1821–28)
Cash Account: (1 volume) December 7, 1821–March 29, 1825
Receipt Book: (1 volume) December 7, 1821–March 21, 1834
Rough Day Book: (1 volume) April 21, 1826–October 24, 1826
Paymaster's Receipt Books for Wages: (5 volumes) 1822–35
Timekeeper's Checklist Showing Days Worked: (2 volumes) 1822–32

Board of Inspectors

Minute Books: (7 volumes) May 19, 1829 through 1914

Wardens

Journals: (11 volumes with Volume 3 [1878–81] missing) 1829–1917
Report to Visiting Inspectors: 1873–83; also 1 volume "Returns to
  Board of Charities"
Warden Samuel R. Wood's Receipt Book: July 24, 1830–November
  4, 1840
Visitors' Register, consisting of signatures of those who visited the
  institution (5 volumes) October 25, 1829–March 29, 1871.

Prisoners' Records

Several oversize volumes listing the prisoners sent to the institution
  from its opening date, October 25, 1829, through 1918. Each prisoner is identified by number followed by such items as height,
  foot measurement, age, place of birth, distinctive marks, offense,
  place of conviction, sentence, degree of literacy, trade, and date
  of discharge. These volumes overlap as to inmate numbers and
  dates. There is a volume giving names of prisoners with their corresponding numbers, also an alphabetical list of inmates.
Commutation Books: May 9, 1873–February 12, 1883; January 13,

1898–August 12, 1901; dates between January 1883 and January
    1898 not available
Physicians' Monthly Reports: (2 boxes) 1829–72
Moral Instructors' and Teachers' Monthly Reports: irregular dates
Joint Legislative Committee Testimony: 1. Investigation, 1834–35,
    11 fascicles; 2. Investigation, 1897, 12 fascicles

Appendix II

PARTIAL WORDING OF MEMORIALS SENT TO THE LEGISLATURE BY THE PHILADELPHIA PRISON SOCIETY, SHOWING THE INTERCHANGE OF IDEAS OF "SEPARATE" AND "SOLITARY" CONFINEMENT AND THE USE OF "LABOR" IN THEIR PHILOSOPHY.

January 29, 1788
Punishment by more *private* or even *solitary labour* would more successfully tend to reclaim the Unhappy Objects as it might be Conducted more Steadily and uniformly and the kind and Portion of Labour better adapted to the different Abilities of the Criminals.[1]

January 12, 1789
Solitary Confinement to hard Labour . . . will prove the most effectual means of reforming these unhappy creatures.[2]

December 14, 1801
Ever since the establishment of the prisons we have wished to make a fair experiment of *Solitude with Labour* on the Convicts . . . We are therefore induced to request that you will devise such means as may appear to you most adequate to separate the Convicts from all other descriptions of prisoners in order that a full opportunity of trying the effects of *Solitude and Labour* may be afforded.[3]

January 12, 1818
[Calling for the erection of penitentiaries throughout the State]. . . . respectfully request the legislature to consider the Propriety and expediency of erecting *effectual employment and separation of prisoners,* and of proving the efficacy of Solitude on the Morals of those unhappy objects.[4]

January 22, 1821
[Urging the erection of a New Prison]. Your Memorialists respect-

[1] See Negley K. Teeters, *They Were In Prison* (Philadelphia, 1937), p. 447, for complete wording of this Memorial.
[2] *Ibid.,* p. 451. As a result of these two memorials the legislature passed the act of April 5, 1790, creating the penitentiary in Walnut Street Jail.
[3] *Ibid.,* p. 453.   [4] *Ibid.,* p. 456.

fully request . . . you pass a law providing for the erection of a Penitentiary for the Eastern Section of the State, in which the benefits of *solitude and hard labour* may be fairly and effectually provided.[5]

December 1827

[After the Penitentiary at Pittsburgh was in operation and the new prison at Philadelphia was nearing completion]. The system of prison discipline which your Memorialists have always been anxious to establish possesses two strongly marked distinctions (from those found in "another prominent system in our country"): 1st. The recognition of moral reform as a principal aim of penitentiary punishment; 2nd. The complete separation of prisoners, as the only mode by which this end can be obtained. As our system advances toward, or recedes from a strict separation . . . do we experience a diminution or increase of the miseries of promiscuous intercourse . . .

[From the following words of the same Memorial, we see for the first time the uneasiness of the Philadelphia Prison Society as it viewed the arguments of other powerful individuals and groups for some other system of prison discipline.]

Perhaps the term *separate* rather than *solitary* confinement, would more appropriately describe the kind of durance which we propose to inflict. Completely to separate one prisoner from another; to take away every possible chance of communication in prison, and mutual recognition, after discharge, is what we greatly desire. Suitable books and private religious instruction we would afford to all; but if labour should be introduced, we hope no other will ever be permitted than such as can be performed in their private separate apartments, and that this will be employed as an alleviation, not an aggravation of their punishment.[6]

[5] *Ibid.*, p. 458.   [6] *Ibid.*, p. 461.

Appendix III

C. and T. Pleasants: offer two adjoining lots containing eleven acres, 100 perches situate on the Passyunk and Bucks Tavern Roads in adjoining Moyamensing township, avout two miles from the Court House—Lowest price, $450 per acre.

Israel Israel: offers his place Cherry Green in Passyunk township, two miles from Cedar Street—12 acres with considerable improvements—situate at the forks of the roads leading to Penrose's Ferry and Banks of Schuylkill. Price, $10,000.

Rebecca Blodget: offers 8 acres on the west bank of Schuylkill about one miles west of Permanent bridge, between Lancaster turnpike and West Chester Road, price $12,000.

E. S. Sergeant: offers 11 acres adjoining the west of Mrs. Blodget's property. Price, $15,000.

Austin Mathew: executor of George Honey offers a lot on the south side of Race street, bounded by Schuylkill second on the west—Schuylkill third on the east, being 495 on Race, 556 on second and 467 on third street. Price, $28,000. The lot on the south of this extending to Arch street may be had says the writer. If price is too high is willing to leave to men to fix.

Frederick Bruner: offers a lot on Schuylkill fourth street adjoining the public Burying Ground of 11 acres, some perches. Price, $1,000 per acre; will give one year's credit.

Thomas Cadwallader: offers a lot on the north west corner of Pine and Schuylkill about 15 acres. Price, $2,500 per acre—also a lot of about ten acres bounded by Old York Road—Sixth street continued Masters street and Camac street in length 1,100 feet and in depth East and West 415. Price, $15,000; a stream of water passes through this lot from north to south.

Lemuel Green: offers his farm of 10 acres 47 perches on Germantown Road opposite Two Mile Stone—considerable improvements. Price, $10,000. He represents the situation as elevated and healthy.

James Lyle: offers several properties. Part of Bushhill estate; No. 1, Sixteen acres or any part bounded on the west by Schuylkill fourth street, north by Francis Lane, east by Sixth street and south by Hunter street. Price, $3,500 per acre. Gravel on this lot.

No. 2, Eleven acres laying to the eastward of the above bounded west by Schuylkill sixth street, north by Francis Lane, south by Hunter street and east by Methodist Burial Ground. Price, $3,000 per acre.

No. 3, Nine acres and a half bounded by Vine street on the south; by Callowhill street on the north, by Schuylkill fourth street on the west and by Schuylkill sixth street on the east. Price, $5,000 per acre.

William Lehman: offers two squares containing together 16 acres situate about 900 feet north of Callowhill street between second and fourth streets from Schuylkill. The south side contains 545 feet, west side 1,000 feet, north side 1,000 feet and east side 400 feet. Price for whole or any part $1,750 per acre.

Henry Nixon and Henry Williams: offer two lots;

1. Five acres and a half bounded by Francis Lane Schuylkill second;

2. Seven acres and a half [——] street, Hunter and Washington streets; soil is fine gravel; other squares can be had. Price, $1,500 per acre; the place is called Morrisville.

James and William Caldwell: offer a lot at Springetsberry adjoining Bush Hill estate situate between Schuylkill second and fourth streets and Hamilton and Morris streets, two squares each 473 and 470; Price, $7,000. Gravel on the premises and near to a run of water.

John Fulmer: offers two lots of ground in Penn township;

1. Eight acres, 70 perches nearly square situate near Bush Hill hospital—Price, $8,000.

2. Twelve acres near the above for $10,000; water can be obtained at 18 feet.

Eliza Crumpston: offers 8 or 12 acres at $900 per acre formerly the property of Doct. Magaw. Buildings are on this property which are to be valued if included in what may be purchased—situate near public water works west of Mr. Pratts and adjoining the farm of John Fulmer. Through it runs a stream of never failing water; the whole place consists of 18 acres 44 perches and if the whole is taken considerable reduction will be made.

Joseph and Benjamin Warner: offer two lots;

    1. Eleven acres—Two dwelling houses in Francis street, first street above Callowhill, running from Ridge Road to Schuylkill—north and south lines 627 feet, east and west lines 750 feet. Two sides bounded by Public Roads. Price $15,000.

    2. Directly west of the above described and separated by a 33 foot wide road the north and south lines 445 feet east and west line 850 feet containing eight acres 70 perches; Price, $10,000; situation, high surface generally level.

George Harrison: offers ten acres 95 perches adjoining Warners. First described lot on the north at $550 per acre and a lot of ten acres 95 perches belonging to Charles Francis lying to the Eastward of Harrison and Warner, as by reference to the plan will appear. Price, $550 per acre.

Elizabeth R. Fisher and Dorothy Francis by T. Morris: offer two lots adjoining each other each containing ten acres and 95 perches lying to the north of Harrison lot as by reference to the plan will appear. Price, $500 per acre.

Respectfull submitted,
Thomas Bradford, Jun.
Caleb Carmalt [1]

June 1, 1821.

[1] Minute Book, Building Commission, I. In State Record Office, Harrisburg, Pennsylvania.

Appendix IV

EARLY GROUND PLANS AND ENGRAVINGS OF THE EASTERN PENITENTIARY
WITH EXPLANATION OF DISCREPANCIES.

JOHN HAVILAND wrote in 1824 that his prison was to consist of seven ranges, or cell blocks, each to contain 36 rooms or cells with exercise yards attached. The Building Commission added two cells to each block so we find 38 in the first three blocks constructed. Blocks 4, 5, 6, and 7 were later constructed of two stories; 4 and 6 with 100 cells each (50 on each floor) and 5 and 7 consisting of 136 cells each (68 on each floor). The discrepancies observed in the various early prints do not apply to these last four blocks.

When William Crawford, the English commissioner, visited the prison in 1833, only the first three blocks were completed. Yet in the report he drew up, published in 1834, he shows these blocks with many more cells than they actually had.[1] For Blocks 1 and 3 he shows "136 cells and 4 work shops"; and for Block 2, "100 cells and 4 work shops." This is completely out of line; how he could have possibly drawn the Philadelphia prison as he did is a mystery.

A few years later a faithful reproduction of the ground plan was drawn by Guillaume A. Blouet, architect, aided by his colleague, Frederic Demetz, jurist, both French commissioners. Their drawings were published in 1837.[2] Their plan shows 38 cells in each of the first three blocks which is correct.

The reproduction of the interior of Cherry Hill that is most frequently seen in books, showing the arrangement of the seven original blocks (see engraving, Fig. 8), cannot be accurately drawn. In this engraving the first three blocks indicate more cells than were built at that time. There was an addition made to Block 1 in 1869–70 but this engraving was done prior to that date.[3]

[1] Crawford, *The Penitentiaries of the United States* (London, 1834), p. 56. See Fig. 6.

[2] Blouet and Demetz, *Rapports sur les pénétenciers des Etats-unis* (Paris, 1837), p. 44. See p. 68 of this book.

[3] Richard Vaux, *Brief Sketch of the Origin and History of the State Penitentiary for the Eastern District of Pennsylvania at Philadelphia* (Philadelphia,

The engraving referred to was drawn by an inmate of Cherry Hill.[4] The legend appearing at the bottom of the engraving states that the original was by No. 2954, that the engraving was done by P. S. Duval & Co., Philadelphia, "Steam lithographer printer" and that it was "entered in the year 1853 by Richard Vaux in the clerk's office of the District Court for the Eastern District of Pennsylvania." This engraving appears first (so far as the authors can learn) in the *Journal of Prison Discipline and Philanthropy* (Vol. XI, No. 1, 1856), as a frontispiece. This engraving depicts 50 cells for each of the first three blocks rather than the correct number of 38.

It cannot be accurately determined why No. 2954 interpreted the interior of the prison as he did. It is possible that there existed one or more "proposed" or "model" plans in which more cells were drawn; or he may have merely wished to present a more symmetrical plan than the actual size of the cell blocks justified. In 1853 the first three blocks were remodeled but the authors can find no evidence that additional cells were added.

1872), pp. 69–71. He states that 20 new cells were added to Block 1, making the total number 50. Because some of the cells were double (made so by knocking out the stone partitions between some of the single cells) the discrepancy of 38 plus 20 equalling 50, is explained. He adds that Blocks 2 and 3 still had the original number of 38 cells each. Block 2 still has only 38 cells (in 1956). For further information concerning the erection of these cells, see *Fortieth Annual Report* of the Board of Inspectors, 1869, pp. 34–38.

[4] No. 2954, Samuel Cowperthwaite. From the prison records we find that this prisoner, under an earlier number, 2354 had been convicted of manslaughter, was sent to Cherry Hill on May 27, 1848, and was pardoned on August 7, 1849. He was a youth of 19 at the time of that conviction. As No. 2954 he was sent to the prison from Philadelphia on December 3, 1852 to serve 7 years 11 months for second degree murder. He was a "copperplate engraver" but was an umbrella maker by trade. While in the prison he was a weaver. He belonged to the Society of Friends. The chaplain wrote in his Journal of this man that "he belonged to one of the rowdy clubs of Skinners [*sic*]." He also wrote that his prevailing vice was intemperance and his predominant passion destructiveness. He served his full time for this second offense and was released on November 3, 1860.

Index